Servius' Commentary on Book Four of Virgil's *Aeneid*

P. VIRG. MARONIS AENEIDOS LIBER QVARTVS.

a At regina, graui iandudum saucia cura
Vulnus alit uenis, & cęco carpitur igni.
Multa uiri uirtus animo, multusq; recursat
Gentis honos, hærent infixi pectore uultus,
Verbaq;, nec placidam membris dat cura quietem.

a At regina graui iamdudum saucia cura. Apolloni[9] Argonautica scripnt: ubi inducit amantem Medeam inde totus hic liber translatus est de tertio Apollonii. Est autem pene totus in affectione: licet in fine pathos habeat: ubi abscessus Aeneæ gignit dolorem. Sane totus & in consiliis, & subtilitatibus. Nam pene comicus stylus est: nec mirum ubi de amore tractatur. Iunctus quoq; superioribus est: quod artis esse uidetur: ut frequenter diximus. Nam ex abrupto uitiosus est transitus: licet stulte quidam dicant hunc tertio nō esse coniunctum. in illo enim nauigationum pericula: in hoc amores exequitur, non uidentes optimā coniunctionē. Cum enim tertius sic clauserit: Factoq; hic fine quieuit, subsequutus est: At regina graui iamdudum saucia cura. Item paulopost: Nec placidam membris dat cura quietem. nam cum Aeneā quieuisse dixerit: satis congrue subiunxit: ut somno amans careret. ¶ IAmdudū. Aut nimiū. ut Terent. iādudū te amat: iādudū illi facile fit, quod doleat. aut iādudum a quo tempore uidit, Aeneam. Legimus enim: Obstupuit primo aspectu Sidonia Dido. ¶ SAucia. Hic subiungit: Vulnus alit. & bene alludit ad Cupidinis tela: ut paulopost ad faculam: Et cæco carpitur igni. nam sagittarum uulnus est, facis incendium. ¶ CVra. Amore: ab eo quod cor urat, ut Veneris iustissima cura. Item: Mea maxima cura. ¶ VEnis. Quia per uenas amor currit, sicut uenenum, inde dictum: Fallasq; ueneno. Item: Lōgumq; bibebat amorem. ¶ CAeco carpitur igni. Agit Virg. ut iuuentas frangat declamationes: ut hoc loco rem dixit sine declamatione. Ouid. Quoq; magis tegitur: tanto magis æstuat ignis. Cæco igitur igni. i. ualidiore: cuius hæc natura est: ut compressus magis conualescat. ¶ MVlta uiri uirtus animo. Bene mediam se facit prębere Didonem inter regalem pudorem, & amoris impulsum. Simulat enim se uirtutem mirari: cuius pulchritudine mouebatur. Multa autem uirtus figurate dixit. nam ad numerum transtulit quod est quātitatis. ¶ REcursat. Bene frequentatiuo usus est uerbo in frequenti amantis cogitatione. ¶ GEntis. Nō Aeneæ: ut sit uelut excusatio: sed Dardani a numinib[9], aut Veneris. ¶ INfixi pec. u. Verbaq;. Tale & illud est: Illū absens absentē, auditq;, uidetq;. ¶ NEc placidā m. d. c. q. Aut penit[9] qete caruit: ut Placida epithetō qetis sit. aut habuit qdē qetē: sed nō placidā, i. turbatā ī somniis. uñ ipsa paulopost: Quæ me suspēsā insomnia terrēt?

Postera Phœbea lustrabat lampáde terras,
Humentemq; Aurora polo dimouerat umbram,
Cum sic unanimem alloquitur male sana sororem:
Anna soror, quæ me suspensam insomnia terrent?
Quis nouus hic nostris successit sedibus hospes?
Quē sese ore ferēs? quàm forti pectore, & armis?
Credo equidē (nec uana fides) genus esse deorū:
Degeneres animos timor arguit. heu quibus ille
Iactatus Fatis? quæ bella exhausta canebat?
Si mihi non animo fixum, immotumq; sederet:
Ne cui me uinclo uellem sociare iugali:

¶ POstera Phœbea lu. lam. ter. Circunlo quutio orientis diei. Secundum enim, & tertium librum Aeneas per noctem in conuiuiis Didonis narrauerat: licet (ut supra diximus) Virg. ista quæ per naturam necesse est fieri, plerunq; contemnat. ¶ LVstrabat. Aut illustrabat, aut reuera, lustrabat, i. purgabat.

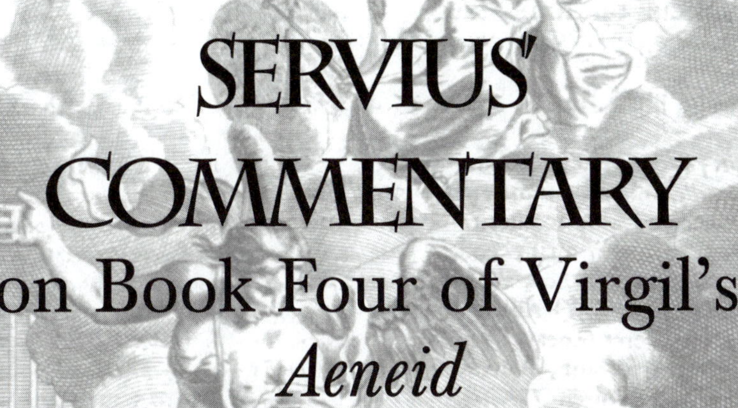

SERVIUS' COMMENTARY on Book Four of Virgil's *Aeneid*

AN ANNOTATED TRANSLATION BY
Christopher M. McDonough, Richard E. Prior
and Mark Stansbury

Bolchazy-Carducci Publishers, Inc.
Wauconda, IL
2004

General Editor: Laurie Haight Keenan
Contributing Editor: D. Scott VanHorn
Cover Design: Cameron Marshall and Megan Burns

Cover Illustration: "The Death of Dido" from Pub. Virgilii Maronis, *Operum Tomus Secundus continens sex priores Libros Aeneidos.* Ludg. Batavorum: Apud Jacobum Hackium. Amstelodami, Apud Abrahamum Wolfgang, 1680, p. 640. John J. Burns Library, Boston College.

Latin text: Latin text reproduced by permission of the American Philological Association, from *Servianorum in Vergilii carmina commentariorum,* vol. 3., edd. Arthur Stocker and Albert Travis. Lancaster, PA, Societatis Philologicae Americanae cura et impensis, 1965, pp. 247–467.

Facsimile text (frontispiece): "Servius' Commentary on Aeneid Four," from *Pvblii Virgilii Maronis, Bvcolica, Georgica, Aeneis: cvm Servii Probiqve commentariis ac omnibvs lectionvm varationibvs in antiqvis codicibvs repertis.* Venitiis : Pietro de Nicolini, 1534, p. 151 (verso). John J. Burns Library, Boston College.

Bolchazy-Carducci Publishers, Inc.
1000 Brown Street
Wauconda, IL 60084 USA
http://www.bolchazy.com

ISBN: 0-86516-514-9

Printed in the United States of America
by United Graphics
2004

Library of Congress Cataloging-in-Publication Data

Servius, 4th cent.
[In Vergilii carmina commentarii. Selections. English & Latin]
Servius' commentary on Book Four of Virgil's Aeneid : an annotated translation / [edited by] Christopher Michael McDonough, Richard Edmon Prior, Mark Stansbury.
p.cm.
Includes bibliographical references.
Virgil's Aeneid, Book 4 and Servius' commentary in Latin and English with English introd.
ISBN 0-86516-514-9 (pbk. : alk paper)
1. Virgil. Aeneis. Liber 4. 2. Epic poetry, Latin—History and criticism. 3. Aeneas
(Legendary character) in literature. I. McDonough, Christopher Michael. II. Prior, Richard E. III. Stansbury, Mark. IV. Virgil. Aeneis. Liber 4. English & Latin. V. Title.

PA6823.S5 S67 2002
873'.01—dc21 2002018948

"For better or worse, it is the commentator who has the last word."

Vladimir Nabokov
Pale Fire

Contents

Preface

As Robert Kaster pointed out, Servius' approach to Virgil does little to endear him to the modern reader. Yet acquaintance with Servius remains essential to students of Virgil and of the late-antique commentary tradition. With this annotated translation of his commentary on Book Four of the *Aeneid* we hope to make Servius (not the thornier *Servius auctus*) accessible to more of these readers: first to those who, though they may have an interest in his Virgil commentary, have neither the Latin nor the patience to deal with Servius in the raw; second, to students of late-antique and medieval history, for whom Servius is an invaluable source. We have chosen to translate the commentary on the fourth book because it is so often taught and because the story of Dido and Aeneas has such resonance in later works of art, from Ovid to Berlioz.

In the course of this project we have incurred many debts of gratitude. Two scholars were especially generous with their advice and encouragement in the early stages of our work, and to them—Professor Raymond Starr of Wellesley College and the late Professor Peter Marshall of Amherst College—we owe special thanks. Professor James Halporn read the completed manuscript and gave valuable advice. Professor James Zetzel also helped shed light on several obscure passages. For their help in preparing the manuscript for publication our thanks to Kim Uyen Dang, Christopher Hydal and Kathleen Kienzle. Finally, to Dr. Ladislaus (Lou) J. Bolchazy and Laurie Haight Keenan of Bolchazy-Carducci Publishers our thanks for their patience and encouragement. We would also like to thank the American Philological Association for permission to reprint the text of Book Four from the "Harvard Servius," as well as John Atteberry of the John J. Burns Library of Boston College, which kindly granted permission for the reproduction of the Niccolini *Aeneid* in its collection. We would especially like to thank the Costa and Mary Maliotis Charitable Foundation, which defrayed many of the expenses incurred in the course of our work.

Introduction

by Mark Stansbury

SERVIUS' commentary on the *Aeneid* is important not only as a source of information on Virgil's poem but also for the countless other gems about Roman life and literature it contains. Indeed, Servius' value as a guide has remained unquestioned from the time of Macrobius to the present day, as a glance through the *Saturnalia* and the notes of any modern edition of Virgil will confirm. In that spirit it seems proper to follow our author's own advice at the beginning of his commentary on Virgil: "In commenting on writers, these things should be considered: the life of the poet, the title of the work, the quality of the poem, the aim of the writer, the number of books, the order of the books, the commentary."[1]

The life of the poet

We know almost nothing of Servius' life except that he was a *grammaticus* teaching in Rome and that he was active in the late-fourth or early-fifth century AD.[2] The oldest manuscript witnesses of the Virgil commentary give the author's name as Servius[3] and, according to a late grammatical catalogue, he came from Sicily.[4] We can determine when he lived by citations: Servius cites the fourth-century Roman *grammaticus* Aelius Donatus and is cited by Priscian, a *grammaticus* teaching in Constantinople in the fifth or sixth century. In addition, our Servius is

1. Harvard Servius vol. 2, p. 1, *In exponendis auctoribus haec consideranda sunt: poetae vita, titulus operis, qualitas carminis, scribentis intentio, numerus librorum, ordo librorum, explanatio.*

2. For the best summary and analysis of what is known, see the prosopography in Robert Kaster, *Guardians of Language: The Grammarian and Society in Late Antiquity* (Berkeley, Los Angeles, and London, 1997) 356–59.

3. The author of *De Finalibus* calls himself Servius Honoratus, and the Naples manuscript of the *De Centum Metris* Marius Servius. Because these two works and the Virgil commentary are attributed to the same author, his name became, in many works, Marius Servius Honoratus. See Ulrich Schindel, *Die lateinischen Figurenlehren des 5. bis 7. Jahrhunderts und Donats Vergilkommentar* (Göttingen, 1975) 34–5.

4. Hermann Hagen, *Anecdota Helvetica* (Keil, *Grammatici Latini* vol. 8), cxlix.

assumed to be the Servius who appears in the *Saturnalia*, Macrobius' dialogue set in ad 383.[5]

Grammatici were an important part of education in the Latin world. Their instruction came after the *litterator*, who taught basic knowledge of letters and syllables, and before the *rhetor*, who taught the composition and delivery of speeches. The *grammaticus* had two related goals: first, to teach the correct forms and syntax of the language and second, to introduce students to the reading and interpretation of authors. We can see how *grammatici* went about achieving these goals by looking at Priscian's *Partitiones*, which are exercises on the first line of each book of the *Aeneid*. In these excercises, the *grammaticus* and pupil march through a series of questions and answers such as 'How many prepositions are there in the line?'[6] Although these dialogues surely represent an imaginary situation, the constant, merciless drill and repetition evident in the *Partitiones* were a large part of the real work of the *grammaticus*. *Enarratio*, the explanation of literary works, no doubt offered some respite from the tedium of this approach: for Augustine, Servius' near-contemporary, the emotions aroused by reading Dido's story with his *grammaticus* remained vivid years later.[7] Servius' Virgil commentary, then, is the work of a teacher closely connected not only with educating young people in language and literature but also in providing a model for other teachers.

The following works are generally attributed to Servius:[8]

1. Commentary on the works of Virgil.
2. Commentary on the *Artes* of Aelius Donatus. Donatus' *Ars Minor* and *Ars Maior* formed the foundation of Latin grammar teaching until modern times.
3. *De finalibus*. A short treatise on the quantity of final syllables.
4. *De centum metris*. Examples of 100 lines of different meter.
5. *De metris Horatii*. Examples of the different meters used by Horace.

5. See Kastner, *Guardians*, 171–175 and the articles cited there. Since Macrobius played with the characters' ages, it is difficult to draw firm conclusions, but having the youthful Servius attend the dialogue in ad 383, the approximate date, would be consistent with everything else we know.

6. Priscian's *Partitiones duodecim uersuum Aeneidos principalium* are edited in Heinrich Keil, *Grammatici Latini*. The *partitio* on Book Four begins vol. 3, 478. Augustine also parodied such instruction in his dialogue *De magistro*. See also Manfred Glück, *Priscians Partitiones und ihre Stellung in der spätantiken Schule* (Spudasmata 12) Hildesheim, 1967.

7. *Confessions* 1.13. Augustine remembers the lessons of the *litterator* with distaste but those of the *grammaticus* with fondness (only to have these values reversed after his conversion to Christianity).

8. In addition, more tenuous connections exist with a set of Greek-Latin glosses (*Glossae Servii grammatici*) and an *Expositio in Terentium*. RE IIA 1848.

We see in this short catalogue the concerns of the *grammaticus*. The writings on meter and the commentary on Donatus show us the teacher concerned with correct usage. The Virgil commentary shows us the teacher applying his knowledge to the *enarratio* of a standard text. We should remember that by Servius' time Virgil had been a school text for centuries.[9]

The title of the work

The grammarian Priscian cites Servius' work as a *commentum*, *commentarius,* or *commentarium* and the manuscripts call it an *expositio* or *explanatio*.[10] In any case, unlike many other genres, the titles of commentaries seem to tell us little about expectations for them, i.e. could Servius' work have been a successful *commentum* but a failed *expositio*?

The quality of the work

Servius' commentary on Virgil is a set of scholia containing a line-by-line treatment of the *Aeneid*, *Georgics*, and *Eclogues*. One of Servius' main sources is the now-lost commentary on Virgil by Aelius Donatus.[11] Two forms of the Servius commentary have come down to us: the first and shorter form is called S, the second, longer, form called DS.

The S scholia form a consistent set of comments transmitted in a large number of manuscripts from the ninth century and later. This is the form of the commentary that most readers of Servius would have known until 1600, and it is the version we have printed and translated.

DS is a more extensive set of scholia, first edited by the French humanist Pierre Daniel, and first printed in 1600.[12] Daniel called this longer set of comments *Servius auctus* ('expanded Servius'), but since

9. Perhaps the best sign of this is in Pompeii, where lines (and parodies of lines) from the *Aeneid* are still visible as graffiti. Virgil dies and the *Aeneid* first circulated in 19 BC. When Pompeii was destroyed some 100 years later in AD 79, lines from Virgil's poetry could be found as graffiti in fifty-six places around the city. Each of the poems is represented: six lines of the *Eclogues* (found in thirteen places), one line of the *Georgics* (found in two places), and thirteen lines of the *Aeneid* (found in forty-one places). The first line of Book One, famous even in Antiquity, was parodied as 'Launderers and the owl I sing, not arms and the man.' (CIL 4.1913 '*fullones ululamque cano non arma uirumque*'.) The owl was the symbol of the *fullones*, whose activities are depicted under the watchful eye of such a bird on the 'Pilaster of the Fullers' in the laundry of Veranius Ipseus in Pompeii.

10. RE IIA 1836. The Harvard Servius chooses *explanatio*.

11. This Aelius Donatus, the grammarian and teacher of St Jerome and author of the *Artes* that were also the subject of a Servian commentary, is not to be confused with Tiberius Claudius Donatus, the author of the extant *Interpretationes Vergilianae,* yet another commentary on the *Aeneid,* on which see below p. xvii.

12. Daniel was a legal scholar in Orléans whose library was enriched in 1562 when the nearby monastery of Fleury (Saint-Benoît-sur-Loire) was pillaged during the wars of religion. For more, see Elisabeth Pellegrin, *Bibliothèques retrouvées* (Paris, 1988) and Marco Mostert, *The Library of Fleury* (Hilversum, 1989).

their publication the more common name has been Servius Danielis. These scholia are found in only seven ninth-century manuscripts and in none of them is it attributed to an author.

The relationship between Servius and Servius Danielis has fevered philological brains since the time of Daniel. In a better world, S would simply be an abbreviation of DS; alas, it is not so. Instead, as Thilo and Barwick showed, DS is an amalgam of S and a second group of Virgil scholia.[13] In other words, DS was created when a medieval scholar sat down with at least two sets of manuscripts: one containing the S scholia and the other containing a different group of scholia. Our medieval scholar then went verse-by-verse using the S scholia as a base and adding and incorporating comments from the second set of scholia. DS is the result of this scholar's work.

Because we have one of the groups of scholia available to the compiler (the S commentary), by comparing S and DS we can peer over the compiler's shoulder. For example, this is the S comment on '*cura*,' 'by care,' in the first line of Book Four:

> BY CARE by love, from that which burns the heart, as 'the most justified care of Venus,' [10.132] likewise, 'my greatest care.' [1.678][14]

This is vintage Servius: striving for *brevitas*, he simply puts the synonym in apposition to the lemma without further explanation. Then he explains the etymology of the word (that *cura* comes from *cor urat*) and gives two examples of Virgil's usage of it in the *Aeneid*. Now observe how the medieval scholar has taken this *scholium* (in bold below) and built upon it:

> **BY CARE by** intolerable **love**, which she cannot bear, as 'and free me from these cares.' [652] Therefore 'care' **from that which burns the heart, as 'the most justified care of Venus,'** [10.132] **likewise, 'my greatest care.'** [1.678] Clearly this is said through confusion of noun and verb, for 'care' is also a verb, as 'I care, you care,' when it is not a noun.[15]

Here, the compiler has expanded on the synonym by adding an adjec-

13. Karl Barwick, "Zur Serviusfrage," *Philologus* 70 (1911): 106–45.

14. Servius on *Aeneid* 4.1: *CVRA amore; ab eo quod cor urat, ut "Veneris iustissima cura," item "mea maxima cura."*

15. Servius Danielis on *Aeneid* 4.1: ***CVRA amore** intolerabili, quem ferre non posset, ut "meque his absolvite curis." "cura" ergo, **ab eo, quod cor urat, ut "Veneris iustissima cura," item "mea maxima cura."** sane per confusionem verbi et nominis dictum est; nam "cura" est et verbum, ut "cura, cures," cum non est nomen.*

tive, an explanatory phrase, and a quotation from the end of Book Four. Then, realizing that the reader might have been thrown off the track, included a transition and repeated the lemma in order to lead into the S comment, which is repeated in full. Finally, the compiler added a comment that offers an entirely different view, namely, that this is all said because of confusion about whether *cura* is a noun or a verb.

On the one hand, the compiler has carefully edited the new comments into the earlier text, mindful of leading the reader back to the lemma.[16] On the other hand, however, the compiler has added a suggestion that is inconsistent with the preceding ones: if the only problem is confusing *cura* the noun and *cura* the imperative, why offer any other explanation? Part of the answer lies in our expectations. Today, we expect that a commentator will examine many possible interpretations of a line or word and then compose the commentary by, for the most part, choosing the best of them according to his or her judgment. Yet for the compiler and Servius,[17] it was often not so. They placed value on including many possibilities—even contradictory ones—without indicating which might be best. In doing so, they are following an accepted practice. As Servius' contemporary St. Jerome, the student of Aelius Donatus, asked a critic of his own biblical commentaries:

> What is the purpose of commentaries? They should offer the words of another, clarify what is obscurely written in plain language, repeat the opinions of many and say: 'Some offer this opinion of this passage, others interpret it that way; some support their own opinion and understanding with these texts, others with argument,' so that the wise reader, when he reads divergent explanations and learns of the many interpretations that must be approved or disapproved, can judge what is more likely and, like a good banker, reject the counterfeit.[18]

For Jerome (and Servius), weighing conflicting opinions was often, but not always, a matter to be left to the reader, following what Jerome some-

16. This careful editing is not always evident in the compiler's work.

17. For example, see Servius' comment on *iamdudum* in line 1 below 3.

18. Jerome *Contra Rufinum*, ed. Pierre Lardet (*Corpus Christianorum Series Latina* vol. 79) 1: *Commentarii quid operis habent? Alterius dicta edisserunt, quae obscure scripta sunt plano sermone manifestant, multorum sententias replicant, et dicunt: Hunc locum quidam sic edisserunt, alii sic interpretantur, illi sensum suum et intellegentiam his testimoniis et hac nituntur ratione firmare, ut prudens lector, cum diuersas explanationes legerit et multorum uel probanda uel improbanda didicerit, iudicet quid uerius sit et, quasi bonus trapezita, adulterinae monetae pecuniam reprobet.*

what grandiosely called the "laws of commentaries."[19] As Jerome's defense of the practice shows, and as we will see below, this was only one way of writing commentaries and it had its critics.

In the *Aeneid* commentary Servius industriously collects the opinions of others and often seems reticent to offer his own. These two qualities correspond to two virtues Macrobius praised in a *grammaticus*: *diligentia* and *verecundia*. Best translated as 'modesty' or 'propriety,' *verecundia* is discussed at length by Kaster, who argues for its importance as a social virtue of the late-antique *grammaticus*.[20] *Diligentia*, perhaps best described as a combination of "care" and "industry," is the basis of scholarship and produces the thoroughness so evident in Servius' commentary. Nor are these uniquely late-antique virtues, as any user of Arthur Stanley Pease's monumental work on Book Four of the *Aeneid* can testify.[21] Thus, when Servius gives a list of seemingly contradictory possibilities for a line of poetry he is fulfilling his duty as a commentator, not shirking it.[22]

The aim of the writer

Because Servius' aim is to be useful to other *grammatici*, he does not fulfill another of our expectations of a commentator. We expect a commentator to paint a harmonious vista in which the minute objects in the foreground are set within the pleasant landscape of larger issues. R.D. Williams, for example, begins his excellent commentary on the fourth

19. Jerome *In Hieremiam*, ed. Siegfried Reiter (*Corpus Christianorum Series Latina* vol. 74) prologus. Jerome repeats the idea that commentaries let the reader judge in *Contra Rufinum, Epistula aduersus Rufinum*, and the commentary on Jonah. For the ideal of clarity in commentaries, see Jerome's letters 36, 37, and 49 in *Epistulae*, ed. Isidore Hilberg (vol. 54).

20. Kaster, *Guardians* 60 and Kaster's other work cited there.

21. *Publii Vergili Maronis Aeneidos Liber Quartus*, ed. Arthur Stanley Pease (Cambridge, MA, 1935). As Pease writes in the preface (p. vii): "Since, as Servius asserts, all Virgil is *scientia plenus*, it has seemed proper to assemble, for teachers and other interested scholars, something of that wealth of exegesis which is largely inaccessible to those remote from large libraries."

22. For more on early commentaries, see Mark Stansbury, "Early-Medieval Biblical Commentaries, Their Writers and Readers," *Frühmittelalterliche Studien* 33 (1999): 49–82.

book of the *Aeneid* with a background essay on the importance of Virgil's Dido in world literature.[23] Then in the middle distance we find comments on individual scenes, and in the foreground questions like manuscript readings. Servius, on the other hand, lacks this sense of proportion. As Henri-Irénée Marrou described Servius' approach, "One read Virgil not in the way one contemplates a vast landscape from a height, but as one admires a pearl necklace held between the fingers, examining one grain after another for its own beauty."[24] In fact, it is precisely this obsessive accumulation of detail that makes Servius such a valuable source for us.

Yet Servius is not representative of all late-antique commentators. Three roughly contemporary commentaries take widely divergent approaches: the *Expositio Vergilianae continentiae secundum philosophos moralis* of Fabius Planciades Fulgentius, the *Commentarii in somnium Scipionis* of Macrobius, and the *Interpretationes Vergilianae* of Tiberius Claudius Donatus. In the *Expositio*, Virgil appears to Fulgentius, insults him, and then proceeds to reveal the inner meaning (*continentia*) of his poem. Macrobius, again writing for his son, managed to shoehorn much Neoplatonic philosophy into his commentary on a short episode from Cicero's *Republic*, commenting, he tells us, not on all Cicero's words, but only those worthy of it.[25] It is with the *Interpretationes*, however, that we can see an approach that seems written specifically to oppose the techniques of *grammatici* like Servius.

Very little is known about Tiberius Claudius Donatus, but he is thought to have lived in the late-fourth or early-fifth century; the *Inter-*

23. *The Aeneid of Virgil* ed. Robert Deryck Williams (Glasgow, 1972): 332–4.

24. Henri-Irénée Marrou, *Augustin et la fin de la culture antique* (Paris, 1958): 25. "On lisait Virgile non comme on contemple de haut un vaste paysage, mais comme on admire un collier de perles tenu entre les doigts, examinant chaque grain l'un après l'autre pour sa beauté propre."

25. Macrobius, *Commentarii in Sominum Scipionis* 1.5, in *Opera,* ed. James Willis (Leipzig, 1970): vol. 2: "*nunc iam discutienda nobis sunt ipsius somnii verba, non omnia sed ut quaeque videbuntur digna quaesitu.*"

pretationes is his only extant work.[26] He tells his son in the preface that after his own education he thought it was better to remain silent than to write about Virgil's poetry. The commentaries of his contemporaries, however, made him change his mind, "when I perceived that teachers bestowed on their students nothing that made sense, moreover that commentary writers left many complicated things written in a pleasing style not so much in eagerness for teaching as for the sake of their own memory."[27] It may even be, as Heinrich Georgii suggested, that Servius was the intended object of these words, though it is not altogether clear whether either of them knew the other's writing.[28] In any case, Tiberius Claudius Donatus' views about *grammatici* teaching Virgil are clear: he assures his son that "If you adequately pay attention to Virgil's poetry and suitably understand its purpose, you will find in the poet a great *rhetor* and hence you will understand that orators especially should teach Virgil, not *grammatici*."[29]

The effect of this is that Tiberius Claudius Donatus approaches the *Aeneid* as a poem of praise, an example of the rhetorical *genus laudatiuum*. That Virgil praised Augustus through Aeneas was not a new insight—Servius acknowledges in his preface that Virgil had two aims in his poem, to imitate Homer and praise Augustus through his ancestors.[30] Yet the way Tiberius Claudius Donatus uses this idea throughout the *Interpretationes* is quite unlike the way Servius does. As Raymond Starr has shown, Tiberius Claudius Donatus is rigorously consistent in applying this idea to every aspect of the *Aeneid*, with the result that Virgil's

26. For a summary, see Kaster, *Guardians*, 400. The latest study is Marisa Squillante Saccone, *Le Interpretationes Vergilianae de Tiberio Claudio Donato* [*Studi e Testi dell'antichità* 17] (Naples, 1985).

27. Tiberius Claudius Donatus, *Interpretationes Vergilianae*, ed. Heinrich Georgii (Stuttgart, 1905) vol. 1, 1.5–8: *sed cum adverterem nihil magistros discipulis conferre quod sapiat, scriptores autem commentariorum non docendi studio, sed memoriae suae causa quaedam favorabili stilo, multa tamen involuta reliquisse…*

28. Tiberius Claudius Donatus, *Interpretationes*, vol. 1, xv. On the question of dependence, see Saccone, *Le Interpretationes*, 27–61 and D. Daintree, "The Virgil Commentary of Aelius Donatus—Black Hole or 'Éminence Grise'?" *Greece and Rome* n.s. 37 (1990): 65–79.

29. Tiberius Claudius Donatus, *Interpretationes*, vol. 1, 4.24–28: *si Maronis carmina competenter attenderis et eorum mentem congrue conprehenderis, invenies in poeta rhetorem summum atque inde intelleges Vergilium non grammaticos, sed oratores praecipuos tradere debuisse.*

30. Servius, *In Aen.* praef.: *intentio Vergilii haec est, Homerum imitari et Augustum laudare a parentibus; namque est filius Atiae, quae nata est de Iulia, sorore Caesaris, Iulius autem Caesar ab Iulo Aeneae originem ducit, ut confirmat ipse Vergilius a "magno demissum nomen Iulo."*

epic is reduced to a one-trick pony.[31] Servius, on the other hand, notes that this is Virgil's aim but reserves his commentary primarily for dealing with words and short phrases divorced from a much larger context.

Instead of considering the poem word by word, Tiberius Claudius Donatus considers groups of lines, often by paraphrasing them. Here, for example, is his commentary on the first two lines of Book Four:

> The story demanded that after all the necessities, Aeneas withdrew to rest; for he had both completed what he himself seemed to have promised and what the queen wanted to hear. The troubled spirit of Dido, however, was long since more inflamed with care by remembering the conversation and was scorched by a hidden fire. This what he says: 'But the queen, long since pierced by painful care, feeds the wound in her veins and is consumed by an unseen flame.'[32]

Tiberius Claudius Donatus has summarized the action, sketched the motivation of the characters, and then quoted the first two lines of the book, seeming to use Virgil to validate his own telling of the story. Compare this with Servius, who by the end of two lines has already commented individually on four words and a phrase, quoting the *Aeneid* six times and Terence and Ovid once each. The *Interpretationes* offers an instructive contrast to Servius in another way as well. Servius is relentlessly focused on line-by-line explanation and his gaze rarely wanders. Even in a book filled with memorable scenes and beautiful poetry, his praise is often reserved for how accurately Virgil describes natural phenomena or how cleverly he can represent the views of philosophical schools. Tiberius Claudius Donatus, on the other hand, always seems to have a sense for the characters as actors in a story, not simply as names with interesting etymologies.[33]

31. Raymond J. Starr, "An Epic of Praise: Tiberius Claudius Donatus and Vergil's *Aeneid" Classical Antiquity* 11 (1985): 159–174.

32. Donatus, *Interpretationes* 1.354.1–7: *Conclusis omnibus quae necessaria narratio exigebat secessit Aeneas ad requiem; complevit enim vel quod ipse pollicitus videbatur vel quod regina desiderabat audire: Didonis tamen animus intolerabili iam dudum cura commotus accendebatur magis recordatione loquentis et secreto incendio torrebatur. hoc est quod ait "at regina graui iamdudum saucia cura / uulnus alit uenis, et caeco carpitur igni."*

33. For this aspect of Tiberius Claudius Donatus, see Raymond J. Starr, "Explaining Dido to Your Son: Tiberius Claudius Donatus on Vergil's Dido," *Classical Journal* 87 (1991): 25–34.

The number and order of books

Servius wrote one book of commentary for each book of Virgil's works, which is to say that there are twelve books on the *Aeneid*. Servius follows Virgil in the order of his commentary.

Our translation

Servius' commentary, as it has come down to us, is like an annotated edition of Virgil and has all the virtues and difficulties of that genre. As in all notes, the writing is telegraphic, the goal to pack the greatest amount of information into the fewest words. We have not expanded this shorthand in our translation. At times, however, this style makes Servius' point difficult to see, and in those cases we have clarified matters in notes at the back of this volume. We have followed the text of the Harvard Servius, *Servianorum in Vergilii carmina commentariorum editionis Harvardianae volumen III*, Oxford, 1965, edited by Arthur Stocker and Albert Travis. We have incorporated the following changes suggested by Charles Murgia.[34]

	Harvard	**Our text**
57	quae aptae	quae sunt aptae
82	aliter 'militat' significat,	aliter 'militat,'
215	qui sustulit † pactum.	qui sustulit alii pactum.
228	descendo ab ducente deo.	descendo abducente deo.
323	recitauit uoce optima primum libros tertium et quartum	recitauit primum quartum et sextum
331	corporis stabilitate aut mobilitate	corporis mobilitate
379	de his dicit	de dis dicit
	ait *ea cura quietos.*	ait *ea cura quietos sollicitat.*
402	ab eo quod micas ferat.	ab eo quod ferat micas.
415	RELINQVAT frustra rogabat,	RELINQVAT rogabat,
577	et *formam* et *uultum*	et *forma* et *uultu*
592	absentibus, ut *ite, ferte tela,*	absentibus, *ferte tela,*
620	Cato dixit iuxta	Cato dicit iuxta
	lapsus est et eius nec cadauer	lapsus est nec eius cadauer
654	definiuit, † *supra spoliatus*	definiuit, *spoliatus*

34. Charles E. Murgia, "Critical Notes on the Text of Servius' Commentary on the Aeneid III–V", *Harvard Studies in Classical Philology* 72 (1967); 311–50.

Because it is difficult to read Servius without also having the text of the Aeneid at hand, we have included Latin and English versions of Virgil. These are both idiosyncratic texts, however. In the Latin text we have thrown out many centuries of Virgil scholarship to present a text that conforms to Servius' suggested readings. As for the English, although there are several good translations of the Aeneid, this is not one of them. At its heart lies a nineteenth-century 'literal' translation of Virgil intended as a trot for those being flogged through the Aeneid.[35] We offer this solely as an ugly crutch to our readers. We have presented the text on the page so that the reader has (as nearly as possible) all four texts available at once.

Abbreviations and sources of the Book Four commentary

Servius' *Aeneid* is resonant with Virgilian references. He cites Virgil more than any other author to explain the sense of a line or the use of a word. The effect—and this is one of Servius' most amazing—is constantly to have before the reader's mind Virgil passages that illuminate the text being discussed. Since Book Four continues the story of Aeneas and his companions after the shipwreck and banquet of Book One (lines 494–756), it is not surprising to find the majority of citations from that book, followed in descending order by books six, two, and three.[36] When he cites authors other than Virgil, Servius' examples tend to come from the schoolroom—that is, they come not from his contemporaries, but from the authors that had already become classics: Horace, Juvenal, Lucan, and Terence are the only authors other than Virgil that he cites more than five times in the commentary on the fourth book. Servius uses citations in a very focused way to clarify Virgil's language and to explain concrete details of Virgil's text. Servius' commentary is not interested in comparing Virgil's treatment of Dido with Ovid's in the seventh letter of the *Heroides*. Servius' first goal is to connect the lines being read first with other lines in the *Aeneid*, then with other Virgilian poems.

When Servius uses quotations he almost always indicates the author (if it is not Virgil), but rarely the work. This may have been enough for his contemporaries, but it is not for ours. Accordingly, we have tried to

35. *The First Six Books of Virgil's Aeneid Literally Translated with Notes by Davidson* (New York n.d. ca. 1900).

36. Here are the number of citations: *Aeneid* Book 1, 38; Book 2, 17; Book 3, 16; Book 5, 8; Book 6, 19; Book 7, 10; Book 8, 11; Book 9, 10; Book 10, 7; Book 11, 2; Book 12, 7; *Bucolica* 15; *Georgica* 17.

indicate Servius' sources unobtrusively but completely by adopting these conventions:[37]

References follow quotations in square brackets. (In the Latin text, quoted words are in italics.)

References to lines in Book Four of the *Aeneid* are given only with line numbers, such as [435], which refers to line 435 of Book Four of the *Aeneid.*

References to lines in *Aeneid* outside Book Four are given with book and line number separated by a period, such as [6.234], which refers to line 234 of Book Six of the *Aeneid.*

References to the *Georgics* or *Eclogues* use *G* or *E* respectively, followed by book and line number.

Below are other authors and their works cited or mentioned by Servius in the commentary on Book Four with the line number in parentheses.

ANAXAGORAS, 500–420 BC (625)

ANNIANVS, 2nd-century AD
Carm = *Carmina* (291)

APOLLONIVS Rhodius, 3rd-century BC (preface)

Marcus Porcius CATO, 234–149 BC (427, 620)

Gaius Valerius CATVLLVS, 84–54 BC (409)

Marcus Tullius CICERO 106–43 BC (379)
In Cat = *In Catilinam* (486)
Tusc = *Tusculanae disputationes* (20)
Verr = *In Verrem* (608, 685)
Phil = *Philippicae* (653)

Quintus ENNIVS, 239–169 BC (9, 404)
Ann = *Annales* (576)

HOMER, 8th-century BC
Il = *Iliad* (33)
Od = *Odyssey* (654)

Quintus HORATIVS Flaccus, 65–8 BC
Ars Poet = *Ars poetica* (412)
Carm = *Carmina* (76, 135, 171, 242, 266, 301, 384, 558, 559, 585, 610, 654)
Ep = *Epistulae* (224, 409)
Epo = *Epodes* (667)
Serm = *Sermones* (54, 345, 402, 403)

37. We have usually not noted places where Servius reuses his own commentary or where Servius is quoted by later writers—these the reader must seek in the critical editions and elsewhere.

Decimus Iunius IVVENALIS, 2nd-century AD
Sat = *Saturae* (33, 77, 98, 209, 215, 228, 237, 331, 402, 516, 609, 698)

Titus LIVIVS, 59 BC–AD 7 (242)

Marcus Annaeus LVCANVS, AD 39–65
BC = *Bellum ciuile* (8, 72, 168, 253, 358, 462)

Titus LVCRETIVS Carus, 94–55 BC
DRN = *De rerum natura* (250, 486, 625, 654)

Publius OVIDIVS Naso, 43 BC–AD 17
Met = *Metamorphoses* (2, 462)

Marcus PACVVIVS, 220–130 BC (9, 469, 473)

Aulus PERSIVS Flaccus, AD 34–62
Sat = *Saturae* (331)

PLATO, 429–347 BC (653)

Titus Maccius PLAVTVS, 205–184 BC
Amph = *Amphitruo* (82)
MG = *Miles gloriosus* (149)

Gaius PLINIVS Secundus, AD 23–79 (9)
NH = *Naturalis historia* (261, 516, 551)

Gaius SALLVSTIVS Crispus, 86–35 BC (336)
Bell Iug = *Bellum Iugurthinum* (415)
Cat = *Bellum Catilinae* (62)
Hist Frag = *Historiae fragmentae* (132, 213, 270)

Septimus SERENVS, 3rd-century AD (pro Anniano) (291)

Publius Papinius STATIVS, AD 45–95
Theb = *Thebais* (132, 681)

TERENTIANVS Maurus, 2nd–3rd century AD
Syll = *De Syllabis* (413)

Publius TERENTIVS Afer, 2nd-century BC
Adel = *Adelphoe* (83, 335, 381, 590)
Andr = *Andria* (318, 335)
Eun = *Eunuchus* (1, 96, 166, 534)
Heau Tim = *Heauton timorumenos* (133)
Phorm = *Phormio* (295)

TITIANVS,
Chorographia (42)

Plotius TVCCA et Rufus VARIVS, 436

VRBANVS, 2nd–4th century AD (384, 469, 548, 624)

Marcus Terentius VARRO, 116–27 BC (427)
LL = *De Lingua Latina* (167)

Servius' Commentary on Book Four of Virgil's *Aeneid*

Liber IV

AT regina graui iamdudum saucia cura
uulnus alit uenis, et caeco carpitur igni.

Apollonius *Argonautica* scripsit et in tertio inducit amantem Medeam; inde totus hic liber translatus est. est autem paene totus in affectione, licet in fine pathos habeat, ubi abscessus Aeneae gignit dolorem. sane totus in consiliis et subtilitatibus est; nam paene comicus stilus est; nec mirum, ubi de amore tractatur. iunctus quoque superioribus est, quod artis esse uidetur, ut frequenter diximus; nam ex abrupto uitiosus est transitus. licet stulte quidam dicunt hunc tertio non esse coniunctum—in illo enim nauigium, in hoc amores exsequitur—non uidentes optimam coniunctionem; cum enim tertium sic clauserit *factoque hic fine quieuit,* [3.718] subsecutus *at regina graui iamdudum saucia cura,* [1] item paulo post *nec placidam membris dat cura quietem;* [5] nam cum Aenean dormire dixerit, satis congrue subiunxit ut somno amans careret.

1. IAMDVDVM aut 'nimium,' ut Terentius 'iamdudum' *te amat; iamdudum illi facile sit quod doleat;* [*Eun* 3.1.58] aut *iamdudum,* a quo tempore uidit Aenean; legimus enim *obstipuit primo aspectu Sidonia Dido.* [1.613]

SAVCIA hinc subiungit *uulnus alit.* et bene adludit ad Cupidinis tela, ut paulo post ad faculam, *et caeco carpitur igni:* [2] nam sagittarum uulnus est, facis incendium.

CVRA AMORE; ab eo quod cor urat, ut *Veneris iustissima cura,* [10.132] item *mea maxima cura.* [1.678]

2. VENIS quia per uenas amor currit sicut uenenum; inde dictum *fallasque ueneno,* [1.688] item *longumque bibebat amorem.* [1.749]

CAECO CARPITVR IGNI agit Vergilius ut inuentas frangat declamationes, ut hoc loco rem dixit sine declamatione; unde Ouidius *quoque magis tegitur, tanto magis aestuat ignis.* [*Met* 4.64] *caeco* ergo *igni* 'ualidiore,' cuius natura est ut compressus magis conualescat.

Book 4

BUT the queen, long since pierced by painful care, feeds the wound in her veins and is consumed by an unseen flame.

Apollonius wrote the *Argonautica* and in the third book portrays Medea in love; this book [of the *Aeneid*] was carried over entirely from there. It is, moreover, almost wholly concerned with feelings [of love], although it does have pathos at the end, when Aeneas' departure produces her grief. Of course the entire book is concerned with plots and contrivances, for its style is nearly comic; and not surprisingly where the subject of love is treated. This book is also joined to the preceding ones, which is part of [Virgil's] skill, as I have said frequently, for an abrupt transition is faulty. Some people foolishly claim that this book is not joined to the third book (in that book he relates a sea voyage, in this one love), not seeing the excellent link to this book. Virgil ends Book Three like this: "and having made an end [to his story] here he rested," [3.718] followed immediately [in Book Four] by, "but the queen, long since pierced by painful care,' [1] and likewise shortly after, "nor does care grant peaceful rest to her limbs;' [5] since when he said that Aeneas was sleeping he quite fittingly added that the one who loved him did not sleep.

1. LONG SINCE [meaning] either "excessively," as Terence wrote, "excessively does he love you; excessively easy may it be for him to grieve" [*Eun* 3.1.58] or [meaning] long since the time she saw Aeneas; in fact, we read, "Sidonian Dido was astonished at first sight."[1.613]

PIERCED he adds to this "feeds the wound." The poet also alludes well to Cupid's weapons, as he does to the little torch shortly after, "she is consumed by an unseen flame," [2] since a wound comes from arrows, the fire from the torch.

BY CARE by love, from that which burns the heart [*cor urat*], as, "the most justified care of Venus," [10.132] likewise, "my greatest care." [1.678]

2. IN HER VEINS because love runs through the veins just like poison (*venenum)*; thus it is said, "and you may deceive [her] with poison," [1.688] and likewise, "she drank love in deeply." [1.749]

IS CONSUMED BY AN UNSEEN FLAME Virgil strives to reduce contrived rhetoric, as in this passage he has stated the matter without declamation; hence Ovid, "the more a fire is covered, the more it heats up." [*Met* 4.64] By "an unseen fire," therefore, means "by a fairly strong fire," the nature of which is to grow stronger when suppressed.

multa uiri uirtus animo, multusque recursat
gentis honos: haerent infixi pectore uultus
uerbaque, nec placidam membris dat cura quietem.
postera Phoebea lustrabat lampade terras,
umentemque Aurora polo dimouerat umbram,

3. MVLTA VIRI VIRTVS ANIMO bene mediam se facit praebere Didonem inter regalem pudorem et amoris inpulsum. simulat enim se uirtutem mirari, cuius pulchritudine commouetur. *multa* autem *uirtus* figurate dixit; nam ad numerum transtulit quod est quantitatis.

RECVRSAT bene frequentatiuo usus est uerbo in frequenti amantis cogitatione.

4. GENTIS non Aeneae, ut sit uelut excusatio, sed Dardani a numinibus aut Veneris.

INFIXI PECTORE VVLTVS VERBAQVE tale et illud est *illum absens absentem auditque uidetque.* [83]

5. PLACIDAM MEMBRIS DAT CVRA QVIETEM aut penitus quiete caruit, ut *placida* epitheton sit quietis, aut habuit quidem quietem, sed non placidam, id est, turbatam somniis; unde et ipsa paulo post *quae me suspensam insomnia terrent.* [9]

6. POSTERA PHOEBEA LVSTRABAT LAMPADE TERRAS circumlocutio orientis diei—secundum enim et tertium librum Aeneas per noctem convivio Didonis narrauerat—licet, ut supra diximus, [ad 1.223] Vergilius ista quae per naturam necesse est fieri plerumque contemnat.

LVSTRABAT aut 'inlustrabat,' aut re uera 'lustrabat,' id est 'purgabat'; nam nox quodammodo polluit mundum.

7. VMENTEM VMBRAM quia nox omnis umida est, ut *noctis lentus non deficit umor.* [*G* 1.290] et nihil interest utrum umbram an noctem dicat; nox enim umbra terrae est, ut supra *inuoluens umbra magna terramque polumque.* [2.251] est etiam hysteroproteron in sensu; Aurora enim solem praecedit.

The many virtues of the man, the many honors of his race, recur to her thoughts; his looks and words dwell fixed in her soul; [5] nor does care grant peaceful sleep to her limbs. Returning Aurora now illumined the earth with the lamp of Phoebus and had chased away the dewy shadow from the sky,

3. THE MANY VIRTUES OF THE MAN...TO HER THOUGHTS he admirably makes Dido represent herself as [caught] between royal modesty and the impulse of love. She pretends to admire the virtue of him by whose beauty she is moved. Also, Virgil said "many virtues" figuratively, applying an adjective normally used to express "how much" to something better expressed by "how great."

RECUR He has used this frequentative verb admirably in the repeated thoughts of a lover.

4. OF HIS RACE not of Aeneas, so that it would be almost a justification, but of Dardanus (the son of a god) or of Venus.

HIS LOOKS AND WORDS DWELL FIXED IN HER SOUL this is like, "absent sees and hears the absent one." [83]

5. NOR DOES CARE GRANT PEACEFUL SLEEP TO HER LIMBS either she was entirely without sleep, so that "peaceful" modifies sleep, or she did indeed have sleep, but it was not peaceful, i.e., it was disturbed by dreams, thus her own comment shortly after, "what dreams terrify and distract my mind."[9]

6. RETURNING AURORA NOW ILLUMINED THE EARTH WITH THE LAMP OF PHOEBUS a circumlocution for daybreak (Aeneas had recited the second and third books over the course of the night), although, as we said above [on 1.223], Virgil often does not concern himself with what must happen according to nature.

ILLUMINED either "illumined" or really "purified," i.e. "cleansed," since night in a certain way pollutes the world.

7. DEWY SHADOW because all of the night is moist, as, "at night the softening moisture is always there." [*G* 1.290] Also, there is no difference whether he says "shadow" or "night," since night is the shadow of the earth, as earlier, "wrapping both earth and sky in its huge shadow." [2.251] There is also hysteron-proteron in the sense here, since Aurora [Dawn] precedes the sun.

cum sic unanimem adloquitur male sana sororem:
'Anna soror, quae me suspensam insomnia terrent!
quis nouus hic nostris successit sedibus hospes,
quem sese ore ferens, quam forti pectore et armis!

8. CVM SIC VNANIMEM de re pudenda locuturam parum fuerat sororem eligere nisi etiam unanimem. dicimus autem et 'unanimus' et 'unanimis,' sicut 'inermus' et 'inermis.'

MALE SANA non plene sana, amore uitiata; 'male' enim plerumque 'non,' plerumque 'minus' significat, sicut 'ue,' ut 'uecors,' 'uesanus.' quamquam 'male' et 'perniciose' significat, ut Lucanus *sic male deseruit.* [*BC* 9.310]

9. INSOMNIA TERRENT et 'terret' et 'terrent' legitur. sed si 'terret' legerimus, 'insomnia' erit uigilia; hoc enim maiores inter uigilias et ea quae uidemus in somnis interesse uoluerunt, ut 'insomnia' generis feminini numeri singularis uigiliam significaret, 'insomnia' uero generis neutri numeri pluralis ea quae per somnum uidemus, ut *sed falsa ad caelum mittunt insomnia manes.* [6.896] sciendum igitur quia, si 'terret' dixerimus, antiqua erit elocutio; 'insomnia' enim, licet et Pacuuius et Ennius frequenter dixerit, Plinius tamen exclusit et de usu remouit. sed ambiguitatem lectionis haec res fecit, quod non ex aperto uigilasse se dixit, sed habuisse quietem inplacidam, id est somniis interruptam, ut intellegamus eam et insomniis territam et propter terrorem somniorum uigilias quoque perpessam.

10. NOVVS magnus, ut *Pollio et ipse facit noua carmina.* [*E* 3.86]

SUCCESSIT SEDIBVS ut *succedoque oneri* [2.723] et *succedunt tecto.* [2.478]

11. QVEM SESE ORE FERENS ut *obstipuit primo aspectu Sidonia Dido,* [1.613] et *namque ipsa decoram caesariem nato genetrix lumenque iuuentae.* [1.589]

FORTI PECTORE ET ARMIS ut etiam ab Ilioneo audierat dicente *nec bello maior et armis.* [1.545] sane subaudis 'est.' et bene uirtutis commemoratione excusat supra dictam pulchritudinis laudem.

when she, hardly sound, thus addresses her sympathizing sister: "Sister Anna, what dreams terrify and distract my mind! [10] What think you of this wondrous guest who has come to our abodes? How noble in appearance! In fortitude and warlike deeds how great!

8. WHEN SHE...THUS ADDRESSES HER SYMPATHIZING SISTER it would not be sufficient for her, about to discuss a shameful matter, to choose a sister unless she were also sympathizing. We say, however, both *unanimus* and *unanimis*, just like *inermus* and *inermis*.

HARDLY SOUND not completely sound, debilitated by love. Sometimes *male* means "not," sometimes it means "less," just as the prefix *ve-* as in *vecors* (senseless), *vesanus* (insane), although *male* also means "ruinously," as Lucan's, "thus ruinously he left." [*BC* 9.310]

9. DREAMS TERRIFY both [singular] *terret* and [plural] *terrent* are found in manuscripts. But if we read *terret*, then *insomnia* [must be singular, which] would mean "wakefulness." Our ancestors wanted to make a distinction between periods of wakefulness and the things that we see in our sleep, so that *insomnia* as a feminine singular noun would mean, "wakefulness," but as a neuter plural noun *insomnia* would refer to the things we see in our sleep, as, "but the shades send false dreams to the heavens."[6.896] Therefore it must be understood that if we say *terret* here it will be an archaic way of speaking, since, although both Pacuvius and Ennius often employed *insomnia* [as a singular], Pliny excluded it and forbade its usage. But this situation has created an ambiguity in the reading because she did not say clearly that she had been awake, rather that she had unpeaceful rest, i.e., rest interrupted by dreams, so that we may understand that she was both terrified by her dreams, and, due to the terror of her dreams, endured wakefulness as well.

10. WONDROUS great, as, "and Pollio too makes wondrous songs." [*E* 3.86]

HAS COME TO OUR ABODES as, "and I come to the burden" [2.723] and "they come to the house." [2.478]

11. HOW NOBLE IN APPEARANCE as, "Sidonian Dido was stunned at first sight," [1.613] and "for his mother herself [had shed] handsome locks on her son and the brightness of youth." [1.589]

IN FORTITUDE AND WARLIKE DEEDS as, she had also heard from Ilioneus who said, "nor [anyone] greater in war and arms." [1.545] Of course you must supply "he is." Also, in mentioning his fortitude, she cleverly justifies her earlier praise of his physical beauty.

credo equidem, nec uana fides, genus esse deorum.
degeneres animos timor arguit: heu, quibus ille
iactatus fatis! quae bella exhausta canebat!
si mihi non animo fixum immotumque sederet,
ne cui me uinclo uellem sociare iugali,
postquam primus amor deceptam morte fefellit;
si non pertaesum thalami taedaeque fuisset,
huic uni forsan potui succumbere culpae.
Anna, fatebor enim, miseri post fata Sychaei

12. CREDO EQVIDEM genus deorum esse, nec enim *uana fides* est, id est 'falsa,' nam *degeneres animos timor arguit,* [13] id est 'probat,' 'inpugnat.'

13. HEV per haec amoris impulsus ostenditur.

14. QVIBVS IACTATVS FATIS ut *quis te, nate dea, per tanta pericula casus.* [1.615]

BELLA EXHAVSTA CANEBAT finita, terminata, quod nimiae uirtutis est; nam inchoare bella quorumlibet est, uincere uel finire paucorum.

15. FIXVM IMMOTVMQVE SEDERET cogi se optat quae sic negat.

SEDERET placeret, ut *et sedet hoc animo.* [2.660]

16. VINCLO IVGALI synaeresis est pro 'uinculo.' 'iugali' autem propter iugum quod imponebatur matrimonio coniungendis; unde et 'Iuno iugalis' dicitur.

17. PRIMVS AMOR id est, maritus.

DECEPIT MORTE FEFELLIT figurate dixit 'morte sua deceptam me et fefellit.'

18. PERTAESVM THALAMI TAEDAEQUE FVISSET 'pertaesus' participium est sine uerbi origine et regit genetiuum, ut hoc loco; nam genetiuus singularis est.

19. HVIC VNI FORSAN POTVI SVCCVMBERE CVLPAE singula pronuntianda sunt; ingenti enim dicta sunt libra, quibus confessioni desiderii sui quandam inicit refrenationem.

CVLPAE propter antiquum ritum, quo repellebantur a sacerdotio bis nuptae.

20. FATEBOR ENIM bene uno sermone et culpam expressit et necessitatem; 'fateri' enim et coactorum est et culpabilium.

MISERI POST FATA SYCHAEI aut muliebriter dixit *miseri,* aut 'mortui,' secundum Ciceronem, qui in Tusculanis 'miseros' mortuos uocat; [*Tusc* 1.5.9] aut certe ob hoc *miseri,* cuius iam obliuiscitur; aut sic occisi.

Indeed I believe (nor is my faith groundless) that he is the offspring of the gods. Fear betrays an ignoble mind. Ah! by what fates has he been tossed! What toils of war he sang, endured to the last! Had I not been fixed and steadfast in my resolution never to join myself to any in conjugal bond since my first love by death mocked and cheated me; had I not been weary of the bridal bed and torch, to this one fault I might perhaps give way. Anna, (for I will admit it) after the fate of poor Sychaeus

12. INDEED I BELIEVE [She believes that] he is the offspring of the gods, nor is her "faith groundless," i.e. false, since, "fear betrays an ignoble mind," [13] i.e. "tests," or "assails."

13. AH! the impact of love is shown in these words.

14. BY WHAT FATES HAS HE BEEN TOSSED as, "what fates, goddess born, [drive] you through such great perils." [1.615]

WHAT TOILS OF WAR HE SANG, ENDURED TO THE LAST finished, ended, which [requires] great valor, since anyone can start wars, but few can win or finish them.

15. HAD I NOT BEEN FIXED AND STEADFAST IN MY RESOLUTION she who makes such a denial longs to be compelled.

FIXED pleased, as, "and this is fixed in mind." [2.660]

16. IN CONJUGAL BOND *vinclo* is synaeresis for *vinculo* (bond). And *iugali* (of the yoke) is taken from the *iugum* (yoke) that used to be placed on those about to be joined in matrimony. This is also why she is called *Juno iugalis* (Juno of the yoke).

17. FIRST LOVE i.e. her husband.

BY DEATH MOCKED AND CHEATED ME she said figuratively, "by his death he mocked and cheated me."

18. HAD I NOT BEEN WEARY OF THE BRIDAL BED AND TORCH "weary" is the participle of an impersonal verb and governs the genitive, as in this passage, since this is a genitive singular.

19. TO THIS ONE FAULT I MIGHT PERHAPS GIVE WAY these words must be pronounced one at a time, as they were said with weighty measure, through which she applies a certain restraint to the confession of her desire.

FAULT on account of an ancient rite by which women who married again were barred from being priestesses.

20. FOR I WILL ADMIT IT she expressed both guilt and necessity admirably in this single utterance; "to admit" is used both of those who compel and those who are guilty.

AFTER THE FATE OF POOR SYCHAEUS either she said "poor" in a womanly way or, "dead" as Cicero did in the *Tusculan Disputations* [1.5.9] calling the dead "poor ones"; or else she could have called him "poor" because she is now forgetting about him, or [because] he was thus "killed."

coniugis et sparsos fraterna caede Penatis,
solus hic inflexit sensus, animumque labantem
impulit: adgnosco ueteris uestigia flammae.
sed mihi uel tellus optem prius ima dehiscat,
uel pater omnipotens adigat me fulmine ad umbras,
pallentis umbras Herebo noctemque profundam,
ante, pudor, quam te uiolo aut tua iura resoluo.
ille meos, primus qui me sibi iunxit, amores
abstulit; ille habeat secum seruetque sepulchro.'
sic effata sinum lacrimis impleuit obortis.

21. SPARSOS FRATERNA CAEDE PENATES si Didonis, dispersos per fugam intellegimus; si fratris, pollutos cruore.

22. INFLEXIT quia supra ait *fixum inmotumque sederet.* [15] *inflexit* a rigido proposito deuiauit.

LABANTEM IMPVLIT impulit et labare fecit. non enim lababat qui antea immobilis fuerat. cauendum sane ne ‘abentem’ contra metrum legamus; nam ‘la’ longa est, ut *labere, nympha, polo.* [11.588]

23. VETERIS VESTIGIA FLAMMAE bene inhonestam rem sub honesta specie confitetur, dicens se agnoscere maritalis coniugii ardorem.

24. SED MIHI VEL TELLVS OPTEM PRIVS IMA DEHISCAT callide, ac si diceret posse se coniungi Aeneae, si mors secuta non fuerit.

26. PALLENTES VMBRAS HEREBO in Erebo. alii ‘Erebi’ legunt.

27. AT TVA IVRA RESOLVO propter *uinclo iugali.* [16]

28. AMORES ABSTVLIT cum illo consumpta sunt desideria et uoluptates.

30. SINVM LACRIMIS IMPLEVIT OBORTIS sinus dicimus orbes oculorum, id est palpebras, quae a palpitatione dictae sunt; nam semper mouentur. *impleuit* autem ideo, quia lacrimae plerumque se intra oculos tenent. et bene praemisit excusationem his *lacrimis* commemoratione prioris mariti.

and since the household gods were stained with his blood shed by a brother, this [man] alone has swayed my inclinations and overthrown my wavering mind: I recognize the traces of my former flame. But I would rather the earth gape open for me to its depths, or the almighty father hurl me with his thunderbolt to the shades, the pale shades in Herebus and deep night, than I violate you, modesty, or break your laws. He who first linked me to himself has borne away my love; may he possess it still and retain it in his grave." This said, she filled the rounds of her eyes with welling tears.

21. HOUSEHOLD GODS WERE STAINED WITH HIS BLOOD SHED BY A BROTHER if this refers to the household gods of Dido, we understand that they were scattered by flight; if it refers to those of her brother, then they were defiled by his blood.

22. HE HAS SWAYED because above she says, "had I not been fixed and steadfast in my resolution." [15] "He has swayed"; she has deviated from her inflexible purpose.

HE HAS OVERTHROWN MY WAVERING [HEART] he has stirred her and made her waver. A person who had been immovable before was not tottering. Of course we must be on guard not to read *labentem* (gliding). This would be contrary to the meter since the *la* in *labentem* is long, as, "glide, o nymph, from heaven." [11.588]

23. TRACES OF MY FORMER FLAME she cleverly discloses an ignoble thing under a noble guise, saying that she recognizes the ardor of marital union.

24. BUT I WOULD RATHER THE EARTH GAPE OPEN FOR ME TO ITS DEPTHS, cleverly put, as if she were to say she would be able to marry Aeneas, if death were not to follow.

26. PALE SHADES IN HEREBUS in Erebus; others read "of Erebus."

27. OR BREAK YOUR LAWS because of her "conjugal bonds." [16]

28. HE HAS BORNE AWAY MY LOVE her desires and pleasures were consumed with him.

30. SHE FILLED THE ROUNDS OF HER EYES WITH WELLING TEARS we call the covering of the eyes the rounds of the eyes, i.e. the eyelids (*palpebras*), which were so called from their blinking (*palpitatione*) because they are always in movement. Although, "she filled" because tears very often hold themselves back inside the eyes. Also, she cleverly gave prior justification for these tears by mentioning her previous husband.

Anna refert: 'o luce magis dilecta sorori,
solane perpetua maerens carpere iuuenta,
nec dulcis natos, Veneris nec praemia noris?
id cinerem aut Manis credis curare sepultos?
esto: aegram nulli quondam flexere mariti,
non Libyae, non ante Tyro; despectus Iarbas

31. ANNA REFERT suasoria est omni parte plena; nam et purgat obiecta, et ostendit utilitatem, et a timore persuadet.

O LVCE MAGIS DILECTA id est 'dilectior'; nam antiqui frequenter pro comparatiuo iungebant particulam 'magis.' tale et illud est *nate, mihi uita quondam, dum uita manebat, care magis.* [5.724]

32. SOLANE *solane maerens* in omni carperis *iuuenta*?

33. NEC DVLCIS NATOS propter liberos, quae fuit causa secundi matrimonii, ut Iuuenalis *sed placet Vrsidio lex Iulia, tollere dulcem cogitat heredem.* [*Sat* 6.38] alii male iungunt *natos* Veneris, Cupidinem et Aenean.

VENERIS NEC PRAEMIA uoluptates; Homerus, τά τε δῶρ' Ἀφροδίτης. [*Il* 3.54]

34. ID CINEREM AVT MANES CREDIS CVRARE SEPVLTOS propter illud, quia marito iurauerat, ut *non seruata fides cineri promissa Sychaeo.* [552] et bene extenuat dicendo non animam, sed cineres et manes sepultos. dicit autem secundum Epicureos, qui animam cum corpore dicunt perire.

35. ESTO aduerbium concedentis est Graecum.

FLEXERE MARITI non qui erant, sed qui esse cupiebant. alii intellegunt *aegram mariti,* ut sit genetiuus singularis.

36. NON ANTE TYRO aut 'in Tyro,' ac si diceret 'Tyri,' aut certe Τυρόθεν, id est 'de Tyro,' ut *Dardanus Hesperia.* [3.503]

DESPECTVS IARBAS rex Libyae, qui Didonem re uera uoluit ducere et, ut habet historia, cum haec negaret, Carthagini intulit bellum; cuius timore cum cogeretur a ciuibus, petiit ut ante placeret manes mariti, et exaedificata pyra se in ignem praecipitauit. ob quam rem 'Dido' id est 'uirago,' appellata est; nam 'Elissa' proprie dicta est.

Anna replies: "O more dear to your sister than the light, will you thus in solitude waste away through all your youth, nor know the dear delights of offspring nor rewards of Venus? Think you that the ashes and the buried dead care for that? [35]What though no husbands moved you before, when your sorrows were green, neither Libya nor before Tyre? What though Iarbas was scorned,

31. ANNA REPLIES her *suasoria* is complete in every way, for it clears away the charges, offers a purpose, and also dissuades from fear.

O MORE DEAR TO YOUR SISTER THAN LIGHT i.e. "dearer," since the old writers often added "more" instead of using the comparative, such as, "child, more dear to me than life, when I was alive." [5.724]

32. IN SOLITUDE will you, weeping and lonely, waste away throughout your entire youth?

33. NOR KNOW THE DEAR DELIGHTS OF OFFSPRING for children, which was the reason for a second marriage, as Juvenal wrote, "but Ursidius likes the Julian law, he plans to raise a sweet heir." [*Sat* 6.38] Others mistakenly take *natos Veneris* (the children of Venus) together, Cupid and Aeneas.

NOR THE REWARDS OF VENUS pleasures; in Homer, "the gifts of Aphrodite." [*Il* 3.54]

34. THINK YOU THAT ASHES AND THE BURIED DEAD CARE FOR THAT? because of what she had sworn to her husband, as, "I have not kept the pledge I had promised to the ashes of Sychaeus." [552] Also, she minimizes this admirably by saying not "soul," but "ashes" and "buried dead." However, she speaks in accordance with the Epicureans, who maintain that the soul perishes with the body.

35. THOUGH this concessive adverb is Greek.

HUSBANDS MOVED YOU not those who were husbands, but those who wanted to be. Others understand it as, "sad for her husband," so that *mariti* is genitive singular.

36. NOR BEFORE TYRE either "in Tyre," as if she said "at Tyre," or else "from Tyre," as, "Dardanus from Hesperia." [3.503]

IARBAS WAS SCORNED the king of Libya who truly wanted to marry Dido and, so the story goes, when she refused, waged war against Carthage; when out of fear of him she was forced by the citizens, she sought to appease the shades of her husband, and, after a pyre had been built, hurled herself into the fire. On account of this she was called Dido, i.e. "heroic woman"; for she was properly called Elissa.

ductoresque alii, quos Africa terra triumphis
diues alit: placitone etiam pugnabis amori?
nec uenit in mentem, quorum consederis aruis?
hinc Gaetulae urbes, genus insuperabile bello,
et Numidae infreni cingunt et inhospita Syrtis;
hinc deserta siti regio, lateque furentes

37. DVCTORESQVE ALII ergo et Iarbas ductor.

QVOS AFRICA TERRA deriuationes frequenter maiores sunt a principalitate, interdum pares inueniuntur, raro minores; unde supra, *Lacaena* [2.601] notandum diximus.

TRIVMPHIS DIVES id est 'bellicosa.'

38. PLACITONE ETIAM PVGNABIS AMORI ac si diceretur 'contempsisti eos qui displicebant; num quid etiam placito amori repugnabis?' et est Graecum 'pugno tibi'; nam nos 'pugno tecum' dicimus.

40. HINC GAETVLAE VRBES ad terrorem 'urbes' posuit; nam in mapalibus habitant.

41. INFRENI aut 'saeui,' aut quia equis sine freno utuntur.

INHOSPITA barbara, aspera.

42. DESERTA SITI inhabitabilis. dicit autem Xerolibyen, quae est inter Tripolin et Pentapolin. et bene terret dicens iuxta esse aut bellicosas gentes aut deserta loca, unde non speratur auxilium.

LATEQVE FVRENTES BARCEI hi prope sunt a Carthagine; unde addidit *late furentes.* hi secundum Titianum in *Chorographia* Phoenicen nauali quondam superauere certamine. Barce autem ciuitas est Pentapoleos, quae hodie Ptolemais dicitur; nam Cyrene et Barce reginae fuerunt quae singulis dederunt ciuitatibus nomina.

as well as other princes whom Africa, a land rich in triumphs, maintains? Will you also fight against pleasing love? Will you not reflect in whose country you now reside? [40] On this side the Gaetulian cities (a race invincible in war), unbridled Numidians, and inhospitable quicksands enclose you round; on that side a region by thirst turned into a desert and the wide-ranging

37. OTHER PRINCES thus Iarbas was also a prince.

WHOM AFRICA, A LAND words derived from other words are frequently longer than the words from which they are derived, sometimes of equal length, rarely shorter. This is why we said above [on 2.601] that "Laconian" was noteworthy.

RICH IN TRIUMPHS i.e. "warlike."

38. WILL YOU ALSO FIGHT AGAINST PLEASING LOVE? as if she said, "you disdained those who were displeasing, will you also repel pleasing love?" This construction using the dative is Greek, "I fight against you"; in Latin we say "I fight with you" (using the ablative with a proposition).

40. ON THIS SIDE THE GAETULIAN CITIES she used the word "cities" to instill fear since they live in huts.

41. UNBRIDLED either [because they are] savage or because they use horses without bridles.

INHOSPITABLE barbarous, harsh.

42. BY THIRST TURNED INTO A DESERT uninhabitable. She means Xerolibya, which is between Tripolis and Pentapolis. She also quite cleverly inspires fear when she says they are next to warlike peoples or empty places from which there is no hope of help.

AND THE WIDE-RANGING BARCAEANS these people are close to Carthage, thus she added "wide-ranging." According to Titianus in his *Geography* they once conquered Phoenicia in a naval engagement. Barce is also a city of Pentapolis, which is called Ptolomais today; Cyrene and Barce were the queens who gave their names to these individual cities.

Barcaei. quid bella Tyro surgentia dicam,
germanique minas?
dis equidem auspicibus reor et Iunone secunda
hunc cursum Iliacas uento tenuisse carinas.
quam tu urbem, soror, hanc cernes, quae surgere regna
coniugio tali! Teucrum comitantibus armis
Punica se quantis attollet gloria rebus!
tu modo posce deos ueniam, sacrisque litatis
indulge hospitio, causasque innecte morandi,
dum pelago desaeuit hiems et aquosus Orion,
quassataeque rates, dum non tractabile caelum.'
His dictis incensum animum inflammauit amore,
spemque dedit dubiae menti, soluitque pudorem.

44. GERMANIQVE MINAS propter aurum quod ei, ut in primo diximus, tulerat. [1.363]

45. DIS EQVIDEM AVSPICIBVS hoc dicit: 'dii, qui sunt auspices matrimonii, Aenean huc uenire fecerunt'; nuptiae enim captatis fiebant auguriis, ut *contentique auspice Bruto.* [Lucan *BC* 2.371]

IVNONE SECVNDA quae praeest coniugiis.

46. TENVISSE perfecisse, inplesse.

48. CONIVGIO TALI id est, uiri fortis; quod ideo non dicit, quia scit a Didone praedictum.

50. VENIAM aut 'beneficium,' aut re uera 'ueniam,' periurii scilicet, ut *non seruata fides cineri promissa Sychaeo.* [552]

SACRISQVE LITATIS 'diis litatis' debuit dicere; non enim sacra, sed deos sacris litamus, id est placamus; ergo noue dixit.

51. INDVLGE da operam, ut *indulgent uino et uertunt crateras aenos.* [9.165]

52. ORION corripuit ratione supra dicta. [ad 1.535]

53. NON TRACTABILE asperum, intractabile.

54. INCENSVM INFLAMMAVIT ut Horatius *oleum adde camino.* [*Serm* 2.3.321]

55. SOLVITQVE PVDOREM propter uincula castitatis.

Barcaeans. Why should I mention the kindling wars from Tyre and your brother's threats? [45] It was surely, I think, under the auspices of the gods and by the favor of Juno that the Trojan ships held their course to this our coast. O sister, how flourishing shall you see this city, how potent your kingdom rise from such a match! By what high exploits shall the Carthaginian glory be advanced when the Trojan's arms join them! [50] Do you but supplicate the mercy of the gods, and, after the sacrifices are appeased, indulge in hospitality and devise one pretence after another for detaining [your guest], while winter's fury rages on the sea and Orion is charged with rain; while his ships are shattered and the sky is not clement."

With these words she inflamed the fire of love burning in Dido's breast, [55] buoyed up her wavering mind with hope, and broke down modesty.

44. AND YOUR BROTHER'S THREATS because of the gold she had taken from him as we noted in the first book. [1.363]

45. SURELY…UNDER THE AUSPICES OF THE GODS she means this: the gods, who are the auspices of marriage, have made Aeneas come here. Weddings used to take place after the auguries were taken, as, "and they being satisfied with Brutus as taker of auspices." [Lucan, *BC* 2.371]

BY THE FAVOR OF JUNO she is patron of marriages.

46. HELD completed, discharged.

48. FROM SUCH A MATCH i.e. to a brave man. She does not say it because she knows it had been said before by Dido.

50. MERCY she means either "favor" or indeed "forgiveness"—for perjury, of course—as "the pledges vowed to the ashes of Sychaeus have not been kept." [552]

AND AFTER THE SACRIFICES ARE APPEASED she should have said "after the gods are appeased" since we do not appease sacrifices but appease the gods with sacrifices, i.e. we please them; therefore she spoke unusually.

51. INDULGE attend to, as, "they attend to the wine and tip the bronze bowls." [9.163]

52. ORION [the first syllable is] shortened for the reason given above. [on 1.535]

53. NOT CLEMENT harsh, inclement.

54. SHE INFLAMED THE FIRE OF LOVE BURNING as Horace says, "add oil to the furnace." [*Serm* 2.3.321]

55. AND BROKE DOWN MODESTY on account of her bonds of chastity.

principio delubra adeunt, pacemque per aras
exquirunt; mactant lectas de more bidentis
legiferae Cereri Phoeboque patrique Lyaeo,

56. DELVBRA ADEVNT 'delubrum' dictum, ut supra diximus, [ad 2.225] propter lacum in quo manus abluuntur, uel propter tectum coniunctum, quia una opera abluitur; aut certe ligneum simulacrum 'delubrum' dicimus a 'libro,' hoc est, raso ligno factum, quod Graece ξόανον dicitur.

PACEMQVE beneuolentiam.

PER ARAS EXQVIRVNT id est, sacrificando explorant an dii uellent huic rei consentire. dicendo autem *per aras,* aruspicalem artem ostendit, ut *spirantia consulit exta.* [64]

57. MACTANT uerbum sacrorum, κατ' εὐφημισμόν dictum, ut 'adolere'; 'mactare' proprie est 'magis augere.'

LECTAS BIDENTES non uacat 'lectas'; moris enim fuerat ut ad sacrificia eligerentur oues quibus nihil deesset, ut in sexto *nunc grege de intacto septem mactare iuuencos.* [6.38] 'bidentes' autem dictae sunt quasi biennes, quia neque minores neque maiores licebat hostias dare. sunt etiam in ouibus duo eminentiores dentes inter octo, qui non nisi circa bimatum apparent; nec in omnibus, sed in his quae sunt aptae sacrificiis inueniuntur.

58. LEGIFERAE CERERI leges enim ipsa dicitur inuenisse, nam et sacra ipsius 'thesmophoria uocantur.' sed hoc ideo fingitur quia, ante inuentum frumentum a Cerere, passim homines sine lege uagabantur; quae feritas interrupta est inuento usu frumentorum, postquam ex agrorum diuisione nata sunt iura.

PHOEBOQVE qui praeest auspiciis, quibus urbes reguntur.

PATRIQVE LYAEO qui, ut supra diximus [ad 3.20], apte urbibus libertatis est deus; unde etiam Marsyas, eius minister, est in ciuitatibus libertatis indicium. et communis hoc habet sensus: sacrificabat, inquit, primo numinibus quae urbi praesunt, quasi nuptura pro utilitate rei publicae, deinde Iunoni, cui curae sunt nuptiae. est etiam sensus altior; nam facturi aliquid ante aduersos placamus deos, et sic propitios inuocamus, ut *nigram Hiemi pecudem, Zephyris felicibus albam.* [3.120] ergo modo nuptura placat ante Cererem, quae propter raptum filiae nuptias exsecratur; Apollinem, qui expers uxoris est; Liberum, qui nisi raptam coniugem habere non potuit. et sic Iunonem conciliat.

First they go to the shrines and peace at the altars they implore: to Ceres the lawgiver, to Phoebus, and to father Lyaeus they offer selected two-toothers according to custom;

56. THEY GO TO THE SHRINES *delubrum* (shrine) is said [either], as mentioned above [on 2.225], on account of the pool in which the hands are washed, or on account of the adjoining building because it is washed at the same time; or else the wooden statue we call a *delubrum* from *liber* (rind), that is, made from wood stripped of bark, which is called *zoanon* in Greek.

PEACE good-will.

AT THE ALTARS THEY IMPLORE i.e. through sacrifice they search out whether the gods are willing to consent to this affair. Moreover, by saying "at every altar" he alludes to the art of haruspicy as in, "she consults the panting entrails." [64]

57. THEY OFFER a word of sacrificial language spoken auspiciously, like "to burn"; strictly speaking, *mactare* means "to make greater."

SELECTED TWO-TOOTHERS "selected" is not superfluous, for it had been the custom that sheep chosen for sacrifice be without defect, as in the sixth book, "now to slaughter seven bulls from the unbroken herd." [6.38] They were called *bidentes* (two-toothers) as though they were *biennes* (two-year-olds), since it was forbidden to offer victims that were younger or older. Also, two of the eight teeth of sheep are more prominent when the sheep is about two years old, and they are not to be found on all sheep, but only on those suitable for sacrifice.

58. TO CERES THE LAWGIVER she herself is said to have invented laws and her sacred rites are called *thesmophoria*. But this is supposed to have happened because, before grain was invented by Ceres, men wandered far and wide without laws; this savagery was broken off when the cultivation of grain was acquired, and after that laws arose from the division of fields.

TO PHOEBUS who is the patron of auspices, by which cities are ruled.

AND TO FATHER LYAEUS who, as noted earlier [3.20], is suitably the god of freedom for cities, so also [statues of] Marsyas, his attendant, are placed in cities as a sign of freedom. And this is the common meaning: he says Dido sacrificed first to the spirits who protected the city, as though she were to wed for the good of the state; then to Juno, for whom marriage is a concern. There is also a deeper meaning, for we placate in advance the gods who would find objectionable anything we intend to do and invoke ones who are well-disposed in this same manner, as, "[he sacrificed] a black sheep to Storm and a white one to the favorable Zephyrs." [3.120] Therefore, since she is about to marry, she appeases in advance Ceres, who curses marriages on account of the kidnapping of her daughter; Apollo, who has no wife; Liber, who could have no spouse without kidnapping her. And in the same way she conciliates Juno.

Iunoni ante omnis, cui uincla iugalia curae.
ipsa, tenens dextra pateram, pulcherrima Dido
candentis uaccae media inter cornua fundit,
aut ante ora deum pinguis spatiatur ad aras,
instauratque diem donis, pecudumque reclusis
pectoribus inhians spirantia consulit exta.
heu, uatum ignarae mentes! quid uota furentem,
quid delubra iuuant? est mollis flamma medullas

59. CVI VINCLA IVGALIA CVRAE quia est Curitis, est matrona, est regina.

61. CANDENTIS candidae; participium est pro nomine.

MEDIA INTER CORNVA non est sacrificium, sed hostiae exploratio, utrum apta sit.

62. ANTE ORA DEVM ante simulacra.

SPATIATVR AD ARAS matronae enim sacrificaturae circa aras faculas tenentes ferebantur cum quodam gestu; unde Sallustius *saltare elegantius quam necesse est probae.* [*Cat* 25.2]

63. INSTAVRATQVE DIEM DONIS muneribus, quae aut diis offerebat aut donabat Tyriis uel Troianis. *instaurat* autem ideo, quia iam supra sacrificauerat, ut *simul Aenean in regia ducit / tecta, simul diuum templis indicit honorem.* [1.631-2]

64. INHIANS intenta per sollicitudinem.

SPIRANTIA palpitantia, quasi adhuc uiua.

65. HEV VATUM IGNARAE MENTES non sacerdotes uituperat quasi nescios futurorum, sed uim amantis exprimit, et inde uituperat sacerdotes qui admonuerunt non credituram; nam omnia futura a sacerdotibus praedicta esse sequens indicat locus, ut *multaque praeterea uatum praedicta priorum.* [464]

66. EST uerbum est indeclinabile; nam frequenter deficit. est autem huius positio 'edo es est.' inuenimus, sed quod abolitum est, 'edo edis edit,' unde est 'edere' et 'comedere,' quod hodie non dicimus; nam ab eo quod est 'es,' 'esse' et 'comesse' facit, quo tempore etiam pro praesenti utimur, ut 'uolo esse'; nam in defectiuis tempora pro temporibus ponimus, ut 'odi noui memini' 'odisse nosse meminisse' etiam pro praesenti ponuntur.

above all to Juno, whose province is the nuptial tie. [60] Dido herself, in all her beauty, holding in her right hand the cup, pours it between the horns of a white-gleaming heifer; or before the faces of the gods in solemn pomp walks around the rich-loaded altars, renews the offerings all the day long and, gaping over the disclosed breasts of the victims, consults their panting entrails. [65] Alas! how ignorant the minds of seers! What can prayers, what can temples, avail a raging lover? The gentle flame all the while eats at her vitals

59. WHOSE PROVINCE IS THE NUPTIAL TIE because she is Curitis and she is The Matron and she is The Queen.

61. WHITE-GLEAMING white; a participle in place of an adjective.

POURS BETWEEN THE HORNS not the sacrifice, but an examination to see whether the sacrificial victim is suitable.

62. BEFORE THE FACES OF THE GODS in front of the statues.

AROUND…THE ALTARS WALKS married women who were about to make sacrifices used to go with a certain posture around the altars holding small torches. Because of this Sallust wrote, "to dance more elegantly than is necessary for an virtuous woman." [*Cat* 25.2]

63. RENEWS THE OFFERINGS ALL THE DAY LONG with gifts that she either offered to the gods or gave to the Tyrians or Trojans. He says "renews" because she had already sacrificed earlier, as, "At once she leads Aeneas into the royal house and calls for an honorary rite in the gods' temples." [1.631]

64. GAPING attentive in her anxiety.

PANTING throbbing, as though still alive.

65. ALAS! HOW IGNORANT THE MINDS OF SEERS! he does not fault priests as though they were ignorant of the future, but expresses the power of a lover, and then he faults the priests who have warned her when she would not believe them. A passage that follows shows that everything that will happen was predicted by the priests, "and many additional things predicted by the earlier seers." [464]

66. EATS AT the verb cannot be [completely] conjugated since it is often defective. It has the forms *edo, es, est* and we find the obsolete forms *edi, edis, edit*, which give the infinitives *edere* and *comedere*, which we do not use today since we use [the infinitives] *esse* and *comesse*, which come from *es*. We also use this tense with a present meaning, as *volo esse*, since the tenses of defective verbs are used in place of other tenses, such as, *odi, novi, memini* and *odisse, nosse, meminisse*, also used for the present tense.

interea, et tacitum uiuit sub pectore uulnus.
uritur infelix Dido, totaque uagatur
urbe furens, qualis coniecta cerua sagitta,
quam procul incautam nemora inter Cresia fixit
pastor agens telis, liquitque uolatile ferrum
nescius; illa fuga siluas saltusque peragrat
Dictaeos; haeret lateri letalis arundo.
nunc media Aenean secum per moenia ducit,
Sidoniasque ostentat opes urbemque paratam;

69. VRBE FVRENS furor enim est amor, in quo nihil est stabile; unde et Cupido puer inducitur quasi instabilis et infans, qui non potest fari; unde paulo post, *incipit effari mediaque in uoce restitit.* [76]

QVALIS CONIECTA CERVA SAGITTA satis congrua conparatio.

70. CRESIA Cretensia; nam Graece Κρής facit, unde et Κρῆτες et Κρήσια facit. Latine 'Cretensis' facit, unde est 'Cretensia.'

71. AGENS TELIS urgens, persequens.

72. NESCIVS ignoratus, latens; non 'qui ceruam nesciret.' et rara sunt uerba quae per contrarium significant; nam 'uector' cum sit proprie qui uehit, inuenimus etiam eum uectorem dici qui uehitur, ut Lucanus *uectoris patiens tumidum supernatat amnem.* [*BC* 4.133] tale est et 'formidolosus'; cum sit 'timidus,' et 'timendum' significat. cum enim exigat ratio ut nomina uerbalia agentis habeant significationem, pro passiua significatione plerumque ponuntur.

FVGA cursu, ut *simul arua fuga, simul aequora uerrit;* [*G* 3.201] nam intellegere non possumus fugam, cum dicat 'peragrat'; peragrare enim est circumire inquirendo.

73. DICTAEOS Cretenses. ceruae uulneratae dictamnum quaerunt, ut in duodecimo legimus *non illa feris incognita capris gramina.* [12.414]

LETALIS HARVNDO propter futurum omen Didonis.

75. SIDONIAS Pygmalionis uel Sychaei.

VRBEMQVE PARATAM *paratam* ad illud pertinet quod Aeneas propter ciuitatem nauigat. sed alii mouent quaestionem quomodo *paratam,* cum paulo post inferat *pendent opera interrupta.* [88] sed *paratum* potest dici cui etiam paululum superest; unde est *minaeque murorum ingentes.* [88]

and the secret wound rankles in her breast. Unhappy Dido burns and frantic is raging through the city. Like a doe wounded by an arrow, [70] whom, off her guard, a shepherd pursuing with his darts has pierced at a distance among the Cretan woods and [in whom] unknowingly left the winged steel, she, flying, bounds over the Dictaean woods and glades; the fatal shaft sticks in her side. Now she conducts Aeneas through the midst of her fortifications; [75] shows him the Sidonian treasures and the prepared city:

69. IS RAGING THROUGH THE CITY the rage, of course, is love, in which nothing is stable. Also, because of this, Cupid is represented as a child, as though he were unable to stand up and, as an infant, unable to speak; thus shortly after, "she begins to talk and halts in mid-speech." [76]

LIKE A DOE WOUNDED BY AN ARROW the comparison is suitable enough.

70. CRETAN in Greek the word is *Kres*, from which come the words *Kretes* and *Kresia*. In Latin the word is *Cretensis* from which comes the form *Cretensia*.

71. PURSUING WITH HIS DARTS driving, following.

72. UNKNOWINGLY unknown, hiding; not "who would not know the doe." Words that take their meaning from the contrary are rare. The word *vector* (carrier), although it strictly refers to one who carries, we also find representing "one who is carried," as Lucan, "supporting his rider he swims across the swollen river." [*BC* 4.133] Another such word is *formidolosus* since it means both "fearful" and "to be feared." Although reason requires that adjectives derived from verbs refer to the person performing the action, at times they are used with a passive meaning.

FLYING in her course, as, "[wind] sweeping fields and seas at the same time in its flight" [*G* 3.201]; for we cannot take it to mean "escape" since he says "she roves." "To rove," means to go around searching.

73. DICTAEAN Cretan. Wounded does will seek out the herb dittany, as we read in the twelfth book, "those herbs not unknown to wild goats." [12.414]

FATAL SHAFT because it is a sign of things to come for Dido.

75. SIDONIAN belonging to Pygmalion, or Sychaeus.

AND THE PREPARED CITY "prepared" refers to the purpose for Aeneas" journey, namely, [to found] a city. But some pose the question of how the city could be "prepared" when shortly after he notes "the work hangs interrupted." [88] But a thing can be called "prepared" on which even a little more remains to be done, thus "and the huge threatening walls." [88]

incipit effari, mediaque in uoce resistit;
nunc eadem labente die conuiuia quaerit,
Iliacosque iterum demens audire labores
exposcit, pendetque iterum narrantis ab ore.
post, ubi digressi, lumenque obscura uicissim
luna premit suadentque cadentia sidera somnos,
sola domo maeret uacua, stratisque relictis
incubat, illum absens absentem auditque uidetque;
aut gremio Ascanium, genitoris imagine capta,
detinet, infandum si fallere possit amorem.
non coeptae adsurgunt turres, non arma iuuentus
exercet, portusue aut propugnacula bello
tuta parant; pendent opera interrupta, minaeque
murorum ingentes aequataque machina caelo.

76. INCIPIT EFFARI MEDIAQVE IN VOCE RESTITIT sic Horatius *cur facunda parum decoro inter uerba cadet lingua silentio?* [*Carm* 4.1.35]

77. LABENTE DIE quia in usu non erant prandia, ut Iuuenalis *exul ab octaua Marius bibit.* [*Sat* 1.49]

78. DEMENS quae ea quae nouerat audire cupiebat.

79. NARRANTIS AB ORE ut eum intueretur. et hoc loco per omnia amantis adfectus exprimitur.

80. OBSCVRA LVNA id est nox; nam nihil tam contrarium lunae est quam obscuritas.

82. SOLA sine eo quem amabat; nam regina sola esse non poterat. est autem Plauti, qui inducit inter multos amatorem positum dicentem quod solus sit. [cf. *Amph* 640]

MAERET si diphthongon habeat, ut hoc loco, 'tristis est' significat; aliter 'militat' ut *aere merent paruo.* sane 'mereor' aliud est.

83. ABSENS ABSENTEM Terentius *praesens praesentem eripi, abduci ab oculis.* [*Adel* 668]

84. IMAGINE CAPTA ob amati similitudinem.

88. MINAE eminentiae murorum, quas pinnas dicunt.

she begins to speak and stops in mid-word. When day declines, she longs to have the same banquets renewed; and, mad, begs again to hear the Trojan disasters and again hangs on the speaker's lips. [80] Now, when they had severally retired, while the dim moon in her alternate course withdraws her light and the setting stars invite sleep, she mourns alone in the deserted hall, presses the couch he had left, and absent sees and hears the absent one; or, captivated with the father's image, hugs Ascanius in her bosom, [85] if possibly she may divert her unutterable love. The towers begun cease to rise; her youth practice not their warlike exercises, nor prepare ports and bulwarks for war; the works and the huge battlements on the walls and the engines equaling the skies are discontinued.

76. SHE BEGINS TO SPEAK AND STOPS IN MID-WORD as Horace writes, "why is my eloquent tongue faltering between words in unseemly silence?" [*Carm* 4.1.35]

77. WHEN DAY DECLINES because a midday meal was not common, as Juvenal, "as an exile Marius starts drinking at the eighth hour." [*Sat* 1.49]

78. MAD she wanted to hear the things she already knew.

79. HANGS ON THE SPEAKER'S LIPS so she could gaze upon him. Also, in every detail of this passage the condition of one in love is expressed.

80. THE DIM MOON i.e. night, since nothing is as contrary to the moon as dimness.

82. ALONE without him whom she loved, since a queen could not be alone. But this is taken from a passage of Plautus in which a lover is portrayed and, although he is surrounded by many people, he says that he is alone. [cf. *Amph* 640]

SHE MOURNS if this word has a diphthong, (*maeret*) as it does in this passage, [it means] "she is sad"; otherwise it means "she performs military service" (*meret*). Of course *mereor* (to earn) is something else.

83. ABSENT...THE ABSENT ONE Terence, "in the presence the present one was snatched up, taken away from before his eyes." [*Adel* 668]

84. CAPTIVATED WITH THE IMAGE because of the likeness to her beloved.

88. BATTLEMENTS the prominences of the walls that they call pinnacles.

Quam simul ac tali persensit peste teneri
cara Iouis coniunx, nec famam obstare furori,
talibus adgreditur Venerem Saturnia dictis:
'egregiam uero laudem et spolia ampla refertis
tuque puerque tuus, magnum et memorabile nomen,
una dolo diuum si femina uicta duorum est.
nec me adeo fallit ueritam te moenia nostra
suspectas habuisse domos Carthaginis altae.
sed quis erit modus, aut quo nunc certamine tanto?
quin potius pacem aeternam pactosque hymenaeos
exercemus? habes tota quod mente petisti:
ardet amans Dido traxitque per ossa furorem.

90. PESTE amore, incendio, ut *et toto descendit corpore pestis.* [5.683]

91. NEC FAMAM honestam scilicet; sane τῶν μέσων est.

FVRORI iam non amori.

92. ADGREDITVR cum calliditate loquitur.

93. EGREGIAM VERO LAVDEM εἰρωνεία est, inter quam et confessionem sola interest pronuntiatio; et ironia est cum aliud uerba, aliud continet sensus.

94. PVER filius. Graece dixit παῖς.

95. DVORVM EST bene cessit masculino femininum.

96. ADEO multum, ut Terentius *adulescentem adeo nobilem.* [*Eun* 880]

VERITAM TE MOENIA NOSTRA propter illud *haud tanto cessabit cardine rerum.* [1.672]

MOENIA NOSTRA Iunonis hospitium.

98. MODVS finis; Iuuenalis *nullo quippe modo millesima pagina surgit.* [*Sat* 7.100]

AVT QVO NVNC CERTAMINE TANTO? quid opus est tanto certamine?

99. PACEM AETERNAM non indutias temporales.

100. HABES TOTA QVOD MENTE PETISTI propter illud *nostram nunc accipe mentem.* [1.676]

[90] When Jove's beloved wife perceived that Dido was thus possessed with the plague and nor could her reputation resist its rage, Saturnia thus artfully addresses Venus: "Distinguished praise, no doubt, and ample spoils, you and your boy carry off, high and signal renown, [95] if one woman is overcome by the wiles of two deities. Nor am I quite ignorant that you apprehend danger from our walls and view the structures of lofty Carthage with a jealous eye. But what will be the limit? Or what do we now propose by such hot contention? Why do not we rather promote an eternal peace, and nuptial contract? [100] You have your whole heart's desire: Dido burns with love, and has sucked the fury into her very bones.

90. WITH THE PLAGUE with love, with fire, as, "and [fire] like a plague eats down through the body [of the ship]." [5.683]

91. NOR...HER REPUTATION good reputation understood; of course "reputation" is ambiguous on its own.

ITS RAGE it is no longer love.

92. ADDRESSES he says this cunningly.

93. DISTINGUISHED PRAISE, NO DOUBT this is irony; the only difference between it and a sincere statement is in the pronunciation. Irony also occurs when the words say one thing and the meaning another.

94. BOY son; in Greek she said "child."

95. OF TWO DEITIES it is fitting for the feminine [gender] to yield to the masculine.

96. QUITE very, as Terence, "a young man, very much a nobleman." [*Eun* 880]

THAT YOU APPREHEND DANGER FROM OUR WALLS because of this, that, "at such a turning point of affairs she will not sit still." [1.672]

OUR WALLS the hospitality of Juno.

98. LIMIT end; Juvenal, "naturally the thousandth column arises with no limit in sight." [*Sat* 7.100]

NOW BY SUCH HOT CONTENTION? what need is there for such contention?

99. ETERNAL PEACE not a temporary truce.

100. YOU HAVE YOUR WHOLE HEART'S DESIRE because of this she said, "now hear my mind." [1.676]

communem hunc ergo populum paribusque regamus
auspiciis; liceat Phrygio seruire marito
dotalisque tuae Tyrios permittere dextrae.'
Olli (sensit enim simulata mente locutam,
quo regnum Italiae Libycas aduerteret oras)
sic contra est ingressa Venus: 'Quis talia demens
abnuat aut tecum malit contendere bello,
si modo, quod memoras, factum fortuna sequatur.
sed fatis incerta feror, si Iuppiter unam
esse uelit Tyriis urbem Troiaque profectis,

102. PARIBVSQVE REGAMVS AVSPICIIS aequali potestate; et ab eo quod praecedit id quod sequitur. dictum est a comitiis, in quibus isdem auspiciis creati, licet non simul crearentur, parem tamen habebant honorem propter eadem auspicia; unde et consules pares sunt, cum necesse esset ut unus prior crearetur.

103. PHRYGIO SERVIRE MARITO ἐμφατικῶς, ac si diceret 'exuli.'

104. DOTALES TYRIOS regalem spectauit personam.

PERMITTERE DEXTRAE quasi per manus conuentionem; secundum ius locutus est.

105. OLLI aut 'illi' aut 'tunc.' cetera per parenthesin dicta sunt.

SIMVLATA MENTE hoc est *talibus adgreditur.* [92]

106. LIBYCAS ADVERTERET ORAS absolutior quidem est haec lectio, sed uerior et figuratior illa est 'Libycas auerteret oras'; nam plerumque trahitur schema ut aliquo ituri non ad locum sed de loco ponamus significationem, ut si dicas 'de Campania abeo in Tusciam,' honestius est quam si 'eo' dixeris. nec hoc tantum hoc loco facit sed pluribus; hinc enim est *ripamue iniussus abibis.* [6.375]

107. INGRESSA VENVS calliditatis est, ut supra [92].

109. FORTVNA SEQVATUR hoc ad casum pertinet.

110. FATIS INCERTA FEROR bene omnia tetigit quibus res humanae reguntur: casum, fata, uoluntatem deorum.

Let us therefore rule this people in common, and under equal auspices: let Dido be at liberty to serve a Phrygian husband and into your hand deliver over the Tyrians by way of dowry."

[105] To whom Venus (for she perceived that she spoke with an insincere mind, with a design to direct the seat of empire to Italy toward the Libyan shores) thus in her turn began: "Who can be so mad as to reject these terms and rather choose to engage in war with you, would fortune but concur with the scheme which you mention? [110] But I am driven to uncertainty by the Fates, [not knowing] whether it be the will of Jupiter that the Tyrians and Trojans should dwell in one city,

102. UNDER EQUAL AUSPICES with equal power. What follows, [power], comes from what preceded, [auspices]. This is taken from the language of the assemblies by which men were elected with the same auspices, who, although they were not elected at the same time, still had equal honor because they were elected under the same auspices. This is why consuls are equal, even though one is necessarily elected before the other.

103. TO SERVE A PHRYGIAN HUSBAND emphatically, as if she were saying "[to serve] an exile."

104. TYRIANS BY WAY OF DOWRY She regards her as a royal person.

INTO YOUR HAND DELIVER as though it were *conventio in manu*; spoken in legal terminology.

105. TO WHOM either "to whom" or "then." The rest was said as a parenthetical remark.

INSINCERE MIND this is how she "artfully addresses" her. [92]

106. DIRECT...TOWARD THE LIBYAN SHORES this reading (*adverteret*) is indeed more accurate, but a truer and more suggestive one is that she might "divert...from (*averteret*) the Libyan shores," for quite often this pattern is used: when we intend to go anywhere we put emphasis not on the place we are arriving, but on the place we are leaving, so saying "I am going from (*abeo*) Campania to Tuscany" is more proper than if you said "I am going." (*eo*) And he does not do this only in this passage, but in many, hence he writes, "or will you go from (*abibis*) the river bank unbidden." [6.375]

107. VENUS...BEGAN this is a mark of cunning, as above [on 92].

109. WOULD FORTUNE BUT CONCUR this refers to happenstance.

110. DRIVEN TO UNCERTAINTY BY THE FATES it is admirable how she touches on all the things by which human affairs are governed: happenstance, the Fates, the will of the gods.

misceriue probet populos aut foedere iungi.
tu coniunx, tibi fas animum temptare precando.
perge; sequar. tum sic excepit regia Iuno:
'mecum erit iste labor: nunc qua ratione, quod instat
confieri possit, paucis, aduerte, docebo.
uenatum Aeneas unaque miserrima Dido
in nemus ire parant, ubi primos crastinus ortus
extulerit Titan, radiisque retexerit orbem.
his ego nigrantem commixta grandine nimbum,
dum trepidant alae, saltusque indagine cingunt,
desuper infundam et tonitru caelum omne ciebo.

112. AVT FOEDERE IVNGI si 'foedera,' per se plenum est; si 'foedere,' ad populos pertinet.

113. TIBI FAS ANIMVM TEMPTARE PRECANDO sic Aeolus *tuus, o regina, quid optes / explorare labor.* [1.76-7]

114. PERGE SEQVAR. bene aliud agens aliud ostendit; ante est enim Iunonis officium ex matrimonio, sic usus Venerius; unde paulo post *adero, et tua si mihi certa uoluntas.* [125]

EXCEPIT subsecuta est.

115. ISTE LABOR scilicet explorationis a Ioue.

116. CONFIERI 'con' abundat, ut *fata renarrabat.* [3.717]

119. RETEXERIT ORBEM quem nox tegebat.

120. NIGRANTEM nigrum; participium pro nomine.

121. TREPIDANT festinant, ut *hic me dum trepidi crudelia limina linquunt.* [3.616]

ALAE equites; ob hoc 'alae' dicti, quia pedites tegunt alarum uice.

INDAGINE ferarum inquisitione.

122. DESVPER INFVNDAM quia aër est Iuno. bene hic se facturam dicit quod habet in potestate.

OMNE CIEBO pro 'totum'; 'omne' enim numeri est, 'totum' quantitatis.

or if he will approve the union of the two nations, or be joined by a treaty. You are his consort: to you it belongs by entreaty to work upon his mind. Lead the way; I will follow." Then imperial Juno thus replied: [115] "That task be mine: meanwhile (mark my words), I will briefly show by what means our present design may be accomplished. Aeneas and most unhappy Dido are preparing to hunt together in the forest as soon as tomorrow's sun shall have brought forth the early dawn and uncovered the world with his beams. [120] I will pour on them from above a blackening storm of rain with mingled hail and with peals of thunder I shall shake all heaven while the [bright-hued] wings flutter and they enclose the thickets with toils.

112. BE JOINED BY A TREATY if "treaties" [accusative] is correct, it refers to the treaties themselves; if "by a treaty" [ablative] is correct, it refers to the people joined by the treaty.

113. TO YOU IT BELONGS BY ENTREATY TO WORK UPON HIS MIND so Aeolus says, "Your task, O queen, is to examine what you desire." [1.76–7]

114. LEAD THE WAY; I WILL FOLLOW the way she refers to one thing and alludes to something else is clever, for Juno's role comes first and, after the wedding, the Venerial exercise; thus shortly after Juno says, "I will be present if I have your firm consent." [125]

REPLIED followed closely.

115. THAT TASK namely of exploring Jupiter's attitude.

116. ACCOMPLISHED *con-* (in *confieri*) is redundant, as is the prefix *re-* in "[Aeneas] recounted (*renarrabat*) his destiny." [3.717]

119. UNCOVERED THE WORLD that night was covering.

120. BLACKENING black. He uses a participle for the adjective.

121. FLUTTER they hurry, as, "Here, while the flying men left the cruel thresholds, [they abandoned] me." [3.616]

WINGS horsemen. They are called "wings" because they give cover to the soldiers like wings.

WITH TOILS in hunting wild animals.

122. POURED ON THEM FROM ABOVE because the lower air is Juno. It is appropriate here that she say that she will do what is in her power.

I SHALL SHAKE ALL instead of "the whole heaven," for "all" expresses how many, "the whole" expresses how much.

diffugient comites et nocte tegentur opaca:
speluncam Dido dux et Troianus eandem
deuenient; adero et, tua si mihi certa uoluntas,
conubio iungam stabili propriamque dicabo.
hic hymenaeus erit.' non aduersata petenti
adnuit atque dolis risit Cytherea repertis.
Oceanum interea surgens Aurora reliquit.
it portis iubare exorto delecta iuuentus;
retia rara, plagae, lato uenabula ferro,

123. NOCTE OPACA nubium caligine.

125. TVA SI MIHI CERTA VOLVNTAS hoc est 'si etiam tuum subsequatur officium.'

126. CONVBIO 'nu' naturaliter longa est ab eo quod est 'nubere,' ut *conubia nostra reppulit;* [213] sed modo metri causa corripuit.

127. NON ADVERSATA legitur et 'auersata.'

130. IVBARE EXORTO nato lucifero. nam proprie 'iubar' lucifer dicitur, quod iubas lucis effundit; unde etiam quicquid splendet iubar dicitur, ut argenti, gemmarum. est autem lucifer interdum Iouis plerumque Veneris stella; unde Veneris dicta est, ut *quem Venus ante alios astrorum diligit ignis.* [8.590] sane modo hysteroproteron in sensu est; iubar enim praecedit auroram. et facit 'hoc iubar, huius iubaris.'

131. RETIA RARA, PLAGAE multi diuidunt ut sit *retia rara* maiora, *plagas* uero minora intellegamus. alii 'plagas' per definitionem accipiunt, ut intellegamus 'quae sunt retia rara, plagae.' sciendum tamen proprie plagas dici funes illos quibus retia tenduntur circa imam et summam partem.

LATO VENABULA FERRO lati ferri. uenabula ob hoc dicta, quod sunt apta uenatui.

Their retinue shall fly different ways and be covered with a dark night. Dido and the Trojan prince shall repair to the same cave: there will I be present, and, if I have your firm consent, I will join them in lasting marriage and consecrate her to be his forever. The god of marriage shall be there." Venus without opposition agreed to her proposal and smiled at the fraud she discovered.

Meanwhile Aurora, rising, left the ocean. When the radiance shot forth, the chosen youth issue through the gates: the fine nets, the toils, the broad-pointed hunting spears,

123. WITH A DARK NIGHT with a bank of clouds.

125. IF I HAVE YOUR FIRM CONSENT this is, "if you would carry out your duty quickly."

126. IN MARRIAGE (*conubio*) the syllable "*nu*" is long by nature coming from the verb *nubere* (to marry), as, "she rejected marriage with me" [213]; but here, for the sake of the meter, it is short.

127. WITHOUT OPPOSITION [*ADVERSATA*] the reading "disgusted" (*aversata*) is also found.

130. WHEN THE RADIANCE SHOT FORTH when the light-bringer rose. Since "radiance" is properly called the light-bringer because it pours out rays of light; so radiance is also said of whatever sparkles, like silver or gems. "Light-bringer" sometimes means [the planet] Jupiter or more commonly Venus; thus it was said to be Venus in, "whom Venus delights more than the other fires of stars." [8.590] Of course here the meaning is hysteron-proteron, for radiance precedes the dawn. Also, *iubar* is neuter and declined *iubar, iubaris*.

131. THE FINE NETS, THE TOILS many make a distinction, as though we should understand "fine nets" as larger and "toils" as smaller. Others say they mean the same thing so that we should understand "the fine nets, i.e. the toils." In any case, it should be understood that the ropes by which the nets are stretched around the bottom and top are properly called the toils.

BROAD-POINTED HUNTING SPEARS of broad iron. Hunting spears are so called because they are designed for the hunt.

Massylique ruunt equites et odora canum uis.
reginam thalamo cunctantem ad limina primi
Poenorum exspectant, ostroque insignis et auro
stat sonipes, ac frena ferox spumantia mandit.
tandem progreditur, magna stipante caterua,
Sidoniam picto chlamydem circumdata limbo.

132. MASSYLI Massylorum gens est non longe a Mauritania. et *Massyli* legendum per unum 'i,' ne non stet uersus; 'sy' enim longa est, ut *hic mihi Massylae gentis monstrata sacerdos.* [483]

ET ODORA CANVM VIS plus est quam si diceret 'multitudo,' unde Sallustius *qua tempestate ex ponto uis piscium erupit.* [*Hist Frag* 3.53] *odora* autem inproprie dixit: nam 'odorum' est quod ex se odorem emittit, non quod odorem sequitur, ut Statius *et odoro uulnere pinus.* [*Theb* 6.104] sic est et '*inter odoratum lauri nemus*' [6.658] pro 'odorum'; nam 'odoratum' est quod aliunde odorem accipit, ut 'odoratum templum.' tria ergo sunt: 'odorum' quod per se olet, 'odoratum' quod aliunde accipit odorem, 'odorisecum' quod odorem sequitur; sicut modo de canibus debuit dicere.

133. CVNCTANTEM morantem. atqui amatrix debuit festinare; sed pathos natura superarat, ut Terentius *dum moliuntur, dum conantur, annus est.* [*Heau Tim* 240] deinde haec morabatur studio placendi.

AD LIMINA ante, uel apud.

135. STAT SONIPES adest, praesens est; nam si *stat* simpliciter acceperis, uituperatio est, nam legimus *stare loco nescit.* [*G* 3.84] denique sequentia dictum hoc explanant, ut *ac frena ferox spumantia mandit.* [135]

SPVMANTIA spumas mouentia, ut *naufragum mare,* [Hor., *Carm* 1.16.10] quod naufragos facit.

137. LIMBO limbus est, sicut supra diximus [ad 2.616], fascia, quae ambit extremitatem uestium secundum antiquum ritum, ut *uictori chlamydem auratam, quam plurima circum / purpura.* [5.250–1]

the Massylian horsemen, and a pack of scenting hounds pours forth together. At the threshold of the palace-gate the Carthaginian nobles await the queen lingering in her alcove: [135] her steed, richly caparisoned with purple and gold, ready stands and fiercely champs the foaming bit. At length she comes attended by a numerous retinue, wearing a Sidonian cloak with embroidered hem:

132. MASSYLIAN the Massylian nation is not far from Mauritania. Also, the word *Massyli* must be read with a single *i,* otherwise the line will not scan; the syllable *sy* is long, as in "a priestess of the Massylian nation was pointed out to me."[483]

AND A PACK OF SCENTING HOUNDS this is stronger than saying "many," as in Sallust's phrase "because of this storm a pack of fish burst out of the sea." [*Hist Frag* 3.53] Also, he used "scenting" incorrectly, for "scenting" means something that emits a scent, not something that tracks a scent, as Statius writes "and the pine tree with its scenting wound." [*Theb* 6.104] So, too, he writes: "within the scented grove of laurel,"[6.658] instead of "scenting," since "scented" refers to something that takes its scent from something else, like a "scented temple." So there are three words: "scenting" meaning something that smells of itself, "scented" meaning something that receives a smell from something else, and "scent-tracking" meaning something that tracks scent, as he ought to have said here about the dogs.

133. LINGERING delaying. Indeed, a woman in love ought to hurry, but her nature has overcome her emotion, as Terence wrote: "while they strive, while they try, a year passes." [*Heau Tim* 240] Then she was delaying in her eagerness to please.

AT THE THRESHOLD "in front of," or "near."

135. HER STEED...STANDS is at hand, is present, for if you take "stands" literally, it would be a criticism, since he writes [of a spirited horse], "he does not know how to stand in place." [*G* 3.84] And then the words that follow clarify this passage: "and fiercely champs the foaming bit." [135]

FOAMING, creating foam as a "shipwrecked sea" [Hor. *Carm.* 1.16.10] makes shipwrecks.

137. HEM a hem, as we said above [on 2.616], is a fringe that goes around the edge of clothing in the ancient style, as, "to the winner, a cloak embroidered with gold which had much purple around its edge." [5.250–1]

cui pharetra ex auro, crines nodantur in aurum,
aurea purpuream subnectit fibula uestem.
nec non et Phrygii comites et laetus Iulus
incedunt. ipse ante alios pulcherrimus omnis
infert se socium Aeneas atque agmina iungit.
qualis ubi hibernam Lyciam Xanthique fluenta
deserit ac Delum maternam inuisit Apollo,
instauratque choros, mixtique altaria circum
Cretesque Dryopesque fremunt pictique Agathyrsi;
ipse iugis Cynthi graditur, mollique fluentem
fronde premit crinem fingens atque implicat auro;
tela sonant umeris: haud illo segnior ibat

138. CRINES NODANTVR IN AVRVM ueluti retiolum, quod colligit comas.

141. IPSE ANTE ALIOS quia amatur, ideo ei dat pulchritudinem, licet Ascanio magis congruat.

143. HIBERNAM LYCIAM non asperam, sed aptam hiemare cupientibus; sic enim se habet natura regionis. et bene aliud agens aliud ostendit; nam constat Apollinem sex mensibus hiemis apud Pataram, Lyciae ciuitatem, dare responsa, unde Patareus Apollo dicitur, et sex aestiuis apud Delum.

144. INVISIT APOLLO Apolloni Aenean uel propter sagittas quibus in uenatu utebatur comparat uel certe propter futurum infelix matrimonium—ut enim supra diximus [ad 58], nuptiis est hoc numen infensum.

145. CRETES ab eo quod est 'Cres.'

146. DRYOPESQVE populi iuxta Parnasum, ut *Dryopumque trahens Erasinus aristas.* [Statius, *Theb* 4.122]

PICTIQVE AGATHYRSI populi sunt Scythiae colentes Apollinem hyperboreum, cuius 'logia,' id est responsa, feruntur. *picti* autem non 'stigmata habentes,' sed 'pulchri,' hoc est 'cyanea coma placentes.'

147. CYNTHI montis Deli.

FLVENTEM unguentatum.

148. FINGENS componens, ut *et corpora fingere.* [8.634]

149. TELA SONANT ut in nono *pharetramque fuga sensere sonantem.* [9.660]

HAVD ILLO SEGNIOR id est 'non illo deformior'; nam plerumque uirtus et pulchitudo pro se inuicem ponuntur. hinc est *satus Hercule pulchro / pulcher Auentinus;* [7.656-7] nam Herculi satis est incongrua pulchritudo. sic Plautus in *Pyrgopolinice* de muliere *quidnam, fortis est?* id est 'pulchra.' [*MG* 1106]

she has a quiver of gold; her hair is knotted in gold; a golden buckle binds up her purple robe. [140] The Trojan youth, too, and sprightly Iulus accompany the procession. Aeneas himself, distinguished in beauty above all the rest, mingles with the retinue and adds his train to hers: as when Apollo, leaving wintry Lycia and the streams of Xanthus, revisits his mother's island Delos and [145] renews the dances, so the Cretans, and Dryopes, and painted Agathyrsi mingle their acclamations around his altars: he himself moves majestic on Cynthus' top and, adjusting his flowing hair, crowns it with a soft wreath and enfolds it in gold; his weapons rattle on his shoulders. With no less active grace Aeneas moved:

138. HER HAIR IS KNOTTED IN GOLD Like a little net that gathers up the hair.

141. HIMSELF...ABOVE THE REST because he is loved, and for that reason Virgil gives him beauty, although it is more appropriate for Ascanius.

143. WINTRY LYCIA not harsh, but suited to those desiring to spend the winter, for that is the climate of the region. Also, he cleverly refers to one thing and alludes to another, for it is agreed that Apollo gives responses at his oracle for the six months of winter at Patara—a city in Lycia (which is why he is called Apollo Patareus)—and spends the six months of summer at Delos.

144. APOLLO...REVISITS he compares Aeneas to Apollo, either on account of the arrows he was using in the hunt or surely on account of the unhappy marriage to come—as we said earlier [58], this god is embittered toward marriage.

145. CRETANS formed from the word *Cres*.

146. AND DRYOPES a people near Parnassus, as, "Erasinus dragging away the grain crops of the Dryopes." [Statius, *Theb* 4.122]

AND PAINTED AGATHYRSI a people of Scythia worshiping northern Apollo, whose *logia*, i.e. responses, are recorded. Also, "painted" does not mean "tattooed," but "beautiful," that is, "pleasing because of their dark blue hair."

147. CYNTHUS mountain on Delos.

FLOWING anointed.

148. ADJUSTING arranging, as, "and shapes the bodies." [8.634]

149. WEAPONS RATTLE as in the ninth book "and they heard his quiver rattling in his flight." [9.660]

NO LESS ACTIVE GRACE i.e., "not less beautifully than he," for grace and beauty are commonly used interchangeably. So, "beautiful Aventinus born of beautiful Hercules," [7.656] for beauty is inappropriate for Hercules. Thus Plautus, in his *Pyrgopolynices*, wrote of a woman: "What? Is she strong?," [*MG* 1106] i.e. "beautiful."

Aeneas, tantum egregio decus enitet ore.
postquam altos uentum in montis atque inuia lustra,
ecce ferae saxi deiectae uertice caprae
decurrere iugis; alia de parte patentis
transmittunt cursu campos atque agmina cerui
puluerulenta fuga glomerant montisque relinquunt.
at puer Ascanius mediis in uallibus acri
gaudet equo iamque hos cursu, iam praeterit illos,
spumantemque dari pecora inter inertia uotis
optat aprum, aut fuluum descendere monte leonem.
  Interea magno misceri murmure caelum
incipit; insequitur commixta grandine nimbus;
et Tyrii comites passim et Troiana iuuentus
Dardaniusque nepos Veneris diuersa per agros
tecta metu petiere; ruunt de montibus amnes.

152. FERAE CAPRAE hoc est capreae. et bene aptat descriptionem ad species, ut ceruis campos, capreis saxa permittat.

153. DECVRRERE bene praeterito usus est tempore ad exprimendam nimiam celeritatem.

154. TRANSMITTVNT celeriter transeunt.

157. IAMQVE HOS CVRSV id est 'modo,' ut *iam digitis, iam pectine pulsat eburno.* [6.647] et bene puerilem ostendit animum, qui per mobilitatem frequenter optat timenda.

159. MONTE LEONEM per transitum tangit historiam; nam Ascanius praeter Iulum et Ilum, quae habuit nomina, etiam Dardanus et Leontodamas dictus est, ad extinctorum fratrum solacium. ideo nunc eum dicit optare aduentum leonis, paulo post *Dardaniusque nepos Veneris.* [163] constat etiam Aenean Dardanum dictum, ut ostendit in quarto *hauriat hunc oculis ignem crudelis ab alto Dardanus,* [661] item Ilioneus *hinc Dardanus ortus, huc repetit;* [7.240] nam latenter etiam illud nomen ostendit.

161. COMMIXTA GRANDINE NIMBVS secundum Iunonem *his ego nigrantem commixta grandine nimbum.* [120] et bene etiam grando adicitur, quia poterat nimbus contemni.

164. DE MONTIBVS AMNES ne uel inuestigare Tyrii possent reginam.

[150] such comeliness shines forth in his matchless mien. Soon as they reached the high mountains and pathless lairs, lo! From the summit of the craggy cliff the wild goats, dislodged, skipped down the rocks: on the other side stags shoot across the open plain, gather their dust-covered squadrons in flight, and forsake the mountains. Now the boy Ascanius delights in his sprightly courser through the enclosed vales; and now these, now these he outrides and devoutly wishes a foaming boar would cross his way amidst the feeble flocks or a tawny lion descend from the mountain.

[160] Meanwhile the air begins to be disturbed with loud murmurings; a storm with mingled hail succeeds. And here and there the Tyrian train, the Trojan youth, and Venus' grandchild of Dardanian line for fear sought different shelters through the fields. Whole rivers pour down from the mountains.

152. WILD GOATS this is the roe deer. And he fittingly adapts his description to the species, so that he grants the fields to the stags and the rocks to the roe deer.

153. SKIPPED DOWN he cleverly used the past tense here to express great speed.

154. SHOOT ACROSS they go across quickly.

157. AND NOW THESE HE OUTRIDES i.e. "immediately in succession," as, "now with his fingers he strikes the same [notes], now with an ivory pick." [6.647] He shows well a boy's spirit, which in its recklessness often hopes for things that should be feared.

159. LION FROM THE MOUNTAIN through this transition he alludes to a story. Ascanius, in addition to the names Iulus and Ilus, was also called Dardanus and Leontodamas as a consolation for his dead brothers. For this reason Virgil says now that he hopes for the arrival of a lion, and shortly after, "and the Dardanian grandson of Venus." [163] It is also agreed that Aeneas was called Dardanus, as Virgil shows in the fourth book, "let cruel Dardanus drink in this fire with his eyes from the sea," [661] likewise Ilioneus says of him, "from this place Dardanus arose, to this place he returns," [7.240] for he uses the latter name implicitly.

161. STORM WITH MINGLED HAIL according to Juno, "I [will pour down] a storm with hail mixed in." [120] Hail is added cleverly because otherwise the storm might have been disregarded.

164. RIVERS [POUR] DOWN FROM THE MOUNTAINS so that the Tyrians could not even track down the queen.

speluncam Dido dux et Troianus eandem
deueniunt. prima et Tellus et pronuba Iuno
dant signum; fulsere ignes et conscius aether
conubiis, summoque ulularunt uertice Nymphae.
ille dies primus leti primusque malorum
causa fuit; neque enim specie famaue mouetur,
nec iam furtiuum Dido meditatur amorem:

166. DEVENIVNT bene subprimit rem pudendam; sic Terentius *'quid tum' fatue? fateor.* [*Eun* 604]

PRIMA ET TELLVS satis perite loquitur; nam secundum Etruscam disciplinam nihil tam incongruum nubentibus quam terrae motus uel caeli.

ET PRONVBA IVNO quae nubentibus praeest. Iunonem autem dedisse signa per tempestatem constat et pluuias, quae de aëre fiunt.

167. FVLSERE IGNES Varro dicit *aqua et igni mariti uxores accipiebant;* [*LL* 5.61] unde hodieque et faces praelucent et aqua petita de puro fonte per puerum felicissimum uel puellam interest nuptiis, de qua nubentibus solebant pedes lauari.

168. VLVLARVNT bene medium elegit sermonem; nam ait Lucanus *non tu laetis ululare triumphis.* [*BC* 6.261] in luctu autem ululari non dubium est.

170. SPECIE FAMAVE MOVETVR species rerum praesentium est, quod quasi aspicitur, fama autem rerum absentium. hoc ergo dicit: non eam mouit nec praesens deformitas, quod non in thalamo sed in specu concuberat, nec futura mox fama.

171. MEDITATVR exercet; sic Horatius *et horridam cultis diluuiem meditatur agris.* [*Carm* 4.14.27] nec incongrue dictum; actus enim est in ipsa meditatione; nam exercitium est meditatio. sciendum tamen hodie hoc in usu non esse.

[165] Dido and the Trojan prince repair to the same cave. [Then] first both primal Earth and Pronuba Juno gave the signal: fires flashed, the sky was a witness to the alliance, and the nymphs howled on the mountain tops. That day first proved the source of death, [170] the source of woes: for [now] Dido is neither influenced by appearance nor rumor, and she considers a love clandestine no longer:

166. REPAIR well does he omit the shameful act, as does Terence in the exchange:

" 'What then,' stupid?"

"I admit it." [*Eun* 604]

PRIMAL EARTH he speaks quite knowledgeably here, since according to the Etruscan teaching nothing is as inauspicious for a wedding as an earthquake or a storm.

PRONUBA JUNO who presides over weddings. Moreover, it is generally agreed that Juno gave signs with storms and rain, which come from the lower air.

167. FIRES FLASHED Varro says that "husbands used to marry their wives with water and fire," [*LL* 5.61] which is why even today at weddings it is important that torches blaze and a very lucky boy or girl bring water from a clean spring, some of which is customarily used to wash the newlyweds' feet.

168. HOWLED he cleverly chooses a word that could be applied in two ways, for Lucan says, "you do not howl in happy triumphs." [*BC* 6.261] Although, howling is without doubt a part of lamentation.

170. NEITHER INFLUENCED BY APPEARANCE NOR RUMOR "appearance" refers to things present, because it is as though she [Dido] were seen; "rumor," on the other hand, refers to things that are absent. Therefore he means this: the present degradation does not upset her (that she slept with him in a cave instead of a marriage bed) nor does the rumor soon to come.

171. SHE CONSIDERS she carries out; thus Horace, "and the river Aufidus considers again and again a terrible flood for the tilled fields." [*Carm* 4.14.27] Nor was this said inappropriately, as there is action in this *meditatio*, for *meditatio* is practice. This, however, is not now general usage.

coniugium uocat; hoc praetexit nomine culpam.
Extemplo Libyae magnas it Fama per urbes—
Fama, malum quo non aliud uelocius ullum;
mobilitate uiget, uiresque adquirit eundo,
parua metu primo, mox sese attollit in auras,
ingrediturque solo et caput inter nubila condit.
illam Terra parens ira inritata deorum
extremam (ut perhibent) Coeo Enceladoque sororem
progenuit, pedibus celerem et pernicibus alis,
monstrum horrendum, ingens, cui, quot sunt corpore

172. CVLPAM ut supra *succumbere culpae.* [19]

174. FAMA MALVM definitio est, ut *quo* ex praecedenti pendeat nomine; quamquam alii 'qua' legant. sane *quo,* nisi definitio sit, legi non potest; nec enim procedit ut ordo sit 'Fama, quo non aliud malum uelocius.'

175. MOBILITATE VIGET dat ei σωματοποιίαν, et laudat a contrario; cum enim omnia labore minuantur, haec crescit.

176. ATTOLLIT IN AVRAS sumpta licentia, quae minuebatur timore.

177. INGREDITVRQVE SOLO ET CAPVT INTER NVBILA CONDIT hoc uult ostendere, nec humili eam fortunae parcere nec superiori.

178. TERRA PARENS generale est: parens rerum omnium.

IRA INRITATA DEORVM amphibolon est, utrum *sua ira* propter exstinctos gigantas an 'ira deorum inritata,' quae exstinxerat gigantas.

179. EXTREMAM aut post omnes gigantas, quippe ad deorum ultionem nata aut certe 'extrema' pessima, omnes enim qui de medicina tractant dicunt naturale esse ut inutiliores sint qui nascuntur ultimi.

VT PERHIBENT quotienscumque fabulosum aliquid dicit, solet inferre 'fama est.' mire ergo modo, cum de ipsa fama loqueretur, ait ut *perhibent.*

180. PEDIBVS CELEREM ET PERNICIBVS ALIS conuertit rerum epitheta; nam 'pernix' pedum est, ut *pernicibus ignea plantis,* [11.718] 'celeritas' pennarum est, ut *celerique fuga sub sidera lapsae.* [3.243]

181. QVOT SVNT CORPORE PLVMAE non ipsius, sed in omnium corporibus; nam exaggeratio est, ac si diceret 'quot sunt arenae.'

she calls it marriage; she veils her guilt under that name.

Forthwith Rumor through the populous city of Libya runs: Rumor, evil than which nothing is more swift, [175] by exerting her agility grows more active and acquires strength on her way: small at first through fear; soon she shoots up into the skies and walks along the ground and hides her head among the clouds. Parent Earth, incited by the gods' wrath, produced her the last sister, as they say, of Coeus and Enceladus, [180] nimble of foot and with fleet wings: a monster hideous, immense, who (wondrous to relate!) for as many plumes as are on the body,

172. GUILT as above "give way to this fault." [19]

174. RUMOR, EVIL this is a definition, so "than which" refers to the preceding noun ("evil"); although others read *qua* [referring to "rumor"]. Surely *quo* cannot be the reading unless it is not a definition, for the word order cannot be "rumor, an evil than which no other is more swift."

175. BY EXERTING HER AGILITY GROWS MORE ACTIVE he personifies rumor and praises it by contrast; for, while all things weaken through effort, this grows.

176. SHE SHOOTS UP INTO THE SKIES after taking the freedom that had been diminished by fear.

177. AND SHE WALKS ON THE GROUND AND HIDES HER HEAD AMONG THE CLOUDS he wants to show that she spares the fate of neither the humble nor the mighty.

178. PARENT EARTH in general—the parent of all things.

INCITED BY THE GODS' WRATH this is amphibolon; it could mean either "by her own wrath," incited because of the murder of the giants or "by the incited wrath of the gods," which murdered the giants.

179. LAST either born after all the giants, surely for the purpose of seeking revenge upon the gods. Or else "last" meaning worst, for all the medical writers say that it is natural for the last-born to be the least useful.

AS THEY SAY whenever he tells a story he usually adds "rumor has it," so it is surprising that now, when he is talking about rumor, he writes "so they say."

180. NIMBLE OF FOOT AND WITH FLEET WINGS he switches the epithets of things, since "fleet" is said of feet, as, "fiery with fleet feet"; [11.718] and "nimbleness" is said of feathers, "slip under the stars in nimble flight." [3.243]

181. AS MANY PLUMES AS ARE ON THE BODY not just on her body but on everyone's body, for this is an exaggeration, as though he were to say "as many grains of sand as there are."

plumae, tot uigiles oculi subter, mirabile dictu,
tot linguae, totidem ora sonant, tot subrigit aures.
nocte uolat caeli medio terraeque per umbram,
stridens, nec dulci declinat lumina somno;
luce sedet custos aut summi culmine tecti,
turribus aut altis, et magnas territat urbes;
tam ficti prauique tenax, quam nuntia ueri.
haec tum multiplici populos sermone replebat
gaudens, et pariter facta atque infecta canebat:
uenisse Aenean Troiano sanguine cretum,
cui se pulchra uiro dignetur iungere Dido;
nunc hiemem inter se luxu, quam longa, fouere
regnorum immemores turpique cupidine captos.

182. OCVLI SVBTER aduerbium est, ac si diceret 'non sub plumis, sed sub ipsa.'

183. TOT LINGVAE infinitus est numerus; nam re uera quot sunt homines in quibus fama est, tot ora habet quae sunt hominum.

184. NOCTE VOLAT bene naturalem rem dixit; nam quanto celatum est aliquid, tanto magis requiritur. et sine dubio incipiens fama semper obscura est; quae diuulgata conquiescit, unde ait *luce sedet.* [186]

TERRAEQVE PER VMBRAM noctem umbram terrae esse nusquam apertius significauit.

186. CVSTOS speculatrix.

SVMMI CVLMINE TECTI per domos nobilium.

187. TVRRIBVS AVT ALTIS per regum domos.

MAGNAS TERRITAT VRBES magnos populos; et dicit plebeios.

188. TENAX in omnibus perseuerans.

190. GAVDENS propter inuentam materiam.

FACTA ATQVE INFECTA sicut sequentia indicant.

192. DIGNETVR librauit sermonem, quasi personae superioris.

193. LVXV QVAM LONGA id est, nunc hiemem inter se luxu fouere in quantum longa est ipsa hiemps. facit talem etiam alibi figuram, ut *Thybris ea fluuium, quam longa est, nocte tumentem leniit* [8.86] pro 'quam longa est ipsa nox.'

194. REGNORVM IMMEMORES hoc fingit; nam et illi curae est Carthago et Aeneae Italia.

numbers so many wakeful eyes beneath, so many tongues, so many babbling mouths, pricks up so many listening ears. By night, through the mid region of the sky and through the shadow of the earth, [185] she flies buzzing, nor inclines her eyes to sweet rest. A guardian by day, she perches either on the peak of the highest roof or on high towers and frightens great cities; as obstinately bent on falsehood and iniquity as on reporting truth. She then, delighted, with various rumors filled the people's ear [190] and uttered facts and fictions indifferently; [namely,] that Aeneas, sprung from Trojan blood, had arrived, whom Dido, with all her charms, deigned to wed; that now in revelling with each other they enjoyed the winter, in luxury, however long, unmindful of their kingdoms and enslaved by base lust.

182. EYES BENEATH *subter* is an adverb, as if he were saying not "under the feathers," but "under her."

183. SO MANY TONGUES the number is infinite, since truly a rumor has as many mouths as there are people spreading it.

184. BY NIGHT...SHE FLIES he has expressed a natural phenomenon well, for the more something is hidden, the more it is sought out. Without doubt, a rumor at the beginning is always unknown, but once it is well known, it stops spreading, which is why he says, "by day she sits." [186]

AND THROUGH THE SHADOW OF THE EARTH never has he more clearly stated that night is the shadow of the earth.

186. A GUARDIAN watch-woman.

ON THE PEAK OF THE HIGHEST ROOF through the homes of the nobles.

187. OR ON HIGH TOWERS through the houses of the kings.

SHE FRIGHTENS GREAT CITIES great nations; includes plebeians.

188. OBSTINATELY persistent in all things.

190. DELIGHTED because of the material she has found.

FACTS AND FICTIONS as the things that follow show.

192. [SHE] DEIGNED he has measured the word as though it were referring to a superior.

193. IN LUXURY, HOWEVER LONG i.e., now they pamper each other in luxury for the winter, for as long as the winter lasts. Virgil also uses a similar turn of phrase elsewhere, "the Tiber soothed its swelling flood that night, however long it lasted" [8.86] meaning "however long the night lasted."

194. UNMINDFUL OF THEIR KINGDOMS she is dissimulating, for Carthage is Dido's responsibility and Italy is Aeneas'.

haec passim dea foeda uirum diffundit in ora.
Protinus ad regem cursus detorquet Iarban
incenditque animum dictis atque aggerat iras.
Hic Hammone satus, rapta Garamantide Nympha,
templa Ioui centum latis immania regnis,
centum aras posuit uigilemque sacrauerat ignem,
excubias diuum aeternas, pecudumque cruore
pingue solum et uariis florentia limina sertis.
isque amens animi et rumore accensus amaro
dicitur ante aras media inter numina diuum

195. DEA FOEDA crudelis.

196. IARBAN filium Iouis Ammonis. Liber cum Indos peteret et per Xerolibyam exercitum duceret, fatigatus siti Iouis sui patris implorauit auxilium, et statim uiso ariete fons secutus est. unde factum est Ioui Ammoni, ab arenis dicto, simulacrum cum capite arietino.

198. RAPTA stuprata, ut *et rapti Ganymedis honores.* [1.28]

GARAMANTIDE NYMPHA et proprium potest esse et gentile; nam Garamantes sunt iuxta Libyam.

200. CENTVM finitus pro infinito.

201. EXCVBIAS DIVVM AETERNAS definitio est aeterni ignis. quid est ignis peruigilis? excubiae deorum. et sciendum non uacare ratione ut in aliquibus templis sit ignis peruigil; nam potestates aut terrenae sunt aut aëriae aut aetheriae; sed quia aether ignis est, ideo in aetheriarum potestatum templis ignis est, ut reddatur eis imago sui elementi. est autem Iouis, qui aether est, [et] Mineruae, quae supra aetherem est; unde de patris capite procreata esse dicitur.

203. ISQVE AMENS ANIMI et amator et barbarus. sane nomen esse ostendit ponendo genetiuum.

AMARO aspero, ut *hostis amare, quid increpitas?* [10.900]

204. MEDIA INTER NVMINA DIVVM ac si diceret 'diis testibus,' ut Sallustius *quam mediusfidius ueram licet mecum recognoscas.* [*Cat* 35.3]

[195] With such news the foul goddess fills the mouths of the people. To king Iarbas straight she turns her course; inflames his soul by her rumors, and aggravates his rage. This Iarbas, the son of Ammon by the ravished Garamantian nymph, raised to Jove a hundred lofty temples within his extensive realms, [200] a hundred altars; and there had he consecrated the wakeful fire, the eternal vigils of the gods, a piece of ground, fattened with victims' blood, and the gates adorned with wreaths of various flowers. He, maddened in soul, and inflamed by the bitter tidings is said, before the altars, amid the very presence of the gods,

195. FOUL GODDESS cruel.

196. IARBAS is the son of Jupiter Ammon. Liber, when he was on his way to India and leading his army through Xerolibya, became worn out from thirst and begged the help of his father Jupiter. Immediately after a ram was seen, a spring appeared. For this reason, a statue with a ram's head was made for Jupiter Ammon, derived from *harena* (sand).

198. RAVISHED raped, as, "and the honors of ravished Ganymede." [1.28]

THE GARAMANTIAN NYMPH this can be both a proper name and the name of a people, for the Garamantians are next to Libya.

200. A HUNDRED a definite number for an indefinitely large one.

201. ETERNAL VIGILS OF THE GODS this is the definition of eternal fire. What is an undying fire? A vigil of the gods. And it must be understood that it is not without reason that in some temples there is an undying fire because powers are either earthly, heavenly, or aetherial. But since the aether is fire, in the temples of aetherial powers there is a fire so that the image of their element might be given back to them. So this is the fire of Jupiter, who is the aether, and of Minerva, who is above the aether, which is why she is said to have been born from the head of her father.

203. HE, MADDENED IN SOUL both a lover and a barbarian. Of course he shows that it is a noun by putting it in the genitive.

BITTER harsh, as, "bitter enemy, why do you reproach?" [10.900]

204. AMID THE VERY PRESENCE OF GODS as if he were saying "with the gods as witnesses," as Sallust wrote, "god as my witness you can recognize this as true." [*Cat* 35.3]

multa Iouem manibus supplex orasse supinis:
'Iuppiter omnipotens, cui nunc Maurusia pictis
gens epulata toris Lenaeum libat honorem,
aspicis haec? an te, genitor, cum fulmina torques
nequiquam horremus, caecique in nubibus ignes
terrificant animos et inania murmura miscent?
femina, quae nostris errans in finibus urbem
exiguam pretio posuit, cui litus arandum

205. SVPPLEX ORASSE SVPINIS partim precatur, unde ait *supplex;* partim conqueritur, unde ait *orasse,* id est 'dixisse'; hinc et oratores dicimus.

206. MAVRVSIA Maura; nam protentio est.

207. NVNC EPVLATA dum in epulis est; nam eum deseruit participium. et bene 'nunc' dixit; officia enim in deos, licet aeternam habeant gratiam tamen in praesenti plus ualent. semper autem Ioui propter hospitalitatem libatur. et bene conqueritur quia humanas res ne tum quidem curat, cum ei tribuitur honos sacrificii.

LENAEVM Bacchicum; nam Liber 'Lenaeus' dicitur quia lacubus praeest, qui et Graece ληνοί dicuntur; nam, cum sit Graecum, a mentis delenimento non potest accipi.

209. NEQVIQVAM HORREMVS quia non iudicio hoc facis.

CAECIQVE IGNES non quia non uidentur, sed quorum origo non apparet. alii enim de uentis dicunt fieri, alii de nubibus, alii de aëre.

IN NVBIBVS ac si diceret 'non ex te'; Iuuenalis '*nec uentorum rabie / sed iratus cadat in terras et iudicet ignis.*' [*Sat* 13.225-6]

211. FEMINA inuidia a sexu. et iam incipit specialis conquestio. est autem ordo: femina errans, quae in nostris finibus urbem posuit.

212. PRETIO ut ostendat eam nec meruisse per gratiam nec inuasisse uirtute. et si uendidit, quid conqueritur? scilicet uel defraudatus per corium uel de nuptiarum promissione.

LITVS ut et supra diximus [ad 1.3], terram mari uicinam. modo etiam infertilem uult ostendere.

to have addressed Jupiter as suppliant with uplifted hands: "Almighty Jove, to whom the Maurusian race, having banqueted on painted couches, pours the Lenaean offering, do you see these things? Or do we vainly tremble when you, O father, dart your thunderbolts and blind fires in the clouds terrify our minds and mingle with mere idle sounds? A wandering woman, who has built in our dominions a small city on purchased land; whom we assigned a tract of shore for tillage

205. TO HAVE ADDRESSED JUPITER AS SUPPLIANT WITH UPLIFTED HANDS in part he is praying, which is why he says "suppliant"; in part he is making a complaint, which is why he says "addressed," (*orasse*) i.e. "said," which is why we speak of "orators" (*oratores*).

206. MAURUSIAN Moorish; this is a longer form.

207. HAVING BANQUETED while at the banquets, for the [perfect] participle leaves him out. He also rightly said "now," since obligations to the gods, although they show timeless thanks, nevertheless have greater worth in the present. Moreover, libations are always made to Jupiter for hospitality. And he is right to complain because he is not concerned with human affairs although the honor of a sacrifice is made to him.

LENAEAN Bacchic, since Liber is called "Lenaean" because he presides over wine-vats, which in Greek are also *lenoi*; so, since it is a Greek word, it cannot come from [the Latin] *mentis delenimento* (relaxation of the mind).

209. DO WE VAINLY TREMBLE because you do this without consideration.

AND BLIND FIRES not because they are not seen, but because their source is not apparent. Some say that they come from winds, others say from clouds, still others claim they come from the lower air.

IN THE CLOUDS as if he were saying "not from you." Juvenal, "not by the madness of the winds, but fire falls angrily to the ground and passes judgment." [*Sat* 13.225–6]

211. WOMAN hatred on account of her gender. And now the specific *conquestio* begins. The word order is thus: the wandering woman who has put a city on our land.

212. PURCHASED so he can show that she neither merited it through gratitude nor took it by force. And if he did sell it, about what is he complaining? Of course he was either deceived on account of the hide or by a promise of marriage.

SHORE as we said above [on 1.3], this refers to land near the sea. Now he also wants to show that it is infertile.

cuique loci leges dedimus, conubia nostra
reppulit ac dominum Aenean in regna recepit.
et nunc ille Paris cum semiuiro comitatu,
Maeonia mentum mitra crinemque madentem
subnixus, rapto potitur: nos munera templis
quippe tuis ferimus, famamque fouemus inanem.'
Talibus orantem dictis arasque tenentem
audiit omnipotens, oculosque ad moenia torsit
regia et oblitos famae melioris amantis.
tum sic Mercurium adloquitur ac talia mandat:

213. LOCI LEGES DEDIMVS aut quam tributariam fecimus, aut cui ideo concessimus ciuitatem, ut in nostrum ueniret matrimonium.

NOSTRA pro 'mea.' est autem nobilium hic sermo; Numanus '*en qui nostra sibi bello conubia poscunt*'; [9.600] Sallustius '*nos in tanta doctissimorum copia.*' [*Hist Frag* 1.3]

214. DOMINVM ut superius *liceat Phrygio seruire marito.* [103] est autem de iure, quasi per coemptionem.

215. PARIS similis Paridi, iniuria a persona. et bene *Paris,* quasi qui sustulit alii pactum. sic Iuuenalis *et caluo seruiret Roma Neroni.* [*Sat* 4.38]

SEMIVIRO COMITATV ut, *o uere Phrygiae, neque enim Phryges.* [9.617]

216. MAEONIA MITRA Lydia; nam utebantur et Phryges et Lydi mitra, hoc est incuruo pilleo, de quo pendebat etiam buccarum tegimen.

CRINEM MADENTEM SUBNIXVS crinem unguentatum subnixum habens.

217. RAPTO POTITVR stupro fruitur; nam proprie raptus est inlicitus coitus. nec enim hic rapuerat.

218. TEMPLIS QVIPPE TVIS FERIMVS ac si diceret 'non mirum si haec patimur te colentes.'

FOVEMVS INANEM aut quia frustra te credimus mundi esse rectorem aut quia me tuum filium esse confido. *fouemus* autem quasi in se infirmam.

220. OCVLOSQVE AD MOENIA TORSIT REGIA ut inde pellat Aenean. nec uideatur esse contrarium quod turbantur omnia Ioue Africam respiciente; nam utrumque a turpi liberat fama.

and whom we gave laws for the place, rejected our proffered match and has taken Aeneas into her kingdom for her lord: [215] and now this other Paris, with his unmanly train, bound under the chin with a Maeonian cap and perfumed hair propped, gains it by rape: [this we deserved] because [offerings] we bring to your temples, and we foster an empty reputation."

While in such terms he addressed his prayer and grasped the altar, [220] the almighty heard and twisted his eyes toward the royal towers [of Carthage] and the lovers heedless of their better reputation. Then thus he bespeaks Mercury and gives him these instructions:

213. WE GAVE LAWS FOR THE PLACE either we made tributary or to whom for this reason we granted the city, that she might marry us.

OUR in place of "my." This is the way nobles speak; Numanus, "So these are the men who by war seek our brides for themselves!"; [9.600] and Sallust, "we in so great a company of highly learned men." [*Hist Frag* 1.3]

214. LORD as above, "let her serve a Phrygian husband." [103] Moreover, it is legal terminology, as if the marriage had taken place by *coemptio.*

215. PARIS similar to Paris, a personal insult. And Paris is well-chosen, as if he stole a woman pledged to another. Thus Juvenal, "and Rome might serve a bald Nero." [*Sat* 4.38]

UNMANLY TRAIN as, "O you are Phrygian women indeed, for Phrygian men you are not!" [9.617]

216. MAEONIAN CAP Lydian, since both Phrygians and Lydians wear the *mitra.* This is a curved cap from the sides of which hang cheek-pieces.

PERFUMED HAIR PROPPED having anointed hair that was propped-up.

217. GAINS IT BY RAPE enjoys by debauchery; to be accurate, rape means illicit sexual intercourse and here he had not raped.

218. WE BRING TO YOUR TEMPLES as if he were saying "it is no surprise that in worshipping you we endure these things."

WE FOSTER AN EMPTY [REPUTATION] either because we believe in vain that you are the ruler of the world or because I trust that I am your son. "We foster," though, sounds as if [the reputation] were inherently weak.

220. TWISTED HIS EYES TOWARD THE ROYAL TOWERS to drive Aeneas from there. Nor should it seem contradictory that all things were agitated as Jupiter looked upon Africa, for he freed each of a shameful reputation.

'uade age, nate, uoca Zephyros et labere pennis
Dardaniumque ducem, Tyria Carthagine qui nunc
exspectat fatisque datas non respicit urbes,
adloquere et celeris defer mea dicta per auras.
non illum nobis genetrix pulcherrima talem
promisit Graiumque ideo bis uindicat armis;

223. VOCA ZEPHYROS aut quibus Aeneas nauiget, unde est *nec zephyros audis spirare secundos,* [562] aut qui uehant Mercurium, ut *uentosque secabat,* [257] item *rapido pariter cum flamine portant.* [241]

224. TYRIA CARTHAGINE pro 'Carthagini'; et, pro aduerbio in loco, de loco posuit; sic Horatius, *Romae Tibur amem, uentosus Tibure Romam,* [*Ep* 1.8.12] pro 'Tiburi.'

225. EXSPECTAT moratur, deterit tempus.

227. NON ILLVM NOBIS κατὰ τὸ σιωπώμενον intellegimus.

PVLCHERRIMA epitheton perpetuum, nec ad praesens negotium pertinens.

228. GRAIVMQVE IDEO BIS VINDICAT ARMIS alii dicunt *bis* semel a Diomedis singulari certamine in quo a Diomede percussus est saxo—Iuuenalis *uel quo Tydides percussit pondere coxam / Aeneae* [*Sat* 15.66–7]—et item in excidio, sicut legimus *descendo abducente deo.* [2.632] alii dicunt propter Diomedis et Achillis certamina singularia. sed quando cum Achille dimicauit, a Neptuno liberatus est. potest tamen quod pro Venere fit a Venere factum uideri; sic Iuno inputat Veneri quod pro ea factum est dicens *et potes in totidem classes conuertere nymphas.* [10.83] potest etiam alter sensus esse; nam Troia antea ab Hercule, qui et ipse Graecus fuit, capta est, ut intellegamus iam tunc Aeneam natum fuisse; nec enim multum tempus interfuit, cum constet Priamo tunc ab Hercule imperium traditum.

"Fly quick, my son, call the Zephyrs and on your pinions glide: and to the Trojan prince, who now waits from Tyrian Carthage [225] nor regards the cities allotted him by the Fates, address yourself; and bear [this] my message swiftly through the skies. Not such a one did his fairest mother promise us, nor was it for this she saved him twice from the Grecian sword:

223. CALL THE ZEPHYRS either those by which Aeneas sails, thus, "nor do you hear the Zephyrs blowing favorably," [562] or those which carry Mercury, as, "and he was slicing the winds"; [257] likewise "they carry him balanced with their swift blast." [241]

224. FROM TYRIAN CARTHAGE instead of "at Carthage." Also, instead of an adverb of place within which he used one of source; thus Horace, "when at Rome I would love Tibur, and shifty as the wind from Tibur I love Rome," [*Ep* 1.8.12] instead of "at Tibur."

225. WAITS loiters, wastes time.

227. NOT SUCH A ONE that we understand according to a tacit agreement.

FAIREST always her epithet, and not referring to the business at hand.

228. SAVED HIM HIM TWICE FROM THE GRECIAN SWORD some say "twice" means once in single combat with Diomedes in which he was struck by Diomedes with a rock—Juvenal, "or with the weight of which the son of Tydeus struck the hip of Aeneas" [*Sat* 15.66– 7]—and then in the fall of Troy, as we read, "I descend, guided by a god." [2.632] Others say twice on account of his single combats with Diomedes and Achilles. But when he fought with Achilles, he was saved by Neptune. It is possible, however, that what was done for Venus seems to have been done by Venus; thus Juno ascribes to Venus what was done on her behalf saying, "and you can turn fleets into so many nymphs." [10.83] There can even be another sense, since Troy was previously captured by Hercules, who himself was also Greek, so we may conclude that at that time Aeneas had already been born. Nor could much time have passed since it is generally agreed that Hercules handed power over to Priam at that time.

sed fore qui grauidam imperiis belloque frementem
Italiam regeret genus alto a sanguine Teucri
proderet, ac totum sub leges mitteret orbem.
si nulla accendit tantarum gloria rerum,
nec super ipse sua molitur laude laborem,
Ascanione pater Romanas inuidet arces?
quid struit? aut qua spe inimica in gente moratur
nec prolem Ausoniam et Lauinia respicit arua?
nauiget! haec summa est; hic nostri nuntius esto.'

229. GRAVIDAM IMPERIIS unde multi imperatores possent creari, ut *hinc populum late regem.* [1.21] ideo autem 'grauida' ablatiuo iungitur quia etiam 'grauis illa re' dicimus, unde est huius origo sermonis; sic Plautus in *Amphitryone uxor tua non puero, sed peste grauida est.* [cf. *Amph* 719]

BELLOQVE FREMENTEM exceptis temporibus quibus a Latino regebatur, ut *longa populos in pace regebat;* [7.46] nam alias bellicosa fuit Italia.

231. PRODERET modo 'protenderet' hoc est 'propagaret.' 'propago' autem si genus significet, 'pro' breuis est, ut *sit Romana potens Itala uirtute propago;* [12.827] si de arbore dicas, producitur 'pro,' ut *flexos propaginis arcus exspectant.* [*G* 2.26] 'prodere' sane significat et 'decipere,' ut *unius ob iram prodimur.* [1.251] et est in infinitum haec glossula polysemos.

233. SVPER SVA LAVDE pro sua laude. et Graecum est schema; sic enim Demosthenes ὑπὲρ τοῦ στεφάνου, id est 'pro corona.'

MOLITVR praeparat, exercet.

234. ASCANIONE propter illud quod frequenter diximus, ipsi imperium deberi. ideo autem hoc adserit poeta, ut laudando Iulum Caesarem laudet, quia ab eo originem ducit, ut *Iulius a magno demissum nomen Iulo.* [1.288]

ROMANAS INVIDET ARCES honestior elocutio est si addamus quam rem inuidemus, ut *Liber pampineas inuidit collibus umbras.* [*E* 7.58]

235. INIMICA IN GENTE praeoccupat quasi praescius.

236. PROLEM AVSONIAM ut in sexto *nunc age Dardaniam prolem quae deinde sequatur gloria.* [6.756]

237. HAEC SVMMA EST id est 'mei praecepti collectio,' Iuuenalis *in summa, non Maurus erat nec Sarmata.* [*Sat* 3.79]

but that he should be one who should rule Italy, pregnant with commands, and fierce in war, [230] who should hand on his descent from Teucer's noble blood and bring the whole world under his sway. If he is not fired by the glory of such deeds, nor himself attempts any laborious enterprise upon his own renown, will he, the father, begrudge Ascanius Rome's towers? [235] What does he propose? Or with what prospect lingers he so long among an unfriendly race, nor regards his Ausonian offspring, and Lavinian fields? Bid him set sail. In sum; be this our message."

229. PREGNANT WITH COMMANDS from which many commanders could be created, as, "from here a people ruling widely." [1.21] For this reason, moreover, "pregnant" (*gravida*) is used with an ablative because we also say "heavy [*gravis*] with that," which is the origin of this saying. Thus Plautus in the *Amphitryon*, "your wife is pregnant, not with a son, but with a plague." [cf. *Amph* 719]

AND FIERCE IN WAR not counting the time when it was ruled by Latinus, as, "he ruled the peoples in extended peace"; [7.46] since Italy was otherwise warlike.

231. HAND ON here, "that he would extend," meaning "that he would beget." In addition, if it refers to a race, the prefix *pro-* is short, as, "let there be a Roman stock potent with Italic manliness." [12.827] If you are speaking about a tree, *pro-* is long, as, "[some] await the bent arches of a shoot." [*G* 2.26] Of course the verb *prodere* (to hand over) also means "to betray," as, "we are betrayed due to the anger of one." [1.251] Also, this little word has countless meanings.

233. UPON HIS OWN RENOWN "for his own renown." Also, this figure is Greek, as in Demosthenes' *Upon the Crown* (*Hyper tou Stephanou*).

ATTEMPTS prepares, undertakes.

234. ASCANIUS on account of that which we have often noted, that command is owed to him. What is more, the poet adds this so that by praising Iulus he praises Caesar, since he is his ancestor, as, "the name Julius descends from the great Iulus." [1.288]

BEGRUDGE ROME'S TOWERS it is a more proper phrase if we add the thing we begrudge, as, "Liber has begrudged the hills the shady vines." [*E* 7.58]

235. AMONG AN UNFRIENDLY RACE he worries as though he had foreknowledge.

236. AUSONIAN OFFSPRING as in the sixth book, "Now come, what glory will then follow the Dardanian line." [756]

237. IN SUM i.e. "the enumeration of my instruction." Juvenal, "in sum, he was not Maurus nor Sarmata." [*Sat* 3.79]

Dixerat. ille patris magni parere parabat
imperio; et primum pedibus talaria nectit
aurea, quae sublimem alis siue aequora supra
seu terram rapido pariter cum flamine portant;
tum uirgam capit: hac animas ille euocat Orco
pallentis, alias sub Tartara tristia mittit,
dat somnos adimitque, et lumina morte resignat.
illa fretus agit uentos et turbida tranat

238. PARERE PARABAT non respondet quasi numen inferius, sed dictis obtemperat.

239. TALARIA NECTIT Mercurius ideo dicitur habere pennas, quia citius ab omnibus planetis in ortum suum recurrit; unde et uelox et errans inducitur, ut *quos ignis caeli Cyllenius erret in orbes.* [*G* 1.337]

242. VIRGAM CAPIT id est caduceum, quod primo Apollo habuit et donauit Mercurio, lyra sibi tradita; sic Horatius *fraternaque umerum lyra.* [*Carm* 1.24.12] huius autem uirgae haec ratio est: Mercurius et orationis deus dicitur et interpres deorum; unde uirga serpentes diuidit, id est uenena. nam bellantes interpretum oratione sedantur. unde secundum Liuium legati pacis 'caduceatores' dicuntur; sicut enim per fetiales bella indicebantur, ita pax per caduceatores fiebat. 'Ερμῆς autem Graece dicitur ἀπὸ τῆς ἑρμηνείας, Latine 'interpres.'

ANIMAS pro 'umbras' secundum poeticum morem. animae enim in caelo sunt, ut, *uisa dehinc caelo facies delapsa parentis.* [5.722] huius autem rei ratio alterius est scientiae.

244. LVMINA MORTE RESIGNAT claudit, perturbat. est et aliud quod physici dicunt, pupillas, quas in oculis uidemus, morituros ante triduum non habere; quibus non uisis est summa desperatio. hoc ergo dicit *resignat,* hoc est 'aufert signa luminibus.'

245. TRANAT transuolat, ut *nare per aestatem liquidam suspexeris agmen.* [*G* 4.59]

He spoke. Mercury prepared to obey his mighty father's will: and first to his feet he binds his golden sandals, [240] which by their wings waft him aloft, whether over sea or land, swift as the rapid gales. Next he takes his wand: with this he calls from hell the pale souls, dispatches others down to sad Tartarus, gives sleep or takes it away, and unseals the eyes from death. [245] Aided by this, he swims across the winds and breasts the troubled

238. PREPARED TO OBEY he does not respond as though an inferior god, but complies with Jupiter's words.

239. BINDS HIS GOLDEN SANDALS Mercury is said to have wings because he rushes back from all the planets to his own place of rising. This is why he is represented as both swift and wandering, as, "into what circles in heaven wanders the Cyllenian fire." [*G* 1.337]

242. TAKES HIS WAND i.e. the caduceus, which Apollo had first and then gave to Mercury as a gift when he received the lyre; thus Horace, "and with his brother's lyre [on] his shoulder." [*Carm* 1.24.12] This is the explanation of this wand: Mercury is called both god of speech and the spokesman of the gods; thus the rod separates the serpents, i.e. poisons. For instance, warring peoples are pacified by the words of spokesmen. That is why, according to Livy, peace negotiators are called caduceators. That is to say, just as wars used to be declared by fetial priests, so peace was made by caduceators. Also, in Greek, Hermes is derived from the Greek word *hermeneia*, which in Latin means "messenger."

SOULS instead of "shades" as is the usual poetic practice. Souls are in the heavens, as, "then a likeness of his fathers seemed to glide down from heaven." [5.722] The reason for this, however, belongs to another [branch of] knowledge.

244. UNSEALS THE EYES FROM DEATH closes, upsets. There is also something else that natural philosophers say, namely, that three days before their death those who are about to die do not have the pupils which we [normally] see in the eye. When these are not seen, there is the greatest hopelessness. Therefore he says "unseals" (*resignat*) meaning "he removes the signs (*signa*) from the eyes."

245. HE SWIMS ACROSS he flies across, as, "you look up at the column swimming through the clear summer sky." [*G* 4.59]

nubila; iamque uolans apicem et latera ardua cernit
Atlantis duri, caelum qui uertice fulcit,
Atlantis, cinctum adsidue cui nubibus atris
piniferum caput et uento pulsatur et imbri;
nix umeros infusa tegit; tum flumina mento
praecipitant senis, et glacie riget horrida barba.
hic primum paribus nitens Cyllenius alis
constitit; hinc toto praeceps se corpore ad undas
misit, aui similis, quae circum litora, circum

246. APICEM ET LATERA bene ei quae sunt hominis dat; nam rex fuit qui, cum audisset oraculo cauendum esse a Iouis filio et timore nullum susciperet, a Perseo in montem conuersus est uiso Gorgonis capite, eo quod illum noluit suscipere. ut autem in primo [ad 1.741] diximus, peritus astrologiae fuit; nam et Herculem docuit. sane Latine 'Telamo' dicitur, sicut Nilus 'Melo.'

247. FVLCIT sustinet; nam altus est nimis.

250. NIX 'niuis' facit; sed uerbum 'ninguit' non hinc uenit, sed ab eo quod est 'haec ninguis' et 'hae ningues'; Lucretius *albas effundere ningues.* [*DRN* 6.736] 'ninguit' autem prima persona caret et secunda, quia non est in nostro arbitrio.

251. PRAECIPITANT ut *nox umida caelo praecipitat.* [2.8]

SENIS aut propter aetatem aut adlusit ad niues, ut *gelidus canis cum montibus umor liquitur.* [*G* 1.43]

252. PARIBVS ALIS leni uolatu, ut *dixit et in caelum paribus se sustulit alis.* [9.14]

CYLLENIVS aut ab auia, unde paulo post *Cyllenia proles,* [258] aut a Cyllene, Arcadiae monte, ubi dicitur esse nutritus.

253. TOTO CORPORE uno impetu excussus; sic Lucanus *nec se tellure cadauer / paulatim per membra leuat terraque repulsum est / erectumque semel.* [*BC* 6.755-7]

254. AVI SIMILIS incongruum heroo credidit carmini, si mergum diceret; ut alibi ciconiam per periphrasin posuit, *candida uenit auis longis inuisa colubris;* [*G* 2.320] sic est et *testa cum ardente uiderent scintillare oleum.* [*G* 1.391]

clouds. And now in his flight he espies the top and lofty sides of hardy Atlas, who with his summit supports the sky; Atlas, whose head, crowned with pines, is always encircled with black clouds and lashed by wind and rain: [250] large sheets of snow enwrap his shoulders, from the chin of the old man rush torrents and his grisly beard is stiff with icicles. Here first Cyllenius, poising himself on even wings, alighted; hence with his whole body he flings himself headlong to the floods. Like the bird, which [hovering] about the shores,

246. THE TOP AND SIDES Virgil is right to give him human attributes since he was a king. When he heard from an oracle that he needed to be on guard against the son of Jupiter, he would not grant shelter to anyone out of fear and was turned into a mountain by Perseus (the one he did not want to grant shelter) when he saw the Gorgon's head. In addition, as we said in the first book [on 1.741], he was skilled in astrology, for he even taught Hercules. Of course in Latin he is called "Telamo," just as the Nile is called "Melo."

247. SUPPORTS holds up; because he is extremely tall.

250. SNOW [*NIX*] gives *nivis*; but the verb *ninguit* ["it is snowing"] does not come from this word, rather it is from [the noun] *haec ninguis* (this snow) and *hae ningues* (these snows); Lucretius, "pour out these snows." [*DRN* 6.736] Also, the verb *ninguit* (it is snowing) lacks first- and second-person forms since it is not in our power [to snow].

251. RUSH as, "damp night rushes from the sky." [2.8]

OF THE OLD MAN either on account of his age or he alluded to the snow, as, "when icy water flows from the white mountains." [*G* 9.14]

252. ON EVEN WINGS in gentle flight, as, "he spoke and raised himself skyward on even wings." [9.14]

CYLLENIUS either from his grandmother, as shortly after, "Cyllenian offspring," [258] or from Cyllene, a mountain in Arcadia, where it is said he was nursed.

253. WITH HIS WHOLE BODY shot off in one thrust; thus Lucan, "and did not raise himself from the earth slowly limb by limb, but pushed up from the ground and stood upright at once." [*BC* 6.755–7]

254. LIKE THE BIRD he believed it would not be fitting for a heroic poem if he said gull, as elsewhere he refered to a stork by way of a circumlocution: "the white bird comes hated by long snakes." [*G* 2.320] So, too, is "when they saw the oil spark in the burning lamp." [*G* 1.391]

piscosos scopulos humilis uolat aequora iuxta.
haud aliter terras inter caelumque uolabat,
litus harenosum Libyae uentosque secabat
materno ueniens ab auo Cyllenia proles.
ut primum alatis tetigit magalia plantis,
Aenean fundantem arces ac tecta nouantem
conspicit; atque illi stellatus iaspide fulua
ensis erat, Tyrioque ardebat murice laena
demissa ex umeris, diues quae munera Dido
fecerat, et tenui telas discreuerat auro.
continuo inuadit: 'tu nunc Carthaginis altae
fundamenta locas, pulchramque uxorius urbem
exstruis? heu regni rerumque oblite tuarum!
ipse deum tibi me claro demittit Olympo
regnator, caelum ac terras qui numine torquet;

257. LITVS HARENOSVM AD LIBYAE bene *harenosum* addidit; nam in Libya erat, sed non in harenosa. Mauritania enim aspera et siluestris est.

258. MATERNO AB AVO per Maiam, Atlantis filiam.

259. MAGALIA Afrorum casas. et 'mapalia' idem significant; sed 'magalia' 'ma' producit, 'mapalia' uero corripit, ut *et raris habitata mapalia tectis.* [*G* 3.340]

261. IASPIDE FVLVA pro 'uiridi,' ut *fuluaque caput nectentur oliua.* [5. 309] dicit etiam Plinius in *Naturali Historia* multa esse iaspidum genera, in quibus etiam fuluum commemorat. [*NH* 37.115]

262. ENSIS ERAT pro 'uagina' posuit.

LAENA genus uestis. est autem proprie toga duplex, amictus auguralis.

265. INVADIT habitum futurae orationis ostendit. et notandum non eum tantum nuntii sed etiam caduceatoris, id est oratoris, officio fungi; nam et persuadet et nuntiat.

266. VXORIVS uxori seruiens; Horatius *uxorius amnis.* [*Carm* 1.2.20]

268. IPSE dat dictis auctoritatem, ut *quae Phoebo pater omnipotens.* [3. 251]

CLARO DEMITTIT OLYMPO Olympus quasi ὁλολαμπὴς dictus est siue mons sit Macedoniae, qui dicitur esse diuersorium deorum, siue caelum; unde addidit *claro,* ut *Plemyrium undosum.* [3.693] accentus sane Graecus tunc potest esse si sit Graeca declinatio, ut *Olympos Olympon,* nam Latina *Olympi.*

269. TORQVET regit, sustinet, ut *cuncta tuo qui bella, pater, sub numine torques.* [12.180]

NVMINE autem est aut 'nutu' aut 'potestate'.

about the fishy rocks, flies low near the surface of the seas: just so Maia's son, shooting down from his maternal grandsire between heaven and earth, [skimmed along] the sandy shore of Libya and cut the winds. As soon as he touched the *magalia* with his winged feet, he views Aeneas founding towers and raising new structures; and at his side there was, studded with yellow jasper, a sword and, hanging from his shoulders, a mantle glowed with Tyrian purple; presents that wealthy Dido had given, and had interwoven the stuff with threads of gold. Forthwith he accosts him: "Is it for you now to be laying the foundations of stately Carthage and, uxorious, be raising a city [for her], regardless, alas! of your kingdom and nearest concerns? The sovereign of the gods, who governs heaven and earth by his godhood, himself sends me down to you from bright Olympus.

257. THE SANDY SHORE OF LIBYA Virgil was right to add sandy because he was in Libya, but not in a sandy part. Mauritania, in fact, is rugged and forested.

258. MATERNAL GRANDSIRE through Maia, daughter of Atlas.

259. *MAGALIA* cottages of Africans. *Mapalia* also means the same thing, but the *ma* in *magalia* is long while it is short in *mapalia* as, "and scattered huts for dwellings." [*G* 3.340]

261. WITH YELLOW JASPER instead of "green"; as, "and they will tie yellow olive on their head." [5.309] Pliny also says in his *Natural History* that there are many kinds of jasper, among which he even notes a yellow one. [*NH* 37.115]

262. THERE WAS A SWORD he wrote this instead of "scabbard."

MANTLE a kind of clothing. To be accurate, it is a double toga, an augur's cloak.

265. ACCOSTS he reveals the nature of the speech that is about to be given. And it should be noted that he is not only functioning in the role of messenger, but also that of caduceator, i.e. of an orator, since he both persuades and brings a message.

266. UXORIOUS slave to a wife; Horace, "uxorious stream." [*Carm* 1.2.20]

268. HIMSELF he gives authority to his words, as, "what the all-powerful father [told] to Phoebus." [3.251]

SENDS [ME] DOWN FROM BRIGHT OLYMPUS Olympus, as though it were said to be "shining all over" (*hololampes*), whether it is the mountain in Macedonia (which is said to be a stopping place of the gods) or heaven, which is why he added "bright," as, "wavy Plemyrium." [3.693] The accent, of course, can then be Greek if it is a Greek declension, such as *Olympos, Olympon*, since the Latin is *Olympi*.

269. SPINS rules, upholds, as, "you, father, who spins all wars under your godhood." [12.180]

BY HIS GODHOOD this is also either "by his nod" or "by his power."

ipse haec ferre iubet celeris mandata per auras:
quid struis, aut qua spe Libycis teris otia terris?
si te nulla mouet tantarum gloria rerum,
[nec super ipse tua moliris laude laborem,]
Ascanium surgentem et spes heredis Iuli
respice, cui regnum Italiae Romanaque tellus
debentur.' tali Cyllenius ore locutus
mortalis uisus medio sermone reliquit,
et procul in tenuem ex oculis euanuit auram.
At uero Aeneas aspectu obmutuit amens,
arrectaeque horrore comae et uox faucibus haesit.
ardet abire fuga dulcisque relinquere terras,
attonitus tanto monitu imperioque deorum.

270. HAEC quae dicturus est; nam supra dicta ex se dixerat.

271. TERRIS per neglegentiam tempora consumis. Sallustius *ibi triennio frustra trito.* [*Hist* 3 *Frag* 16]

274. SVRGENTEM crescentem, ut *surgentem in cornua ceruum,* [10.725] item *surgentemque nouae Carthaginis arcem.* [1.366]

276. DEBENTVR honestius plurali numero respondit.

CYLLENIVS antonomasiuum est pro proprio.

ORE oratione.

277. MORTALIS VISVS aut oculis se Aeneae sustulit, aut humanam reliquit effigiem quam sumpserat ut ab Aenea posset uideri, quod melius est.

MEDIO SERMONE atqui exsecutus est omnia quae Iuppiter dixerat. sed sermo est consertio orationis et confabulatio duorum uel plurium; medius ergo sermo est cum persona cum qua quis loquitur non respondet, ut nunc fecit Aeneas.

280. ARRECTAEQVE HORRORE COMAE subaudis 'sunt.'

281. DVLCESQVE RELINQVERE TERRAS minus est 'quamquam.' et, ne uideatur ingratus, deorum excusatur imperio; sic ipse in sexto *sed me iussa deum.* [6.461]

The same commanded me to bear these his instructions swiftly through the air. What do you propose, or with what prospect do you waste your peaceful hours in the territories of Libya? If no glory from such deeds moves you, and you will attempt no laborious enterprise for your own renown, have some regard [at least] to the rising Ascanius and the hopes of your heir Iulus, for whom the kingdom of Italy and the Roman territories are destined." When the Cyllenian spoke with such a mouth, he left mortal vision in mid-adddress and far beyond sight vanished into thin air.

Meanwhile Aeneas, entranced by the vision, was struck dumb; his hair stood erect in horror, and his tongue cleaved to his jaws. He burns to be gone in flight and leave the darling lands, awed by the message and dread command of the gods.

270. THESE what he is about to say, since the things he had said earlier had been his own words.

271. YOU WASTE you spend time in negligence. Sallust, "there three years were wasted in vain." [*Hist* 3 *Frag* 16]

274. RISING growing, as, "a stag rising in antlers," [10.725] likewise "and the rising citadel of new Carthage." [1.366]

276. ARE DESTINED he properly responds with a plural.

THE CYLLENIAN this is the epithet instead of his proper name.

WITH SUCH A MOUTH [*ORE*] with such an oration.

277. MORTAL VISION either he removed himself from the eyes of Aeneas or he left the human form that he had assumed so that he could be seen by Aeneas (which is better).

IN MID-ADDRESS and yet he reported everything that Jupiter had said. But an address (*sermo*) is a joining together of speech (*orationis*) and a conversation of two or more; therefore mid-address is when a person with whom someone is speaking does not respond, as Aeneas did now.

280. AND HIS HAIR STOOD ERECT IN HORROR "had [stood]" understood.

281. AND LEAVE THE DARLING LANDS "although" is missing. And, lest he seem ungrateful, he is relieved of blame by an order from the gods. Thus he himelf says in the sixth book, "but orders from the gods [compel] me." [6.461]

heu quid agat? quo nunc reginam ambire furentem
audeat adfatu? quae prima exordia sumat?
atque animum nunc huc celerem, nunc diuidit illuc,
in partisque rapit uarias perque omnia uersat.
haec alternanti potior sententia uisa est:
Mnesthea Sergestumque uocat fortemque Serestum,
classem aptent taciti sociosque ad litora cogant,
arma parent et quae rebus sit causa nouandis
dissimulent; sese interea, quando optima Dido
nesciat et tantos rumpi non speret amores,
temptaturum aditus et quae mollissima fandi
tempora, quis rebus dexter modus. ocius omnes
imperio laeti parent ac iussa facessunt.

283. AMBIRE blanditiis circumuenire. et 'ambio illam rem' dicimus, ut *neu conubiis ambire Latinum.* [7.333]

284. EXORDIA orationem. sed exordium in duo diuiditur, in principium et orationem, sicut in rhetoricis legimus.

287. ALTERNANTI uaria mente tractanti. et per hoc ostenditur cogitasse eum etiam amorem sed praetulisse uoluntatem deorum.

289. TACITI sine strepitu celantes consilia.

290. ARMA PARENT contra impetum iratae forte reginae.

291. QVANDO non est temporis, sed significat 'siquidem' et est coniunctio ratiocinantis. sane *quando* '-do' breuis est naturaliter; sic Serenus *quando flagella ligas ita liga.* [immo Annianus *Carm* frag. 3.1] Vergilius usurpat *si quando Thybrin uicinaque Thybridis arua.* [3.500]

294. QVIS REBVS DEXTER MODVS quis sit optimus rebus euentus.

295. LAETI alacres, festini.

FACESSVNT frequentatiuum est, ut in Georgicis *matris praecepta facessit.* [*G* 4.548] alias 'discedit' significat, ut Terentius *haec hinc facessat, tu molestus ne sies.* [*Phorm* 635]

Ah! What should he do? In what terms can he now presume to solicit the consent of the raving queen? With what prologue shall he begin? [285] And now this way, now that, he swiftly turns his wavering mind, snatches various purposes by starts, and roams uncertain through all. To him wavering, this resolution seemed the best: he calls to him Mnestheus, Sergestus, and the brave Serestus; [and bids them] with silence equip the fleet, summon their companions to the shore, [290] prepare their arms, and artfully conceal the cause of this sudden change: [adding] that he himself, in the meantime, while generous Dido was in ignorance and had no apprehension that their so great loves could be dissolved, would try the avenues [to her heart], what may be the softest moments of address, what means might be auspicious in this situation. [295] With joy they all obey the commands and execute his orders.

283. TO SOLICIT to come around with enticements. We also say "I am soliciting on that issue," as, "nor solicit Latinus for wives." [7.333]

284. PROLOGUE a speech. But a prologue is divided into two parts, the introduction and the speech, as we read in the rhetoricians.

287. TO HIM WAVERING to him considering different things in his mind. This also shows that he thought about love but preferred to follow the will of the gods.

289. WITH SILENCE without din hiding their plans.

290. PREPARE THEIR ARMS against the attack of a queen possibly angered.

291. WHILE not referring to time, instead it means "seeing that" and is a conjunction of inference. Of course in *quando* (while), the last syllable is short by nature, thus Serenus, "while you bind the lashes, bind them like this." [actually Annianus *Carm* frag. 3.1] Virgil has misused it, "if when [I enter] the Tiber and the fields neighboring the Tiber." [3.500]

294. WHAT MEANS MIGHT BE AUSPICIOUS IN THIS SITUATION what outcome would be best for the situation.

295. WITH JOY swiftly, hurriedly.

EXECUTE this verb is frequentative, as, "he does what his mother instructed." [*G* 4.548] Otherwise it means "go away," as Terence, "let her go away from here so you won't be a pest." [*Phorm* 635]

At regina dolos (quis fallere possit amantem?)
praesensit, motusque excepit prima futuros,
omnia tuta timens. eadem impia Fama furenti
detulit armari classem cursumque parari.
saeuit inops animi totamque incensa per urbem
bacchatur, qualis commotis excita sacris
Thyias, ubi audito stimulant trieterica Baccho
orgia, nocturnusque uocat clamore Cithaeron.
tandem his Aenean compellat uocibus ultro:
'dissimulare etiam sperasti, perfide, tantum

297. PRAESENSIT ac si diceret 'antequam ille moliretur.' et nimia in hoc uis amantis exprimitur.

298. OMNIA TVTA deest 'etiam'; et est exaggeratio.

EADEM FAMA quae et Iarbae nuntiauerat.

299. CVRSVMQVE PARARI nauigationem, ut *ni teneant cursus.* [3.686]

300. INOPS ANIMI sine animo, sine consilio.

301. BACCHATVR furit more Bacchantum. et bene uno sermone praeoccupauit futuram comparationem.

302. THYIAS Baccha; nam sicut a Baccho Bacchae, sic et a Thyoneo Thyiades dicuntur. *commotis* autem *sacris* ideo dixit, quia in sacrorum renouatione commouebantur simulacra; unde Horatius *non ego te, candide Bassareu, / inuitum quatiam.* [*Carm* 1.18.11-12]

TRIETERICA triennalia; Liberi enim sacra tertio quoque anno innouabantur. sane sciendum 'orgia' apud Graecos dici sacra omnia, sicut apud Latinos 'caeremoniae' dicuntur. sed iam abusive sacra Liberi 'orgia' vocantur, vel ἀπὸ τῆς ὀργῆς, id est a furore, vel ἀπὸ τῶν ὀρέων.

303. NOCTVRNVSQVE nocte celebratus; unde ipsa sacra 'nyctelia' dicebantur; quae populus Romanus exclusit causa turpitudinis.

CITHAERON autem mons est ex quo clamor veluti numinis Bacchas vocabat.

305. DISSIMVLARE ETIAM satis artificiosa adlocutio; nam et sibi consulit sub facie utilitatis Aeneae. *dissimulare* autem ideo, ac si diceret 'ita rem pudendam cogitas ut eam fateri nolis'; supra enim dixerat *quae rebus sit causa nouandis / dissimulent.* [290-1]

But the queen (who can deceive a lover?) had foreseen the fraud and was the first to conjecture their future motions, dreading where all seemed to be safe: the same malignant Rumor conveyed the news to her, frantic, that the fleet was being equipped and the course prepared. [300] Destitute in mind she storms burning through the city like a Thyiad worked up into ecstatic fury in celebrating the sacred mysteries of her god when the trieteric orgies stimulate her at hearing the name of Bacchus and the nocturnal howlings on Mount Cithaeron invite her. At length, in these words she first accosts Aeneas: [305] "And did you also hope, you traitor, to conceal from me so wicked a plan and

297. HAD FORESEEN as if he were saying "before he got to work." Also in this verse the excessive power of a lover is expressed.

298. ALL...SAFE "even" is lacking. Also, this is an exaggeration.

THE SAME RUMOR that had taken news to Iarbas.

299. AND THE COURSE PREPARED the sailing route, as, "not to hold their course." [3.686]

300. DESTITUTE IN MIND without thought, without a plan.

301. SHE STORMS she rages in the manner of Bacchantes. Also, the poet cleverly anticipates the coming comparison in one word.

302. THYIAD a Bacchante; for just as Bacchantes from Bacchus, so also Thyiads from Thyoneus. In addition, he said "ritual mysteries" because the statues are moved at the renewal of the sacred rites; thus Horace, "I will not shake you, bright Bassareus, against your will." [*Carm* 1.18.11–12]

TRIETERIC triennial; the sacred rites of Liber used to be celebrated every third year. Of course it must be understood that among the Greeks all sacred rites are called orgies, just as among the Latins they are called ceremonies; but now sacred rites of Liber are loosely called orgies, either from passion (*orges*) (i.e. madness) or from the mountains (*oreon*).

303. AND THE NOCTURNAL celebrated at night; and from this the sacred rites themselves were called *nyctelia*, which the Roman people banned on grounds of depravity.

CITHAERON, moreover, is the mountain from which the Bacchantes were called by a shout as if from the deity.

305. TO CONCEAL a quite artful address, since she looks out for herself under the guise of Aeneas' best interest. In addition, "conceal" as if she were saying "you are thinking about a shameful thing in such a way that you are unwilling to confess it." Earlier, of course, he had said, "they conceal the cause of this sudden change." [290–1]

posse nefas tacitusque mea decedere terra?
nec te noster amor, nec te data dextera quondam,
nec moritura tenet crudeli funere Dido?
quin etiam hiberno moliris sidere classem
et mediis properas aquilonibus ire per altum,
crudelis? quid, si non arua aliena domosque
ignotas peteres, et Troia antiqua maneret,
Troia per undosum peteretur classibus aequor?
mene fugis? per ego has lacrimas dextramque tuam te
(quando aliud mihi iam miserae nihil ipsa reliqui)
per conubia nostra, per inceptos hymenaeos,
si bene quid de te merui, fuit aut tibi quicquam
dulce meum, miserere domus labentis et istam,
oro, si quis adhuc precibus locus, exue mentem.
te propter Libycae gentes Nomadumque tyranni
odere, infensi Tyrii; te propter eundem
exstinctus pudor et, qua sola sidera adibam,

307. DATA DEXTERA foedus amicitiarum.

309. HIBERNO...SIDERE non hieme sed hiemali sidere, aut propter quod ait supra *dum pelago desaeuit hiemps et aquosus Orion.* [52] ergo aut 'tempore,' ut *quo sidere terram / uertere, Maecenas,* [*G* 1.1-2] aut re uera 'sidere' propter Orionem.

311. CRVDELIS etiam in te odio mei; sic Lucanus de Caesare *saeuitia est uoluisse mori.* [*BC* 5.687]

DOMOSQVE IGNOTAS ac si diceret 'Carthago iam tibi nota est, licet et hic aliena sint arua.'

312. TROIA ANTIQVA MANERET 'si' deest; et quasi per interrogationem intellegendum.

314. MENE FVGIS adhuc aperte non uult inputare beneficia, sicut paulo post irata.

315. NIHIL IPSA RELIQVI non pudorem, non regnum.

316. INCEPTOS HYMENAEOS qui nouitate sunt dulces.

318. DVLCE MEVM tegit rem inhonestam; sic Terentius *seu tibi morigera fuit in rebus omnibus.* [*Andr* 294]

320. TYRANNI nihil intererat apud maiores inter regem et tyrannum, ut *pars mihi pacis erit dextram tetigisse tyranni.* [7.266]

to steal away in silence from my coasts? Can neither our love, nor your once promised hand, nor Dido resolved to die by a cruel death, detain you? You prepare your fleet under the winter stars and hurry to launch into the deep amid northern blasts! Cruel one! Suppose you were not bound for a foreign land and settlements unknown and ancient Troy remained. Would Troy be sought by your fleet across the wavy sea? Are you running from me? By these tears, by your right hand, (since there is nothing else left for my sorrow), by our wedding, the marriage we began, if I have deserved any thanks at your hand, or if ever you saw any sweetness in me, take pity, I implore you, on a falling house, and, if there remains any room for prayers, set aside your plan. For your sake I have incurred the hatred of the Libyan nations, of the Numidian tyrants, and made the Tyrians my enemies; for your sake I have sacrificed my honor, and, what alone raised me to the stars,

307. PROMISED HAND the agreement of friendships

309. UNDER THE WINTER STARS not in winter but a wintry star, or on account of what he said earlier, "while winter's fury rages on the sea and Orion is charged with rain." [52] Therefore, either it is "at this time," as, "under what star, Maecenas, to turn the soil," [*G* 1.1–2] or, in fact, "under this star" because of Orion.

311. CRUEL ONE also to yourself because of your hatred of me; thus Lucan on Caesar, "it is savagery to have been willing to die." [*BC* 5.687]

AND SETTLEMENTS UNKNOWN as if she were saying "Carthage is now familiar to you, although the fields belong to someone else."

312. ANCIENT TROY REMAINED "if" is missing; also it should be understood as though it had been stated as a question.

314. ARE YOU RUNNING FROM ME? she still does not want to take into account the favors she has bestowed, just as she becomes angry shortly after.

315. NOTHING ELSE LEFT not shame, not a kingdom.

316. THE MARRIAGE WE BEGAN which is sweet because of its newness.

318. SWEETNESS IN ME she covers up an improper thing; thus Terence, "if she has been compliant to you in all things." [*Andr* 294]

320. TYRANTS as far as our ancestors were concerned, there was no difference between a king and a tyrant, as, "to me it will be a term of peace to have touched the right hand of your tyrant." [7.266]

fama prior. cui me moribundam deseris, hospes
(hoc solum nomen quoniam de coniuge restat)?
quid moror? an mea Pygmalion dum moenia frater
destruat, aut captam ducat Gaetulus Iarbas?
saltem si qua mihi de te suscepta fuisset
ante fugam suboles, si quis mihi paruulus aula
luderet Aeneas, qui te tamen ore referret,
non equidem omnino capta ac deserta uiderer.'

323. FAMA PRIOR quae melior fuit sine dubio.

HOSPES Aeneas et hospes fuerat et maritus, sed modo maritum se negat, hospitem confitetur; unde nunc Dido hoc dicit 'cui me deseris, hospes, quoniam hoc solum nomen restat de coniuge,' hoc est 'superest.' alii *restat* intellegunt 'resistit,' id est 'contrarium tibi est.' non nulli dicunt 'hoc solum nomen quoniam superest, ut te coniugem dicam.' dicitur autem ingenti adfectu hos uersus pronuntiasse, cum priuatim paucis praesentibus recitaret Augusto; nam recitauit primum quartum et sextum.

327. SALTEM 'uel hoc.' est autem sermo tractus a captiuis, qui cum tenerentur ab hostibus dicebant 'sublatis omnibus, salutem concede.' inde per synaeresin hic natus est sermo, ut in contemptu rerum multarum petituri aliquid 'saltem' dicamus.

328. ANTE FVGAM SVBOLES et amatorie et amare; nam haec fugam dicit, quam ille nominat profectionem. amor autem ex filii desiderio conprobatur.

SI QVIS MIHI bene iterat *mihi.* et secundum ius loquitur; nam ubi non est iustum matrimonium, liberi matrem sequuntur.

329. ORE REFERRET aut sic dixit quasi amatrix, ut supra de Ascanio infandum si fallere possit amorem, [85] aut illud dicit 'optarem filium similem uultui, non moribus tuis.'

my former reputation. For whom do you abandon Dido, soon about to die? 'Guest' I must call you since, instead of a husband's name, only this remains! [325] What do I wait for? Is it until my brother Pygmalion reduces my city to ashes, or Iarbas, the Gaetulian, carries me away as his prisoner? If at least I had enjoyed from you some offspring before your flight, if there were some little Aeneas for me to play in my hall, who would recall your face in his, [330] I would not have thought myself quite a captive and forlorn."

323. FORMER REPUTATION which was without a doubt better.

GUEST Aeneas had been both her guest and her husband, but since he now he denies that he is her husband, he admits to being a guest. Because of this Dido now says, "for whom are you leaving me, guest, seeing that only this remains from the name of spouse," meaning "survives." Some understand remains as, "resists," i.e. "it is the opposite for you." A few say, "since only this name survives, I call you husband." Also, Virgil is said to have read these verses out loud with tremendous emotion when he recited privately for Augustus with only a few other people present—he recited the first, fourth and sixth books.

327. AT LEAST "or even this." This expression was taken from prisoners, who, when held by the enemy, used to say, "since everything else has been taken away, grant me at least my well-being." From this, by way of synaeresis, the expression came into being, so we who are about to ask for something, belittling many things, say *saltem* (at least).

328. OFFSPRING BEFORE YOUR FLIGHT both lovingly and bitterly, since what she calls running away, he calls setting out on a journey. But her love is proven by her longing for a son.

IF THERE WERE SOME LITTLE AENEAS FOR ME she rightly repeats "for me." Also, her speech is in accordance with the law since when a marriage is not lawful, the mother retains custody of the children.

329. WOULD RECALL YOUR FACE either she said this as though a lover, as she did earlier about Ascanius, "if she might possibly divert her unutterable love," [85] or she says this: "I would hope for a son similar to you in appearance, but not in character."

Dixerat. ille Iouis monitis immota tenebat
lumina et obnixus curam sub corde premebat.
tandem pauca refert: 'ego te, quae plurima fando
enumerare uales, numquam, regina, negabo
promeritam; nec me meminisse pigebit Elissae,
dum memor ipse mei, dum spiritus hos regit artus.

331. IOVIS MONITIS bene praescribit, ne ei det impietatem. sane et 'haec monita' dicimus, ut *Carmentis nymphae monita et deus auctor Apollo,* [8.336] et 'hos monitus,' ut Persius *hos pueris monitus patres infundere lippos.* [*Sat* 1.79]

IMMOTA TENEBAT LVMINA physicum enim est ut qualitatem animi ex oculorum aut corporis mobilitate noscamus. ergo modo uult ostendere Aenean a proposito non esse deuiaturum.

333. EGO TE QVAE PLVRIMA FANDO controuersia est plena, in qua et purgat obiecta, remouens a se crimen ingrati, et ueniali utitur statu, profectionem suam retorquens in uoluntatem deorum. habet etiam finem; nam purgat obiectam fugam nomine profectionis.

335. PROMERITAM praestitisse, bene gessisse; et est sermo de his qui per contrarium magis lucent: Terentius *ita me uelim ames promerentem pater,* [*Adel* 681] id est, bene agentem. et congruit ut praestet qui bene agit; contra alibi *quid commerui aut peccaui, pater?* [*Andr* 139] id est 'quid male egi?'

MEMINISSE PIGEBIT ELISSAE 'memini' et 'illius rei' dicimus, ut hoc loco, et 'memini illam rem,' ut *numeros memini, si uerba tenerem.* [*E* 9.45]

336. DVM MEMOR IPSE MEI de futuro dixit et congrue; nam 'piget' ad futurum spectat, 'pudet' ad praeteritum. et, licet paene una sit significatio, tamen dicimus 'piget me illud facere,' 'pudet fecisse'; unde interdum, praecipue a Sallustio, simul ponuntur.

So she spoke, but Aeneas held his eyes unmoved by the commands of Jove and struggled to suppress the anxious care in his heart. At last he briefly replied: "I will never deny that you, O queen, have indebted me for many things, which you could deservedly list at length. [335] Nor will it cause me regret to have memory of Elissa so long as I remember myself, while I have a soul to move these limbs.

331. BY THE COMMANDS OF JOVE the poet is correct to use this as a pretext so that he does not ascribe any impiety to Aeneas. Of course we say both "these warnings" [second-declension neuter plural], as, "the warnings of the nymph Carmentis and our patron the god Apollo," [8.336] and "these commands" [fourth-declension masculine plural], as Persius, "blear-eyed fathers shower these commands on their sons." [*Sat* 1.79]

HELD HIS EYES UNMOVED it is a fact of natural philosophy that we may learn the characteristic of the mind from the motion of the eyes or the body. Therefore, he now wants to show that Aeneas is not about to turn away from his plan.

333. I [WILL NEVER DENY] THAT YOU...MANY THINGS the argument here is complete. In it he both clears away the accusations, relieving himself of the charge of ingratitude, and assumes a pardonable stance, turning his voyage into the will of the gods. He even has a purpose, since he clears away the accusation of running away by calling it voyage.

335. DESERVEDLY to have stood out, to have done well. Also, this is a speach about those things that are more apprarent through their opposites. Terence, "I would have you love me, father, as I deserve," [*Adel* 681] i.e. "as I am doing well." It is also fitting that a person who does well should be outstanding. On the other hand, he wrote elsewhere, "what have I earned or erred, father?" [*Andr* 139] i.e. "what have I done badly?"

WILL IT CAUSE ME REGRET TO HAVE MEMORY OF ELISSA we say "to have memory" and "of that thing" [genitive case], and we also say "I remember that thing," [accusative case] as, "I remember the rhythm if I could hold onto the words." [*E* 9.45]

336. SO LONG AS I REMEMBER MYSELF he spoke of the future, and appropriately since "it is regrettable" looks to the future, "it is shameful" looks to the past. Furthermore, although the meaning is nearly identical, we say "it is regrettable for me to do that," and "it is shameful to have done that"; thus they are sometimes used interchangeably, especially by Sallust.

pro re pauca loquar. neque ego hanc abscondere furto
speraui (ne finge) fugam, nec coniugis umquam
praetendi taedas aut haec in foedera ueni.
me si fata meis paterentur ducere uitam
auspiciis et sponte mea componere curas,
urbem Troianam primum dulcisque meorum
reliquias colerem, Priami tecta alta manerent,
et recidiua manu posuissem Pergama uictis.

337. PRO RE PAVCA LOQVAR remoto ingrati crimine descendit ad causam.

NEQVE EGO HANC 'profectionem' subaudis; nam posteriori non potest iungi, ne sit confessio.

339. PRAETENDI TAEDAS probat non esse matrimonium.

AVT HAEC IN FOEDERA VENI aut matrimonii, et iungendum est superiori, aut certe ad posteriora pertinet et hoc dicit 'non ad hoc ueni, ut hic morarer,' sicut et nunc probat *me si fata meis paterentur ducere uitam,* et dixit in primo *quae me cumque uocant terrae.* [1.610] ergo *ueni* 'consensi,' hoc est 'non ad haec consensi foedera, ut cum uellem discedere non liceret.'

340. MEIS AVSPICIIS argumentum a necessitate. et *auspiciis* ideo, quia maiores omnia auspicato gerebant; ergo *auspiciis* 'dispositionibus.'

341. SPONTE MEA modo nomen est; nam et genus et casum habet. sic et 'mane,' cum ei et genus et casus additur, nomen est, ut *dum mane nouum, dum gramina canent.* [*G* 3.325] sic est et *forte sua Libycis tempestas appulit oris.* [1.377] alias aduerbia sunt. uerum autem dicit non sua sponte; nam supra legimus *hos cape fatorum comites,* [2.294] item *diuersas quaerere terras / auguriis agimur diuum.* [3.4-5]

344. RECIDIVA post casum restituta.

On this point I will say a few things. Believe me, neither did I conspire to conceal this departure, nor did I ever hold out a groom's torches, or enter into these contracts. [340] Had the Fates allowed me to lead my life by my own authority and ease my cares according to my own will, my first thoughts have been for Troy and the dear relics of my country; Priam's lofty palace would still remain and with this hand I would have revived the renascent Pergamum for my conquered people by hand.

337. ON THIS POINT I WILL SAY A FEW THINGS after removing the charge of ingratitude, he moves on to his reason.

NEITHER DID I THIS understand "voyage," since it cannot be joined with the following [flight], otherwise it would be a confession.

339. DID I HOLD OUT TORCHES he demonstrates that there is no marriage.

OR I ENTER INTO THESE CONTRACTS either of marriage, and this should be linked to the above, or else it refers to what follows and says, "I did not come to this place so I could be delayed here," just as he proves in the next line saying: "Had the fates allowed me to lead my life by my own [authority]." Also he said in the first book, "whatever lands call me." [1.610] Therefore "did I enter" is "I agreed," meaning "I did not agree to these contracts so that I would be allowed to leave when I wanted to."

340. BY MY OWN AUTHORITY an argument from necessity. Also, he uses the word *auspiciis* (by auguries or authority) for the reason that our ancestors used to carry on all their business as approved by augury. Thus *auspiciis* (by auguries or authority) "by my own authority" means "by my own arrangement."

341. MY OWN WILL this is a noun since it has both gender and case. *Mane* (in the morning) is also like this—when both gender and case are added to it, it is a noun, as, "when the morning is new, while the grasses are white with frost." [*G* 3.325] as is *forte* (by chance), as, "a storm by its own chance drove [us] to the Libyan shores." [1.377] Otherwise they are adverbs. But he also says not by his own will, for we read above, "take these companions of your fate," [2.294] likewise, "we are driven to seek different lands by the authority of the gods." [3.4–5]

344. RENASCENT restored after the fall.

sed nunc Italiam magnam Gryneus Apollo,
Italiam Lyciae iussere capessere sortes:
hic amor, haec patria est. si te Carthaginis arces,
Phoenissam, Libycaeque aspectus detinet urbis,
quae tandem Ausonia Teucros considere terra
inuidia est? et nos fas extera quaerere regna.
me patris Anchisae, quotiens umentibus umbris
nox operit terras, quotiens astra ignea surgunt,
admonet in somnis et turbida terret imago;
me puer Ascanius capitisque iniuria cari,
quem regno Hesperiae fraudo et fatalibus aruis.
nunc etiam interpres diuum, Ioue missus ab ipso

345. GRYNEVS APOLLO Clazomenae ciuitas est Asiae; unde Horatius *diues agebat / Clazomenis.* [*Serm* 1.7.4-5] iuxta hanc nemus est Gryneum, ubi Apollo colitur, inde ergo nunc epitheton dedit, licet in Delo acceperit oraculum.

346. LYCIAE SORTES nec hinc accepit responsum, sed sic dixit *Lyciae* ac si diceret 'Apollineae.'

347. HIC AMOR, HAEC PATRIA EST eo, inquit, desiderio Italia per uoluntatem deorum circa Italiam teneor quo possem circa Troiam. et ad illud spectat quod dixit *Troia per undosum peteretur classibus aequor.* [313]

350. ET NOS FAS 'nobis fas' dicimus, sed hoc loco non est iungenda elocutio, ne sit uitium; nam legimus 'fas mihi Graiorum sacrata resoluere iura.' [2.157] sed hoc dicit: *fas est etiam nos extera regna requirere.*

352. NOX OPERIT TERRAS a uerisimili, ideo tempus posuit.

QVOTIENS autem, hoc est, per unamquamque noctem.

353. IN SOMNIS more suo pro 'in somniis.'

TVRBIDA terribilis, quod et umbrae conuenit et parentis auctoritati.

354. PVER ASCANIVS amor Ascanii scilicet admonet.

355. QVEM longe repetiit, et ad Ascanium rettulit; et, licet excusetur, tamen σολοικοφανές est.

356. INTERPRES DIVVM Hermes; expressit uerbum de uerbo.

AB IPSO id est 'magno,' ut supra *ipse deum tibi me claro dimittit Olympo.* [268]

[345] But now Grynean Apollo compels me to move on to Italy and the Lycian lots have commanded it. This is my love, this my country. If the towers of Carthage and the sight of a Libyan city hold you, a Phoenician, why should you be dissatisfied that we Trojans settle in the land of Ausonia? [350] And it is right we go in quest of foreign realms as well. As often as the night covers the lands with humid shades, as often as the fiery stars arise, the troubled ghost of my father Anchises warns me in my sleep and with dreadful summons he urges my departure. He calls me from here, as does the injury done to the boy Ascanius, [355] whom I cheat of the Hesperian crown and his destined dominions. Now also the messenger of the gods, sent by Jove himself,

345. GRYNEAN APOLLO the city of Clazomenae is in Asia, whence Horace, "a wealthy man was doing business at Clazomenae." [*Serm* 1.7.4–5] Next to this city is the Grynean grove where Apollo is worshiped, from which he has now applied this epithet, although he received the oracle on Delos.

346. LYCIAN LOTS nor did he receive a response from this place, but he said Lycian as if he were saying "of Apollo."

347. THIS IS MY LOVE, THIS MY COUNTRY he said, "Through the will of the gods I am gripped by a longing for Italy as I could be about Troy." And he refers to what she said, "would Troy be sought by your fleet across the wavy sea." [313]

350. AND IT IS RIGHT WE we say "right for us," but in this passage the expression should not be joined together, otherwise it would be a solecism; for we read, "it is right for me [dative] to break solemn oaths of the Greeks." [2.157] But this says, "it is right that we [nominative] go in quest of foreign realms as well."

352. NIGHT COVERS THE LANDS he put the time to make it sound real.

AS OFTEN AS moreover, that is, each and every night.

353. IN SLEEP his way of saying "in dreams."

TROUBLED frightening, because he meets both the ghost of his father and his father's authority.

354. THE BOY ASCANIUS it is the love of Ascanius, namely, that warns.

355. WHOM he has reached far into the future and has referred back to Ascanius. Also, although he is justified, still, he is a clumsy speaker.

356. MESSENGER OF THE GODS Hermes; he has spoken word-for-word.

BY [JUPITER] HIMSELF i.e. "the great," as above, "the sovereign of the gods…himself sends me down to you from bright Olympus." [268]

(testor utrumque caput) celeris mandata per auras
detulit; ipse deum manifesto in lumine uidi
intrantem muros uocemque his auribus hausi.
desine meque tuis incendere teque querelis:
Italiam non sponte sequor.'
  Talia dicentem iamdudum auersa tuetur,
huc illuc uoluens oculos totumque pererrat
luminibus tacitis et sic accensa profatur:
'nec tibi diua parens generis nec Dardanus auctor,
perfide, sed duris genuit te cautibus horrens
Caucasus Hyrcanaeque admorunt ubera tigres.

357. VTRVMQUE CAPVT meum et tuum, aut Iouis et Mercurii, aut meum et Ascanii.

CELERES MANDATA PER AVRAS ut supra *celeres defer mea dicta per auras.* [226]

358. MANIFESTO IN LVMINE aut 'claro,' aut 'in nimbo', cuius maius est lumen; sic Lucanus *postquam se lumine uero / impleuit.* [*BC* 9.11-12]

359. AVRIBVS HAVSI accepi; et est pleonasmos.

361. SEQVOR ut *Italiam sequimur fugientem.* [5.629]

362. IAMDVDVM ab initio orationis.

AVERSA irata, ut *diua solo fixos oculos auersa tenebat.* [1.482]

364. LVMINIBVS TACITIS ipsa tacita, ut *tacitumque obsedit limen Amatae,* [7.343] pro 'ipsa tacita.' sequitur autem inuectio, quae semper statu caret.

365. NEC TIBI DIVA PARENS non est sola in Aenean obiecta uituperatio sed etiam in se obiurgatio, quia dixerat *credo equidem, nec uana fides, genus esse deorum;* [12] unde nunc dicit *generis nec Dardanus auctor.*

366. PERFIDE amantum uerbo eum increpat; sic supra *dissimulare etiam sperasti, perfide?* [305]

367. CAVCASVS mons Scythiae inhospitalis.

HYRCANAEQVE TIGRES Arabicae; nam Hyrcania silua est Arabiae. et notandum relictis mediis conparationibus eum augmenta fecisse; nam post deos non homines sed saxa intulit.

(I call each head to witness!) bore to me orders through the swift breezes. I myself saw the god in conspicuous light entering your walls and with my ears I drank in his voice. [360] Cease to torment yourself and me by your complaints. I pursue the Italian coasts not out of choice."

She views him saying such things all along turned away, rolling her eyes this way and that, and with silent eyes surveys his whole person, then, thus inflamed, angrily breaks forth: [365] "No goddess was your mother, traitor! Nor is Dardanus the founder of your race, but frightful Caucasus on rocky cliffs brought you forth and Hyrcanian tigers nursed you.

357. EACH HEAD mine and yours, either Jupiter's and Mercury's or mine and Ascanius.'

ORDERS THROUGH THE SWIFT BREEZES as above, "bear [this] my message through the skies." [226]

358. IN CONSPICUOUS LIGHT either "bright" or "in a cloud", the light of which is stronger, thus Lucan, "after he filled himself with the true light." [*BC* 9.11–12]

359. WITH MY EARS I DRANK I received; also, this is a pleonasm.

361. I PURSUE as, "we pursue a fleeing Italy." [5.629]

362. ALL ALONG from the beginning of his speech.

TURNED AWAY angered, as, "the goddess turned away and held her eyes fixed on the ground." [1.482]

364. WITH SILENT EYES she herself is silent, as, "and sits before Amata's silent threshold," [7.343] instead of "she herself is silent." Also, an invective follows, which always lacks [rhetorical] status.

365. NO GODDESS WAS YOUR MOTHER this is not only a criticism leveled against Aeneas, but it is also a reprimand for herself, because she had said, "I am fully persuaded (nor is my faith groundless) that he is the offspring of the gods"; [12] from this she now says, "nor is Dardanus the founder of your race."

366. TRAITOR she assaults him with a word lovers would use, thus above, "And did you also hope, you traitor, to be able to conceal…?" [305]

367. CAUCASUS an inhospitable mountain in Scythia.

AND HYRCANIAN TIGERS Arabian, since the Hyrcanian forest is in Arabia. Also, it should be noted that he has made the contrast stronger by omitting the intermediate comparison, for after he dealt with gods he introduced not humans but rocks.

nam quid dissimulo aut quae me ad maiora reseruo?
num fletu ingemuit nostro? num lumina flexit?
num lacrimas uictus dedit aut miseratus amantem est?
quae quibus anteferam? iam iam nec maxima Iuno
nec Saturnius haec oculis pater aspicit aequis.
nusquam tuta fides. eiectum litore egentem
excepi et regni demens in parte locaui.
amissam classem, socios a morte reduxi

368. QVID DISSIMVLO? tacitae quaestioni occurrit, ne quis eius nimiam iracundiam reprehenderet dicens Aenean posse mitigari forsitan precibus.

370. MISERATVS AMANTEM 'miseratus' accusatiuum regit, ut hoc loco, 'misereor' genetiuum, ut *miserere animi non digna ferentis.* [2.144]

371. QVAE QVIBVS ANTEFERAM amphibolia: 'quid prius, quid posterius dicam?'

NEC MAXIMA IVNO aut in Iunonem male dictum est, ut eam non esse maximam dicat, sicut etiam in Iouem; nam conuicium est, quod eum Saturnium dicit, hoc est, nocentem. aut certe iungitur, ut 'nec Iuno aspicit nec Iuppiter.'

373. NVSQVAM TVTA FIDES hoc est, nec apud rem nec apud hominem; Terentius *quid credas, aut cui credas?* [*Adel* 330] et declamauit per contrarium; nam omnis fides tuta est; *haec* ait *nusquam tuta.*

EIECTUM naufragum; legimus enim *huc pauci uestris adnauimus oris.* [1.538] et est separandum.

LITORE EGENTEM id est, 'egentem litoris,' ut *hospitio prohibemur harenae.* [1.540]

374. REGNI IN PARTE ut *ac dominum Aenean in regna recepit,* [214] quod Iarbas queritur.

375. AMISSAM CLASSEM subaudis 'renouaui.'

Why am I pretending? Why should I hold back? How else could I be injured? Had he pitied his lover? Did he once move his eyes? Was he overcome and shed a tear, or comfort me in my love? What should I put before what? Now neither greatest Juno nor the Saturnian sire considers these things with impartial eyes. Nowhere is there secure trust. He was an outcast needing a shore, a poor wretch. I took him in and, fool that I was, made him partner of my crown. I restored his lost fleet and saved his companions from death.

368. WHY AM I PRETENDING? she replies to an unspoken matter, lest anyone chastise her excessive anger saying that Aeneas could perhaps be assuaged by prayers.

370. HAD HE PITIED HIS LOVER *miseratus* (pitied) takes an accusative object, as in this passage; *misereor* (I pity) takes the genitive, as, "pity a soul that bears undeserved pains." [2.144]

371. WHAT SHOULD I PUT BEFORE WHAT a rhetorical ambiguity: "What should I say first? What last?"

NEITHER GREATEST JUNO either this was said as a curse against Juno, so that she says that she is not the greatest, just as it also is against Jupiter, since it is an insult since she calls him Saturnian, meaning harmful. Or else it is linked like this: "neither Juno considers nor Jupiter."

373. NOWHERE IS THERE SECURE TRUST meaning, neither in the situation, nor among men. Terence, "what can you believe, or whom can you believe?" [*Adel* 330] Also, she declared this by way of its opposite, since all trust is secure; "this" she says, "is secure nowhere."

AN OUTCAST shipwrecked, for we read, "a few of us swam here to your shores." [1.538] Also, it should be separated.

NEEDING A SHORE [ablative] i.e. "needful of a shore" [genitive], as, "we are kept from the hospitality of the beach." [1.540]

374. PARTNER OF MY CROWN as, "and she has taken Aeneas into her kingdom for her lord," [214] about which Iarbas complains.

375. LOST FLEET "I rebuilt" understood.

(heu furiis incensa feror!): nunc augur Apollo,
nunc Lyciae sortes, nunc et Ioue missus ab ipso
interpres diuum fert horrida iussa per auras.
scilicet is superis labor est, ea cura quietos
sollicitat. neque te teneo neque dicta refello:
i, sequere Italiam uentis, pete regna per undas.
spero equidem mediis, si quid pia numina possunt,
supplicia hausurum scopulis et nomine Dido

376. FVRIIS INCENSA FEROR quia multa erat in deos locutura. et bona praemittitur excusatio; nam numina non credere curare mortalia et ab his beneficium non sperare furoris est; subiungit enim *si quid pia numina possunt.* [382]

377. NVNC LYCIAE SORTES inrisio est honesta satis, cum his uerbis fit quibus laus praemissa est, ut *et nobis idem Alcimedon duo pocula fecit,* [*E* 3.44] *necdum illis labra admoui sed condita seruo*'; [*E* 3.47] scimus autem Aenean superius [345] haec uerba dixisse.

379. QVIETOS SOLLICITAT Cicero in libris *De deorum natura* triplicem de dis dicit esse opinionem: deos non esse, cuius rei auctor apud Athenas exustus est; esse et nihil curare, ut Epicurei; esse et curare, ut Stoici, secundum quos paulo post *si quid pia numina possunt.* [382] nam modo secundum Epicureos ait *ea cura quietos.*

380. REFELLO redarguo.

381. I, SEQVERE ITALIAM VENTIS satis artificiosa prohibitio, quae fit per concessionem; quae tamen ne non intellecta sit persuasio, permiscenda sunt aliqua quae uetent latenter, ut *uentis, per undas;* sic Terentius *profundat, perdat, pereat; nihil ad me attinet.* [*Adel* 134]

382. MEDIIS SCOPVLIS aut 'manifestis,' ut *medioque ex hoste recepi,* [6.111] aut illa saxa dicit quae sunt inter Africam et Sardiniam Siciliamque.

383. HAVSVRVM luiturum, daturum.

DIDO potest et uocatiuus esse et accusatiuus.

Ah! I am all on fire, enraged by the Furies! Now the prophetic voice of Apollo, now the Lycian lots, and now the messenger of the gods, sent by Jove himself, brings the horrid orders through the air. A worthy job for the powers above, a concern to disturb them in their peaceful state! [380] I neither detain you nor do I refute what you have said. Go, pursue Italy by the winds, pursue this kingdom of yours over the waves. I hope, however, (if the just gods have any power) you will drink your punishment amid the rocks and often call on the name Dido in vain.

376. I AM ALL ON FIRE, ENRAGED BY THE FURIES because she was about to say many things against the gods. Also, a good justification is put forward, for it is a sign of *furor* not to believe that the gods care about mortal affairs and not to hope for favor from them; for she adds, "if the just gods have any power." [382]

377. NOW THE LYCIAN LOTS her mockery is quite proper, because it comes about with these words, by which praise had been put forward, as, "and the same Alcimedon made two cups for me," [*E* 3.44] "I have not yet put my lips to them, but keep them stored away." [*E* 3.47] Also, we know that Aeneas said these words earlier [345].

379. DISTURB THEM IN THEIR PEACEFUL STATE Cicero in his books *On the Nature of the Gods* says that there are three suppositions about the gods: that the gods do not exist (the author of this opinion was burned at Athens); that they exist and care about nothing, as the Epicureans believe; that they exist and do care, as the Stoics believe, in accordance with whom shortly after, "if the just gods have any power." [382] For now in accordance with the Epicureans she says, "a concern [to disturb] them in their peaceful state."

380. I REFUTE I disprove.

381. GO, PURSUE ITALY BY THE WINDS a quite artful prohibition, made by way of concession. In order that the argument not fail in its persuasiveness, some things opposing it, like "by the winds" and "over the waves" had to be sneaked in; thus Terence, "let him breathe his last, let him fail, let him die. It has nothing to do with me." [*Adel* 134]

382. AMID THE ROCKS or "obvious things," as, "I rescued from the enemy's midst." [6.111] Or she refers to those rocks which are between Africa, Sardinia, and Sicily.

383. WILL DRINK will pay, will give.

DIDO this form can be both vocative and accusative.

saepe uocaturum. sequar atris ignibus absens,
et, cum frigida mors anima seduxerit artus,
omnibus umbra locis adero. dabis, improbe, poenas.
audiam et haec Manis ueniet mihi fama sub imos.'
his medium dictis sermonem abrumpit et auras
aegra fugit seque ex oculis auertit et aufert,
linquens multa metu cunctantem et multa uolentem
dicere. suscipiunt famulae conlapsaque membra
marmoreo referunt thalamo stratisque reponunt.

384. SEQVAR ATRIS IGNIBVS ABSENS alii 'furiarum facibus' dicunt, hoc est, 'inuocatas tibi immittam Diras'; alii 'sociorum,' ut paulo post *ferte citi flammas.* [594] melius tamen est ut secundum Vrbanum accipiamus *atris ignibus* 'rogalibus,' qui uisi tempestatem significant, ut Aeneae, sicut in quinto legimus, contigit [5.7]; hoc ergo nunc quod factura est dicit, id est, 'occidam me et rogalibus te persequar flammis.' *absens* quasi 'mortua.' 'rogalibus' autem mali ominis, quod *atris* dixit; legimus et in Horatio *nigrorumque memor dum licet ignium.* [*Carm* 4.12.26]

385. ANIMA SEDVXERIT ARTVS hypallage pro 'animam artubus seduxerit.'

386. OMNIBVS VMBRA LOCIS ADERO dicunt physici biothanatorum animas non recipi in originem suam, nisi uagantes legitimum tempus fati compleuerint; quod poetae ad sepulturam transferunt, ut *centum errant annos.* [6.329] hoc ergo nunc dicit Dido: 'occisura me ante diem sum; uaganti mihi dabis poenas, nam te persequar semper; si autem fuero recepta in originem, poenas tuas audiam, quas uidere non potero.' hic ergo sensus est: si tempestatem euaseris flammarum rogalium, umbra mea te persequetur; si et hanc euaseris, uel recepta audiet famam suppliciorum tuorum.

388. MEDIVM SERMONEM propter hoc quod sequitur, *multa metu cunctantem et multa uolentem dicere.* [390]

391. SVSCIPIVNT subaudis 'eam.'

I, though absent, will pursue with black flames [385] and, when cold death will have separated these limbs from my soul, as a ghost I will haunt you in every place. Monster! You will pay for this. I will hear it; even in the underworld this news will reach me." With these words she breaks off in the middle of the conversation and, growing ill, she shuns the light of day. She turns away from his sight, [390] leaving holding many things back out of fear and wanting to say many things. Her maids raise up, bear her fainting limbs into her marble bedchamber, and gently lay her on a couch.

384. I, THOUGH ABSENT, WILL PURSUE WITH BLACK FLAMES some say "with the torches of the Furies," that is, "I will summon the Furies and send them against you." Others say with the torches "of allies" as shortly after, "run quick, fetch flames." [594] But it is better that, according to Urbanus, we understand "black flames" as "belonging to funeral pyres," which, when seen, indicate a disaster, as happened to Aeneas as we read in the fifth book. [5.7] So now she says what she is about to do, i.e., "I will kill myself and follow you with the flames of my funeral pyre." "Absent" as though "dead," and "of my funeral pyre" meaning "of bad omen," because she says "black." We also read in Horace: "and mindful of the black fires while possible." [*Carm* 4.12.26]

385. WILL HAVE SEPARATED THESE LIMBS FROM MY SOUL hypallage for "it will have separated my soul from my limbs."

386. AS A GHOST I WILL HAUNT YOU IN EVERY PLACE natural philosophers say that the souls of those who die a violent death are not welcomed at their point of origin unless they have completed the time prescribed by fate as wanderers, which poets translate into burial, as, "they wander for a hundred years." [6.329] So now Dido says: "I will die before my day; you will be punished for my wandering; for I will follow you always. And if I will have been returned to my origin, I will hear your punishment, which I will not be able to see." This, then, is the sense: if you escape the disaster of my pyre's flames, my shade will follow you: and if you escape this as well, or I have been welcomed to my point of origin, my ghost will hear the rumor of your punishment.

388. IN THE MIDDLE OF THE CONVERSATION what follows is because of this, "holding many things back out of fear and wanting to say many things." [390]

391. RAISE UP "her" is understood.

At pius Aeneas, quamquam lenire dolentem
solando cupit et dictis auertere curas,
multa gemens magnoque animum labefactus amore
iussa tamen diuum exsequitur classemque reuisit.
tum uero Teucri incumbunt et litore celsas
deducunt toto naues. natat uncta carina,
frondentisque ferunt remos et robora siluis
infabricata fugae studio.
migrantes cernas totaque ex urbe ruentis.
ac uelut ingentem formicae farris aceruum
cum populant, hiemis memores, tectoque reponunt;

397. TVM VERO TEVCRI INCVMBVNT regis praesentia; sic in nono *tunc uero incumbunt, urguet praesentia Turni.* [9.73]

399. FRONDENTESQVE FERVNT REMOS non qui erant, sed qui esse poterant, ut *quos ego sim totiens iam dedignata maritos.* [536]

400. FVGAE STVDIO celeris profectionis, ut *ille uolans simul arua fuga simul aequora uerrit.* [*G* 3.201]

401. CERNAS honesta figura si rem tertiae personae in secundam referas, ut 'si quis cernat.'

402. FORMICAE ad studium respicit comparatio hoc loco. et notandum cautelam exprimi per hanc comparationem; Horatius *paruula, nam exemplo est, magni formica laboris,* [*Serm* 1.1.33] Iuuenalis *formica tandem quidam expauere magistra.* [*Sat* 6.361] sane 'formica' dicta est ab eo quod ferat micas.

FARRIS solum nomen est quod 'r' geminet in genetiuo; monadicon ergo est, sicut 'sol.' item 'cor cordis' solum in 'dis' mittit genetiuum; item 's' geminat 'as assis.' et haec carent exemplis.

403. CVM POPVLANT antique dixit; nam hoc uerbum apud ueteres actiuum fuit, nunc tantum deponens est.

HIEMIS MEMORES Horatius *quae, simul inuersum contristat Aquarius annum, non usquam prorepit.* [*Serm* 1.1.36]

But pious Aeneas, though he desires to ease her grief, and by words to calm her anguish, [395] heaving many a sigh, and troubled in his mind by mighty love, obeys the commands of the gods and returns to his fleet. Then indeed the Trojans attend to their work and launch the ships all along the shore. The pitchy keel floats [400] and in their eagerness for flight they bring oars with leaves and unhewn timber. You could see them leaving and pouring from all quarters of the town, as when ants, mindful of winter, plunder a large pile of grain and hoard it in their nests.

397. THEN INDEED THE TROJANS ATTEND TO THEIR WORK by the presence of the king as, "then indeed they attend to their work, the presence of Turnus drives them." [9.73]

399. THEY BRING OARS WITH LEAVES not those that actually were oars, but those that could be, as, "whom I have so often disdained as husbands." [536]

400. AND IN THEIR EAGERNESS FOR FLIGHT of a swift departure, as, "flight at the same time sweeps the watery fields." [*G* 3.201]

401. YOU COULD SEE it is correct construction if you change something from third person into second, as, "if anyone should see."

402. ANTS the comparison refers back to the eagerness in this passage, and it should be noted that carefulness is portrayed through this comparison; Horace, "the tiny ant of great labor, for that is their example," [*Serm* 1.1.33] Juvenal, "but an ant certainly fears its queen." [*Sat* 6.361] Of course they were called ants (*formicae*) from the fact that they carry (*fero*) crumbs (*micae*).

GRAIN [*FARRIS*] is the only noun where the *r* doubles in the genitive so it is a *monadicon*, just like *sol* (sun). Likewise, only *cor, cordis* (heart) shows a genitive in *-dis.* Likewise the *s* doubles in *as, assis* (penny). These also lack examples.

403. AS WHEN [THEY] PLUNDER he used this verb in an archaic form because it was active among older authors; now it is only a deponent.

MINDFUL OF WINTER Horace, "which, just as Aquarius saddens the upturned year, slithers to nowhere." [*Serm* 1.1.36]

it nigrum campis agmen praedamque per herbas
conuectant calle angusto; pars grandia trudunt
obnixae frumenta umeris; pars agmina cogunt
castigantque moras; opere omnis semita feruet.
quis tibi tum, Dido, cernenti talia sensus,
quosue dabas gemitus, cum litora feruere late
prospiceres arce ex summa, totumque uideres
misceri ante oculos tantis clamoribus aequor!

404. IT NIGRVM CAMPIS AGMEN hemistichium Ennii de elephantis dictum, quo ante Accius usus est de Indis.

405. CALLE ANGVSTO 'callis' est semita tenuior, callo pecorum praedurata; 'semita' est semis uia, unde et semita dicta est; 'uia' est actus dimidius, qua potest ire uehiculum; nam 'actus' duo carpenta capit propter euntium et uenientium uehiculorum occursum.

GRANDIA TRVDVNT quae portare non possunt.

407. MORAS tardas, morantes.

409. FERVERE LATE infinitus hic a tertia est coniugatione, id est, a 'feruo feruis'; nam secundae coniugationis uerba, perdito 'e' quod habent ante 'o,' in tertiam migrant, ut 'ferueo feruo,' 'fulgeo fulgo.' hinc est *feruere Leucaten auroque effulgere fluctus.* [8.677] sic etiam Horatius *uade, uale, caue ne titubes mandataque frangas;* [*Ep* 1.13.19] nam *caue* '-ue' longa est, nec uocalis sequitur, ut in Vergilio *uale, uale, inquit, Iolla.* [*E* 3.79] sed dicimus a tertia esse coniugatione imperatiuum, ut 'cauo cauis'; hinc etiam Catullus *cauere* dixit. [Frag 10 Lach]

410. ARCE EX SVMMA regum enim fuit habitare in arcibus propter tutelam. denique Romae Valerius, cum in Esquiliis domum haberet altissimam, inuidiae causa eam complanauit. item Augustus post Actiacum bellum Palatium ex suo praecepto aedificatum, cum esset domus priuata, donauit rei publicae.

411. TANTIS CLAMORIBVS nautarum scilicet.

The black battalion marches over the plains and [405] along the narrow track they carry their loot through the meadows; some, shoving with their shoulders, push the heavy seeds; some encourage the slow and chastise those that lag. The path heaves widely with their work. Dido, how were you then affected with so sad a prospect? What groans did you utter when [410] from your lofty tower you watched the shores heaving widely with activity and with your own eyes observed the whole watery plain mixed with such loud shouts?

404. THE BLACK BATTALION MARCHES OVER THE PLAINS a half verse of Ennius about elephants, which Accius used earlier about the Indians.

405. ALONG THE NARROW TRACK a track (*callis*) is narrower than a path (*semita*), hardened by the thick skin (*callum*) of cattle. A path (*semita*) is a half-lane (*semi via*), and from this it is called a *semita*; a lane (*via*) is a half-road (*actus*), on which a vehicle is able to travel: for a road (*actus*) accommodates two carts, for the meeting of coming and going traffic.

PUSH THE HEAVY SEEDS things which they are not able to carry.

407. THOSE THAT LAG slow, dallying.

409. HEAVES WIDELY this [*fervere*] is an infinitive from the third conjugation, i.e. from *fervo fervis*, since verbs of the second conjugation, when they have dropped the *e* that they have before the *o*, change to third, as, *ferveo-fervo*, *fulgeo-fulgo*. Hence, "Leucate heaved and its waves gleamed with gold." [8.677] Thus Horace also, "go, be well, be careful you don't stagger and break orders," [*Ep* 1.13.19] since in *cave* (be careful) the *-ve* is long and a vowel does not follow, as in Virgil, " "farewell, farewell, Iolla," he said." [*E* 3.79]. But we say this is a third-conjugation imperative, like *cavo cavis*. For this reason Catullus said *cavere* (to be careful).

410. FROM YOUR LOFTY TOWER it was the custom of kings to live in citadels for protection. Then in Rome Valerius, since he had a very tall house on the Esquiline, leveled it on account of envy. Likewise Augustus, after the battle of Actium, gave to the republic the *palatium* he had built according to his own instructions, although it was a private residence.

411. WITH SUCH LOUD SHOUTS namely of the sailors.

improbe Amor, quid non mortalia pectora cogis!
ire iterum in lacrimas, iterum temptare precando
cogitur et supplex animos submittere amori,
ne quid inexpertum frustra moritura relinquat.
'Anna, uides toto *properari* litore; circum
undique conuenere; uocat iam carbasus auras,
puppibus et laeti nautae imposuere coronas.

412. INPROBE AMOR exclamatio a poeta contra amorem. et hoc est quod Horatius dicit *hoc amet, hoc spernat promissi carminis auctor.* [*Ars Poet* 45] tale est et illud in tertio *auri sacra fames,* [3.57] id est, cupiditas; nam et illic amoris est increpatio, qui secundum philosophos omnium generalis est rerum. hinc est quod apud inferos Eriphyla inter amantes commemoratur, quae monile concupierat.

413. IRE ITERVM IN LACRIMAS hinc est amoris inprobitas, quae lacrimis cogit rogare dudum superbam. est autem speciosa elocutio 'pergit in lacrimas.'

PRECANDO 'cantando.' in hoc modo '-do' naturaliter breuis est; sic Terentianus *ut uitae dubius uarios renouando dolores.* [*Syll* 1296] plerumque tamen a Vergilio producitur, ut *cantando tu illum,* [*E* 3.25] item *cantando rumpitur anguis.* [*E* 8.71]

414. SVMMITERE AMORI ac si diceret 'non Aeneae'; aut certe Aenean amorem uocauit.

415. NE QVID INEXPERTVM FRVSTRA MORITVRA RELINQVAT rogabat, non spe inpetrandi sed ne esset quod sibi posset inputare si non rogasset, quamquam frustra rogaret. et *frustra* ex iudicio poetae dictum est; sic Sallustius *falso queritur de natura sua genus humanum,* [*Bell Iug* 1.1] ut supra *hoc amet, hoc spernat promissi carminis auctor.* [Horatius, *Ars Poet* 45; cf. ad 412]

416. PROPERARI LITORE CIRCVM circum litus. nam postposita praepositio et accentum mutauit et suas perdidit uires. 'properari' autem inpersonale est.

418. ET LAETI NAVTAE id est, minime timentes.

Shameless love, how irresistible is your power over the mind of mortals! She is once more reduced to tears, once more tries him by prayers, and subjects her soul to love, [415] lest, by leaving any means untried, she should throw away her life in vain.

"Anna, you see the shore all over how they are hurrying. From all sides they gather; the canvas now invites the gales; and the joyful sailors have crowned their sterns with garlands.

412. SHAMELESS LOVE an exclamation by the poet against love. And this is what Horace says, "let him love this, let him scorn this, the author of promised poems." [*Ars Poet* 45] Such, too, is it in the third book, "sacred hunger of gold," [3.57] i.e. desire; since it is that, the rebuking of love, that, according to the philosophers, is shared by all things. This is the reason that Eriphyla, who had desired a necklace, is remembered in the underworld among the lovers.

413. ONCE MORE REDUCED TO TEARS here is the shamelessness of love, which now forces a proud woman to beg with her tears. It is also an impressive expression: "she proceeds into tears."

BY PRAYERS (*PRECANDO*) "by singing" (*cantando*); In this instance the syllable *-do* is naturally short; thus Terentianus, "as he uncertain of life by renewing various pains" [*Syll* 1296] But often it is lengthened by Virgil, as, "you [beat] him in singing?" [*E* 3.25] likewise, "the snake is burst by singing." [*E* 8.71]

414. SUBJECTS TO LOVE as if she were saying "not to Aeneas," or else she called Aeneas [her] love.

415. LEST, BY LEAVING ANY MEANS UNTRIED, SHE SHOULD THROW AWAY HER LIFE IN VAIN she asked, not in hope of succeeding, but so that there would not be any reason for which she could blame herself had she not begged, even though she was begging in vain. "In vain" was said because it is the judgment of the poet. Thus Sallust, "the human race complains about its nature falsely," [*Bel Iug* 1.1] as above, "let him love this, let him scorn this, the author of promised poems." [Horace, *Ars Poet* 45; cf. on 412]

416. FROM ALL SIDES THEY GATHER over all the shore, for the preposition placed after [the noun] both changed its accent and lost its force. Also, the verb *properari* is impersonal.

418. AND THE JOYFUL SAILORS i.e. hardly afraid.

hunc ego si potui tantum sperare dolorem,
et perferre, soror, potero. miserae hoc tamen unum
exsequere, Anna, mihi. solam nam perfidus ille
te colere, arcanos etiam tibi credere sensus;
sola uiri mollis aditus et tempora noras.
i, soror, atque hostem supplex adfare superbum:
non ego cum Danais Troianam exscindere gentem
Aulide iuraui classemue ad Pergama misi,
nec patris Anchisae cineres Manesue reuelli:

419. SPERARE DOLOREM pro 'timere.' et est acyrologia; nam speramus bona, timemus aduersa. hoc autem dicit: si scirem abiturum Aenean, non tantum diligerem; si non dilexissem, minus dolerem.

SI POTVI autem pro 'si potuissem.' et sic est dictum, ut *omnia praecepi atque animo mecum ante peregi;* [6.105] ac si diceret 'nihil mihi nouum contigit.'

421. MIHI pro me exsequere.

422. COLERE colebat, infinitus pro indicatiuo.

423. MOLLES ADITVS faciles, ut *et quae mollissima fandi tempora.* [293]

424. HOSTEM SVPERBVM postquam ex aperto denegauit se Carthagini esse mansurum.

426. AVLIDE IVRAVI Aulis insula est in qua coniurarunt Graeci se non ante reuersuros quam Troia caperetur. et est sensus illud spectans *scio me Danais e classibus unum.* [3.602] *Aulide* autem aut 'in Aulide' aut pro 'Aulidi.'

AD PERGAMA in Pergama, id est, contra Pergama.

427. ANCHISAE CINERES MANESVE REVELLI quod dicitur ex oraculo fecisse Diomedes et secum eius ossa portasse, quae postea reddidit Aeneae, cum multa aduersa perferret; hinc est *saluete recepti nequiquam cineres.* [5.80] sciendum sane Varronem dicere Diomedem eruta Anchisae ossa filio reddidisse, Catonem autem adfirmare quod Anchises ad Italiam uenit. tanta est inter ipsos uarietas et historiarum confusio.

REVELLI non 'reuulsi'; nam 'uelli' et 'reuelli' dicimus. 'uulsus' uero et 'reuulsus' usurpatum est tantum in participiis contra naturam.

O sister, if I were able to foresee this sadness, I will be able to bear it. [420] But, Anna, perform this one request for wretched me. That traitorous man made you alone his confidant and always trusted you with the secrets of his soul. You alone knew his moods and the soft approaches to his heart. Go, sister, and as a suppliant address the arrogant enemy. [425] I did not conspire with the Greeks at Aulis to destroy the Trojan race or sent a fleet to Pergamum. Nor were the ashes or *manes* of his father Anchises torn up.

419. TO FORESEE THIS SADNESS in place of "to fear." Also, this is an acyrology since we hope for good things and fear bad things. However, she says this: if I knew that Aeneas would leave, I would not love him so much; if I had not loved him, I would grieve less.

IF I WERE ABLE [the perfect indicative] instead of "if I had been able" [the pluperfect subjunctive]. And thus it was said, as, "I have foreseen everything, and have already examined it with my mind," [6.105] as if she were saying, "nothing unusual has affected me."

421. FOR [WRETCHED] ME perform this on my behalf.

422. MADE...HIS CONFIDANT he used to make you his confidant; infinitive for the indicative.

423. THE SOFT APPROACHES easy ones, as, "and what [may be] the softest moments of address." [293]

424. ARROGANT ENEMY after he openly denied that he would remain at Carthage.

426. CONSPIRE...AT AULIS Aulis is the island on which the Greeks swore that they would not return before Troy was captured. And this is the meaning he has in mind thinking of "I know that I am one from the Greek fleets." [3.602] In addition, [he uses the ablative] *Aulide* either [for the ablative with preposition] *in Aulide* or for [the locative] *Aulidi.*

TO PERGAMVM toward Pergamum, i.e. in opposition to Pergamum.

427. THE ASHES OR *MANES* OF ANCHISES TORN UP a thing that Diomedes is said to have done (on the advice of an oracle), carrying the bones with him, which he later returned to Aeneas after he had suffered many misfortunes. Whence, "greetings, ashes recovered in vain." [5.80] Of course it should be understood that Varro said that Diomedes had returned to his son the bones of Anchises that he had dug up; Cato, however, asserted that Anchises came to Italy. So great is the diversity and confusion of the stories.

TORN UP (*REVELLI*) not "having been torn up" (*reuulsi*); We say "to be torn" (*uelli*) and "to be torn up." (*reuelli*) But "torn" and "torn up" are only used in participles against their nature.

cur mea dicta neget duras demittere in auris.
quo ruit? extremum hoc miserae det munus amanti:
exspectet facilemque fugam uentosque ferentis.
non iam coniugium antiquum, quod prodidit, oro,
nec pulchro ut Latio careat regnumque relinquat:
tempus inane peto, requiem spatiumque furori,
dum mea me uictam doceat fortuna dolere.
extremam hanc oro ueniam (miserere sororis),
quam mihi cum dederis cumulatam morte remittam.'

429. QVO RVIT properat sine respectu salutis; nam hoc dicit, 'quod peto etiam ipsi prodest,' amoris scilicet inpatientia.

430. FERENTES bene flantes, propitios.

431. QVOD PRODIDIT quod decepit. et bene; ad diruptionem enim coniugii inmutata uoluntas sufficit.

432. PVLCHRO VT LATIO CAREAT quod illi pulchrum uidetur. sic est illud *o tantum libeat mecum tibi sordida rura,* [*E* 2.28] quae tibi sic uidentur.

433. TEMPVS INANE PETO sine officio coeundi; nam 'sine beneficio' non procedit, cum *spatium* petat et *requiem.*

434. DVM MEA ME VICTAM D[OCEAT] F[ORTUNA] D[OLERE] *mea fortuna* id est 'aduersa,' ut *hac Troiana tenus fuerit fortuna secuta;* [6.62] ex eo statu in quo est fortunam dixit. *doceat* autem *dolere,* illud est quia non habet in aduersis patientiam nisi qui dolere consueuit; hoc ergo petit, ut ei praestetur tempus per quod discat aduersa perferre.

435. ORO VENIAM beneficium, ut *orantes ueniam.* [1.519]

MISERERE SORORIS genetiuum tantum regit.

436. QVAM MIHI CVM DEDERIS CVMVLATAM MORTE REMITTAM sensus est: quod beneficium cum mihi cumulatum dederis, sola morte derelinquam. et hic intellectus est melior, *quam mihi cum dederis cumulatam;* quam lectionem Tucca et Varius probant. nam male quidam legunt 'quam mihi cum dederit (id est Aeneas) cumulata morte relinquam', et uolunt intellegi 'acceptum ab illo beneficium morte cumulabo et sic relinquam,' ut amantes dicere consuerunt, ut *aerii specula de montis in undas deferar; extremum hoc munus morientis habeto;* [*E* 8.59] nam si eam odio habet Aeneas, restat ut eius morte laetetur. sed non procedit; nemo enim dicit 'ueniam cumulata,' sed 'cumulatam.'

Why does he block his ears to my words? To what place is he rushing? Let him grant just this one last favor to his unhappy lover; [430] may he wait for an easy escape and fair winds. I plead no more for that old promised wedlock, which he has betrayed, nor that he should deprive himself of fair Latium and relinquish a kingdom. I ask a brief moment, a truce and break from this pain, until my fortune teaches me to grieve in my conquered state. [435] This favor I implore as the last, (pity your sister!) and when you have granted it, I will repay him with interest by my death."

429. TO WHAT PLACE IS HE RUSHING he hurries without concern for safety; for she says this: "what I seek also profits itself," namely the impatience of love.

430. FAIR blowing well, favorable.

431. WHICH HE HAS BETRAYED which he deceived, and well he did since changed desire is sufficient for the dissolution of marriage.

432. DEPRIVE HIMSELF OF FAIR LATIUM which seems beautiful to him. Thus is that, "O how pleasing for you to live with me in the country so sordid to you," [*E* 2.28] which seems that way to you.

433. I ASK A BRIEF MOMENT without conjugal duty; for it cannot be construed as "without favor" since she is seeking a "truce" and a "break."

434. UNTIL MY FORTUNE TEACHES ME TO GRIEVE IN MY CONQUERED STATE "my fortune," i.e. "adverse," as, "may Trojan fortune have pursued us only up to here." [6.62] From the position in which she is, she called it Fortune. Moreover, "teach to grieve" means this, because only one who has become accustomed to grieving has patience in adversity. So she asks that time be furnished for her in which she can learn to endure adversity.

435. THIS FAVOR I IMPLORE a favor, as, "imploring a favor." [1.519]

PITY YOUR SISTER the verb *miseror* takes only the genitive.

436. WHEN YOU HAVE GRANTED IT, I WILL REPAY HIM WITH INTEREST BY MY DEATH the idea is: when you will have granted me the favor with interest, I will leave only by death. This is the better understanding, "when you have granted it with interest," which is the reading Tucca and Varius approve. Some read wrongly, "when he (i.e. Aeneas) will have granted me this I will leave you with the totality of my death," and they wish [this] to be understood, "I will top the kindness received from him with my death and thus leave him," as lovers are in the habit of saying, as, "I will be drawn down from a lofty mountaintop into the waves; take this last gift of the dying." [*E* 8.59] If Aeneas did hate her, it remains that he would be happy at her death. But that does not work, for no one says "she earned a favor with interest" but that it "was earned with interest."

Talibus orabat, talisque miserrima fletus
fertque refertque soror: sed nullis ille mouetur
fletibus aut uoces ullas tractabilis audit;
fata obstant placidasque uiri deus obstruit aures.
ac uelut annoso ualidam cum robore quercum
Alpini Boreae nunc hinc nunc flatibus illinc
eruere inter se certant; it stridor, et alte
consternunt terram concusso stipite frondes;
ipsa haeret scopulis et quantum uertice ad auras
aetherias tantum radicem in Tartara tendit:
haud secus adsiduis hinc atque hinc uocibus heros
tunditur, et magno persensit pectore curas;
mens immota manet; lacrimae uoluuntur inanes.

438. FERTQVE REFERTQVE non ab Aenea, qui nihil dicit, sed a Didone fert et refert, id est, iterum portat.

439. VOCES VLLAS TRACTABILIS AVDIT cur mitis non audit? quasi mirum est, recusat dicendo *fata obstant placidasque uiri deus obstruit aures.* [440] aut certe *uoces tractabilis* accipe, aut alias *tractabilis.*

440. DEVS Iuppiter scilicet, unde et supra Dido ait *Saturnius.* [372]

442. ALPINI BOREAE flantes de Alpibus, quae Gallorum lingua alti montes uocantur.

NVNC HINC NVNC ILLINC sicut Aeneas ab Anna et Didone.

443. IT STRIDOR ad dolorem Aeneae pertinet, de quo ait *magno persensit pectore curas.* [448]

ALTE iugiter, diu.

444. CONSTERNVNT implent, ut *strata iacent passim sua quaeque sub arbore poma.* [*E* 7.54]

FRONDES sicut lacrimae Aeneae.

445. HAERET SCOPVLIS sicut ille in consilio perseuerat.

446. TANTVM RADICEM IN TARTARA TENDIT secundum physicos, qui dicunt parem esse altitudinem radicum et arborum.

449. LACRIMAE INANES quia *mens immota manet.*

To this effect she prayed and her sister, deeply distressed, bears once and again this mournful message to Aeneas; but by none of her mournful messages is he moved, nor listens with calm regard to any words. [440] The Fates stand in his way; and the god renders his ears deaf to compassion. And as the Alpine north winds by their blasts, now on this side, now on that, strive with joint force to overturn a sturdy ancient oak; loud howling goes forth also from on high; leaves strew the ground in heaps, while the trunk is shaken; [445] the tree itself cleaves fast to the rocks; and as high as it shoots up to the top in the ethereal regions, so deep it descends with its root towards Tartarus: just so the hero on this side and that side is plied with importunate remonstrances and feels deep pangs in his mighty soul his mind remains unmoved; unavailing tears are shed.

438. BEARS ONCE AND AGAIN not from Aeneas, who says nothing, but she bears once and again from Dido, i.e. she carries it repeatedly.

439. NOR LISTENS WITH CALM REGARD TO ANY WORDS Why does he not gently listen to her? It is almost a wonder that [Virgil] defends him by saying "the fates stand in his way; and heaven renders his ears deaf to compassion." [440] Either read "calm words," or else "[he is] calm."

440. THE GOD namely Jupiter, which is also why Dido says above "Saturnius."

442. ALPINE NORTH WINDS blowing from the Alps, which means "high mountains" in the language of the Gauls.

NOW ON THIS SIDE, NOW ON THAT just as Aeneas [is buffeted] from Anna and Dido

443. LOUD HOWLING GOES FORTH pertains to the grief of Aeneas, of whom he says "he feels the pain deeply in his great heart." [448]

FROM ON HIGH perpetually, for a long time.

444. STREW they cover, as, "they lie strewn out in every direction each under the apple tree." [*E* 7.54]

LEAVES just like the tears of Aeneas.

445. CLEAVES FAST TO THE ROCKS just as he had remained steadfast to his plan.

446. SO DEEP IT DESCENDS WITH ITS ROOT TOWARDS TARTARUS according to natural philosophers, who say that the height of trees and the depth of their roots are equal.

449. UNAVAILING TEARS because "his mind remains unmoved."

Tum uero infelix fatis exterrita Dido
mortem orat; taedet caeli conuexa tueri.
quo magis inceptum peragat lucemque relinquat,
uidit, turicremis cum dona imponeret aris,
horrendum dictu, latices nigrescere sacros,
fusaque in obscenum se uertere uina cruorem.
hoc uisum nulli, non ipsi effata sorori.
praeterea fuit in tectis de marmore templum
coniugis antiqui, miro quod honore colebat,
uelleribus niueis et festa fronde reuinctum:
hinc exaudiri uoces et uerba uocantis
uisa uiri, nox cum terras obscura teneret;

450. TVM VERO post desperationem.

EXTERRITA praecipitata, turbata.

451. MORTEM ORAT pro 'desiderat,' ut *mortemque miserrimus opto;* [2.655] aut certe ideo *orat,* quia consecrata fuit nec mori poterat nisi soluta consecratione.

CAELI CONVEXA incurua caeli.

453. TVRICREMIS cremantibus tura.

456. HOC VISVM hoc quod uiderat nulli dixit. quid est *nulli?* ne sorori quidem, cui fuerat de amore confessa.

458. CONIVGIS ANTIQVI aut prioris aut cari.

MIRO QVOD HONORE COLEBAT exhibendo ea quae circa uiuos solent fieri. moris enim fuerat ut nubentes puellae, simul uenissent ad limen mariti, postes antequam ingrederentur ornarent laneis uittis, unde ait *uelleribus niueis,* et oleo ungerent, unde uxores dictae sunt, quasi unxores.

459. FESTA FRONDE diuina, tamquam numen coleret. sane hoc loco latenter quam supra diximus tangit historiam; nam si amabat Aeneam, utique non coleret extinctum maritum.

461. VISA VIRI non enim erant uera, ut supra.

NOX CVM TERRAS OBSCVRA TENERET a uerisimili.

[450] Then, indeed, unhappy Dido, struck to the heart by her fate, prays for death; she sickens of beholding the canopy of the sky. The more to prompt her to execute her purpose and to part with the light, while she was presenting her offerings upon the incense-smoked altar she beheld, horrid to relate, the sacred liquors grow black and [455] the outpoured wine turn into inauspicious blood. This vision she revealed to none, not even to her sister. Besides, there was in the palace a marble shrine in honor of her former husband, to which she paid extraordinary veneration, [having] it encircled with snow-white fleece and festal garlands. [460] Hence voices, and the words of her calling husband seemed to be heard, when dim night shrouded the earth;

450. THEN, INDEED after hopelessness.

STRUCK cast down, in disorder.

451. PRAYS FOR DEATH for "desired," as "and most wretchedly I hope for death"; [2.655] or else "she prays" because she was consecrated and could not die unless consecration were removed.

THE CANOPY OF THE SKY the arch of the sky.

453. INCENSE-SMOKED smoked with incense.

456. THIS VISION what she had seen she told no one. What is "to no one?" Not even to her sister, to whom she had confessed her love.

458. OF HER FORMER HUSBAND either the first, or the beloved.

TO WHICH SHE PAID EXTRAORDINARY VENERATION by offering those things that are normally done among the living. For it had been the custom for married girls, as they came to the thresholds of their new husbands, to decorate the doorposts with woolen bands before they entered (so he says "with snow-white fleece") and to anoint themselves with oil, so they are called wives (*uxores*) as though anointed (*unxores*).

459. FESTAL GARLANDS divine, as though she were honoring a divinity. Of course he touches on the story we mentioned above, for if she loved Aeneas, she would certainly not honor her dead husband.

461. OF HER HUSBAND...SEEMED though they were not real, as above.

WHEN DIM NIGHT SHROUDED THE EARTH by verisimilitude.

solaque culminibus ferali carmine bubo
saepe queri et longas in fletum ducere uoces;
multaque praeterea uatum praedicta priorum
terribili monitu horrificant. agit ipse furentem
in somnis ferus Aeneas; semperque relinqui
sola sibi, semper longam incomitata uidetur
ire uiam et Tyrios deserta quaerere terra,
Eumenidum ueluti demens uidet agmina Pentheus,
et solem geminum et duplicis se ostendere Thebas;
aut Agamemnonius scaenis agitatus Orestes,
armatam facibus matrem et serpentibus atris
cum fugit, ultricesque sedent in limine Dirae.

462. SOLA BVBO *sola* contra genus posuit; Lucanus *et laetae iurantur aues bubone sinistro,* [*BC* 5.396] item Ouidius *infandus bubo.* [*Met* 5.550] et hoc est in usu; sed Vergilius mutauit, referens ad auem. plerumque enim genus relicta specialitate a generali sumimus, ut si dicas 'bona turdus' referendo ad auem; item si dicamus 'prima est a,' id est littera, cum 'a' sit neutri generis.

FERALI CARMINE bene hoc addidit. non enim omni modo malum est bubonis omen, sed cum canit. cantus autem eius aut fletum imitatur aut gemitum; tacens ostendit felicitatem. omnes enim aues oscines malae, praepetes bonae sunt; uel econtra malae praepetes, oscines bonae sunt.

464. PRIORVM legitur et 'piorum'; sed illuc spectat *heu uatum ignarae mentes! quid uota furentem.* [65]

465. HORRIFICANT horrorem incutiunt.

466. IN SOMNIS pro 'insomniis,' id est uigiliis.

SEMPERQVE RELINQVI per omnes noctes nauigare uidebatur Aeneas, quasi eam semper desereret.

467. INCOMITATA quod ferale, id est, mortiferum omen est, et praecipue regibus.

469. AGMINA PENTHEVS aut impetus aut secundum Vrbanum 'agmina' serpentium. Pentheus autem secundum tragoediam Pacuuii furuit etiam ipse.

471. SCAENIS AGITATVS famosus, celebratus tragoediis. et 'agitatus' quia et furuit et multae sunt de eo tragoediae, quasi 'frequenter actus.'

472. ARMATAM MATREM causam ipsam furoris.

473. SEDENT IN LIMINE DIRAE a Pacuuio Orestes inducitur Pyladis admonitu propter uitandas furias ingressus Apollinis templum; unde cum uellet exire, inuadebatur a furiis; hinc ergo est *sedent in limine.*

and on the house-tops the solitary owl often complained in doleful song and spun out his long notes in a mournful strain. Besides, many predictions of former prophets [465] terrify her with dreadful forebodings. Aeneas himself, now stern and cruel, disturbs her raving in her sleep; and still she seems to be abandoned in solitude, still to be going on a long tedious journey with no attendance and to be in quest of her Tyrians in some desert country: as frantic Pentheus sees troops of Furies, [470] two suns, and Thebes appear double; or like Orestes, Agamemnon's son, agitated on the stage when he flees from his mother armed with firebrands and black snakes and the avenged Furies are planted at the threshold.

462. THE SOLITARY OWL the gender of *sola* does not agree: Lucan says "and the happy birds swore to the unfavorable owl," [*BC* 5.396] likewise Ovid "the unspeakable owl." [*Met* 5.550] This is also how it is now used, but Virgil has changed it, referring to "bird" [which is feminine]. For often we take the gender from the type of thing, ignoring the specific thing, as if you were to say "a good thrush" (*bona turdus*) by referring to the bird and likewise if we say "the first is *a*" (*prima est a,*) i.e. the first letter, although *a* is neuter.

IN DOLEFUL SONG he added this well: for the omen of the owl is not in every way evil, but only when it sings, for its song imitates wailing, or sighing: being silent it shows good fortune. For all *oscines* are evil, all *praepetes* good; or, on the other hand, all *praepetes* are evil, *oscines* good.

464. FORMER [*PRIORUM*] there is also the reading "pious," (*piorum*) but he is refering to, "Alas! how ignorant the minds of seers! what can prayers ... avail a raging lover?" [65]

465. TERRIFY they produce terror.

466. IN HER SLEEP for *insomniis*, i.e. during her sleeplessness.

STILL ABANDONED Aeneas seemed to sail every night, as if he were abandoning her endlessly.

467. WITH NO ATTENDANCE an omen which is funereal, i.e. death-bearing, especially for rulers.

469. AS PENTHEUS SEES TROOPS either an attack or, according to Urbanus, troops of serpents. Pentheus, however, according to the tragedy of Pacuvius, was himself mad.

471. AGITATED ON THE STAGE celebrated, famous in tragedies. And "agitated" both because he was mad and because there are many tragedies about him, as if he were "frequently acted."

472. MOTHER ARMED the cause itself of the rage.

473. FURIES ARE PLANTED AT THE THRESHOLD Orestes is portrayed by Pacuvius as having entered Apollo's temple on the advice of Pylades in order to avoid the Furies. For this reason, when Orestes wanted to leave, he was assailed by the Furies. For this reason, "they are planted at the threshold."

Ergo ubi concepit furias euicta dolore
decreuitque mori, tempus secum ipsa modumque
exigit, et maestam dictis adgressa sororem
consilium uultu tegit ac spem fronte serenat:
'inueni, germana, uiam (gratare sorori)
quae mihi reddat eum, uel eo me soluat amantem.
oceani finem iuxta solemque cadentem
ultimus Aethiopum locus est, ubi maximus Atlas
axem humero torquet stellis ardentibus aptum:
hinc mihi Massylae gentis monstrata sacerdos,
Hesperidum templi custos, epulasque draconi
quae dabat et sacros seruabat in arbore ramos,

478. VIAM rationem.

GRATARE gratulare, suscipe gaudium pro sorore; sic enim dicimus 'grator tibi honorem.'

479. EVM Aeneam, quem ut notum noluit dicere.

480. OCEANI FINEM IVXTA finem oceani nullus nouit, sed initium; quod et ipsum potest finis uideri, aliunde sumpto principio.

481. AETHIOPVM Aethiopiae duae sunt, una circa ortum solis, altera circa occasum in Mauritania, quam nunc dicit. et dicta Aethiopia a colore populorum, quos solis uicinitas torret.

ATLAS nullum nomen Graecum 'ns' terminatur.

482. TORQVET sustinet.

STELLIS APTVM satis perite loquitur; nam *aptum* 'coniunctum' dicit ἀπὸ τοῦ ἅπτεσθαι, non 'insignitum stellis'; axis enim non habet stellas, qui est medius inter septemtriones, unde et Graece ἄναστρος dicitur. septemtriones autem non occidere axis uicinitas facit, non quia in axe sunt.

483. HINC MIHI MASSYLAE GENTIS MONSTRATA SACERDOS *monstrata* 'praedicta'; quae est oriundo Massyla, aliquando horti Hesperidum sacerdos, nunc habitans circa Atlantem. nam aliter non procedit. Massylia enim mediterranea est; Berenicis ciuitas Libyae, unde haud longe horti sunt Hesperidum; *Atlas* uero *maximus* in Mauritania est.

484. HESPERIDVM TEMPLI CVSTOS Hesperides, Atlantis filiae nymphae, secundum fabulam hortum habuerunt in quo erant mala aurea Veneri consecrata, quae Hercules, missus ab Eurystheo, occiso peruigili dracone sustulit. re uera autem nobiles fuerunt puellae, quarum greges abegit Hercules occiso eorum custode; unde mala fingitur sustulisse, hoc est oues; nam μῆλα dicuntur, unde μηλονόμος dicitur pastor ouium.

When, therefore, overpowered with grief, she had taken the Furies into her breast, [475] and determined to die, she ponders the time and manner with herself; and thus accosting her sister, the partner of her grief, covers her intention in her looks, and puts on a serene air of hope. "Rejoice, O sister, with your sister! I have found a way that will restore him to me, or set my love-sick soul at liberty from him. [480] Near the end of the ocean and the setting sun, the utmost boundary of Ethiopia lies, where mighty Atlas on his shoulder twists the pole, fixed with refulgent stars: hence appeared to me a priestess of the Massylian nation, the guardian of the temple of the Hesperides, [485] who supplied the dragon with food and watched the sacred branches on the tree,

478. A WAY a procedure.

REJOICE give thanks, take joy on behalf of your sister; for thus we say, "I congratulate you on the honor."

479. HIM Aeneas, whom she wished to deny she knew.

480. NEAR THE END OF THE OCEAN no one knows the end of the ocean, only its beginning, which can itself be seen as the end, taking its beginning from somewhere else.

481. ETHIOPIA there are two Ethiopias: one in the east, the other in the west in Mauritania, to which she now refers. And this Ethiopia was named from the color of its people, whom the closeness of the sun scorches.

ATLAS no Greek noun ends in "ns".

482. TWISTS supports.

FIXED WITH STARS spoken quite knowledgeably: for "fixed" (*aptum*) means "joined" from "fastened" (*haptesthai*), not "marked with stars," for the pole, which is in the middle of Ursa Minor, has no stars, which is why in Greek it is called "carrying no star" (*anastros*). The proximity of the pole causes Ursa Minor not to set, not because this constellation is on the pole.

483. HENCE APPEARED TO ME A PRIESTESS OF THE MASSYLIAN NATION "appeared"; foreshadowed. Massylian by descent, a one-time priestess of the garden of the Hesperides, now living near Atlas, for otherwise it does not make sense, for Massylia is inland. Berenicis is a city of Libya not far from which are the gardens of the Hesperides. "Mighty Atlas" is in Mauritania.

484. THE GUARDIAN OF THE TEMPLE OF THE HESPERIDES According to the fable, the Hesperides, the nymph daughters of Atlas, had a garden, in which there were golden apples sacred to Venus, which Hercules, sent by Eurystheus, stole after having slain the ever-watchful dragon. In reality, however, they were noble girls whose flocks Hercules drove off after killing their guard; which is why apples (*mala*) are said to have been stolen, namely sheep, for they are called *mela* [in Greek], from which the shepherd of sheep is called *melonomos*.

spargens umida mella soporiferumque papauer.
haec se carminibus promittit soluere mentes
quas uelit, ast aliis duras immittere curas,
sistere aquam fluuiis et uertere sidera retro;
nocturnosque mouet Manis: mugire uidebis
sub pedibus terram et descendere montibus ornos.
testor, cara, deos et te, germana, tuumque
dulce caput, magicas inuitam accingier artes.
tu secreta pyram tecto interiore sub auras

486. SOPORIFERVMQUE PAPAVER incongrue uidetur positum ut soporifera species peruigili detur draconi. sed dicimus uariam uim praebere uictum diuersis animalibus; nam salices hominibus amarae sunt, dulces capellis, ut *et salices carpetis amaras,* [*E* 1.78] scilicet hominibus. item cicutae secundum Lucretium hominibus uenenosae sunt, cum pingues reddant capellas. [*DRN* 899-900] ergo et papauer, licet det hominibus somnum, draconi adimit forsitan; et est excusatio. potest tamen melior esse sensus si *seruabat in arbore ramos* plena sit distinctio, sequentia uero sic accipiamus 'haec se promittit carminibus curas soluere, spargens umida mella soporiferumque papauer,' id est, 'miscens,' ut Cicero *et spargere uenena didicerunt.* [*In Cat* 2.23] nec incongrue ad amaritudinem amoris mel adhibet, ad obliuionem papauer.

489. SISTERE AQVAM FLVVIIS ET VERTERE SIDERA RETRO quanto magis poterit Aeneam ab incepto retorquere.

490. MVGIRE VIDEBIS uidebit quis, ut *migrantes cernas.* [401]

492. TESTOR, CARA, DEOS quia, cum multa sacra Romani susciperent, semper magica damnarunt; ideo excusat.

493. ACCINGIER praeparari. 'accingier' autem, ut ad infinitum addatur 'er,' ratio efficit metri; nam, cum in eo ultima sit longa, addita 'er' syllaba breuis fit, ut 'audiri audirier.'

494. TV SECRETA sine arbitris. et est bona elocutio rem loci uel temporis ad personam transferre, ut 'nocturnus uenit,' 'secretus fecit.'

PYRAM sub specie sacrificii praeparat mortis exequias.

infusing liquid honey and the sleepy poppy. She undertakes by charms to release any souls whom she will [from the power of love] and to entail on others irksome cares: to stop the course of rivers and turn the stars backward: [490] she summons up the ghosts by night. You shall see the earth bellow under her feet and the wild ashes descend from the mountains. My dear sister, I call the gods, and you, and that dear person of yours, to witness, that it is against my will I set about these magic arts. Do you in secrect erect a funeral pyre in the inner court, under the open air,

486. SLEEPY POPPY it seems out of place that a soporific should be given to an ever-watchful dragon. But we say that what is ingested has different effects on different animals, for willow trees are bitter to humans, sweet to she goats, as, "and you gather bitter willow trees," [*E* 1.78] namely, for humans. Likewise, according to Lucretius hemlock is poisonous to humans, while it restores she goats to plumpness. [*DRN* 899–900] Therefore the poppy, although it induces sleep in humans, perhaps takes it away from the dragon; and it is a justification. Nevertheless the sense is better if we take "it watched the branches on the tree" as a complete statement and take the following phrase as, "she undertakes to release my cares with songs, spreading liquid honey and the sleepy poppy," i.e. "mixing," for as Cicero says "and they learned to scatter poison." [*In Cat* 2.23] Not unsuitably, the honey applies to the bitterness of love, the poppy to forgetting it.

489. TO STOP THE COURSE OF RIVERS AND TURN THE STARS BACKWARD how much more could she have turned Aeneas back from his undertaking.

491. YOU SHALL SEE...BELLOW anyone will see, as, "you could have seen them leaving." [401]

492. MY DEAR SISTER, I CALL THE GODS TO WITNESS because, although the Romans adopted many rites, they always condemned magic; thus he justifies it.

493. SET ABOUT to be prepared. *Accingier*, however, *-er* is added to the infinitive to make the line scan, for, although its last syllable is long, by adding the *-er* it becomes short, as, *audiri–audirier*.

494. YOU IN SECRET without witnesses: and it is proper idiom to apply a statement about place or time to a person, as in "he came at night" (*nocturnus venit*) and "he did it in secret" (*secretus fecit*).

A FUNERAL PYRE she prepares the funeral rite under the appearance of a sacrifice.

erige, et arma uiri, thalamo quae fixa reliquit
impius exuuiasque omnis lectumque iugalem,
quo perii, superimponas: abolere nefandi
cuncta uiri monumenta iuuat, monstratque sacerdos.'
haec effata silet; pallor simul occupat ora.
non tamen Anna nouis praetexere funera sacris
germanam credit, nec tantos mente furores
concipit, aut grauiora timet, quam morte Sychaei:
ergo iussa parat.
At regina, pyra penetrali in sede sub auras
erecta ingenti taedis atque ilice secta,
intenditque locum sertis et fronde coronat
funerea; super exuuias ensemque relictum

495. ET ARMA gladium dicit abusiue; nam est paulo post *ensemque relictum.* [507] proprie enim arma sunt quae armos tegunt.

496. IMPIVS qui gladium reliquit furenti. hoc autem tractum est de Homero, qui dicit gladium Aiaci datum ab Hectore et Hectori ab Aiace balteum, quae eis exitio fuerunt; nam alter tractus est balteo, alter se donato telo interemit.

EXVVIAS uestes Aeneae, quem hostem dixerat supra *i, soror, atque hostem supplex adfare superbum;* [424] item *dulces exuuiae.* [651]

497. QVO PERII propter extinctum pudorem.

500. PRAETEXERE praeuelare, abscondere.

501. TANTOS FVRORES quantos cogitabat Dido.

502. GRAVIORA TIMET QVAM MORTE SYCHAEI aut *quam* detrahimus et stat elocutio, aut subaudimus 'grauiora timet posse contingere.'

504. AT REGINA PYRA notatus est hic uersus; uitiosa enim est elocutio quae habet exitus similes, licet sit casuum dissimilitudo.

506. INTENDITQVE LOCVM SERTIS ligat, ut *et stupea uincula collo intendunt.* [2.236] et est hypallage: 'intendit serta per locum.'

507. FVNEREA cupresso; nam et supra dicta ligna ad funus pertinent, ut *procumbunt piceae, sonat icta securibus ilex.* [6.180]

[495] and lay upon it his arms, which lie, impiously base, left fixed in my bedchamber, with all his clothes, and the nuptial bed in which I was undone. The priestess orders and directs me to destroy every monument of that execrable man." Having thus spoken, she ceases: at the same time, paleness overcasts her whole complexion. [500] Yet Anna imagines not that her sister aimed at death under pretext of these unusual rites, nor once suspects that she had formed such a desperate purpose, nor dreads things worse than had happened at the death of Sychaeus. Therefore she makes the desired preparations.

But the queen, when the pyre was erected high under the open air in the inner court, [505] with torches and bundles of oak, circles garlands around the place and crowns it with funeral boughs: upon the bed she lays his clothes, the sword left behind,

495. HIS ARMS a sword; she says it incorrectly, for shortly after, "the sword left behind"; [507] for the arms (*arma*) are properly what cover the upper arms and shoulders (*armos*).

496. IMPIOUSLY BASE who left his sword to the enraged woman. This however is taken from Homer, who speaks of the sword given to Ajax by Hector, and the belt given to Hector by Ajax, gifts that were ruinous to each: for one was dragged by his belt, the other killed himself with the weapon given to him.

CLOTHES [*EXVVIAS*] the clothes of Aeneas, whom she had called an enemy above: "go sister, and as a suppliant address the arrogant enemy"; [424] likewise "dear remains (*exuuiae*)." [651]

497. IN WHICH I WAS UNDONE because of compromised modesty.

500. UNDER PRETEXT to cover over, to conceal.

501. SUCH A DESPERATE PURPOSE as desperate as Dido was considering.

502. DREADS THINGS WORSE THAN HAD HAPPENED AT THE DEATH OF SYCHAEAS either we delete "than," and the expression remains, or we understand "dreads that worse things can happen."

504. BUT THE QUEEN [WHEN] THE PYRE this verse has been marked, for an expression with similar endings is defective, even though they are not the same case.

506. CIRCLES GARLANDS AROUND THE PLACE binds, as in "and hempen chains surround his neck," [2.236] and it is hypallage: "she circles the place with garlands."

507. FUNERAL from the cypress tree, for also all the above-mentioned woods pertain to funerals, as in "the pitch pines fall, the struck holm oak resounds with the blows." [6.180]

effigiemque toro locat, haud ignara futuri.
stant arae circum et crines effusa sacerdos
ter centum tonat ore deos, Erebumque Chaosque,
tergeminamque Hecaten, tria uirginis ora Dianae.
sparserat et latices simulatos fontis Auerni,
falcibus et messae ad lunam quaeruntur aënis
pubentes herbae nigri cum lacte ueneni;
quaeritur et nascentis equi de fronte reuulsus

508. EFFIGIEMQVE TORO LOCAT exprimitur amoris affectus, quod etiam in morte amati imagini uolebat esse coniuncta, ut paulo post *natumque patremque / cum genere extinxem, memet super ipsa dedissem.* [605-6]

HAVD IGNARA FVTVRI memor suae dispositionis.

510. TER CENTVM TONAT ORE DEOS non 'tercentum deos' sed 'tonat ter centum numina Hecates'; unde Hecate dicta est, ἑκατόν, id est, centum potestates habens. *tonat* autem perite dixit; in aliquibus enim sacris imitabantur tonitrua.

EREBVM inferorum profunditatem.

511. TRIA VIRGINIS ORA DIANAE iteratio est: Lunae, Dianae, Proserpinae.

512. SIMVLATOS FONTIS AVERNI in sacris, ut supra diximus, [ad 2.116] quae exhiberi non poterant simulabantur, et erant pro ueris. bene autem de Auerno, per quem descensus ad inferos dicitur.

513. FALCIBVS ET MESSAE AD LVNAM QVAERVNTVR AENIS herbae enim secundum rationem lunae tolluntur; nec omnes eodem modo: unde perite et *aenis falcibus* dixit, quia aliae uelluntur, aliae inciduntur. et *ad lunam* non ad noctem, sed ad lunae obseruationem.

514. PVBENTES autem quia aliae siccae, aliae uiridiores leguntur. et sciendum inter homines et herbas esse reciprocam translationem; sic enim 'pubentem herbam' dicimus quemadmodum 'florem aetatis.'

NIGRI CVM LACTE VENENI 'nigri' aut 'noxii,' quia nigri fiunt homines post uenenum, aut certe illud est, quia sunt herbae nigri lactis, id est, suci. dicunt autem per periphrasin agreste papauer significari.

and his image, well knowing of the future. Altars are raised around; and the priestess, her hair disheveled, with thundering voice invokes thrice hundred gods, and Erebus, and Chaos, and threefold Hecate, virgin Diana's triple form. She also sprinkled water counterfeiting that of the lake Avernus: grown-up herbs, cut by moonlight with brazen sickles, are searched out, together with the juice of black poison: and, torn from the forehead of a new-foaled colt

508. AND UPON THE BED SHE LAYS HIS IMAGE the emotion of love is expressed, because even in death she wished to be joined to the image of her lover, as shortly after, "I might have extirpated the son, the sire, with the whole race, and flung myselft upon the pile." [605– 6]

WELL KNOWING OF THE FUTURE mindful of what she was arranging.

510. WITH THUNDERING VOICE, INVOKES THRICE HUNDRED GODS not "three hundred gods," but "three times she thunders out the hundred-divinity Hecate," for she is called Hecate from *hekaton*, i.e. having a hundred powers. He expertly says "thunders" for in some rites thunder is imitated.

EREBUS the depths of the lower regions.

511.VIRGIN DIANA'S TRIPLE FORM it is a repetition: of Luna, Diana, and Proserpina.

512. WATER COUNTERFEITING THAT OF LAKE AVERNUS in rites, as we said above [on 2.116], things that could not be procured were simulated and stood for the real things. However it is well said about Avernus, the descent through which is said to lead to the underworld.

513. CUT BY MOONLIGHT WITH BRAZEN SICKLES ARE SEARCHED OUT for herbs are plucked according to the phase of the moon, not all in the same way, so he expertly says "with brazen sickles," because some are plucked and others are cut. Also, "by moonlight" is not at night, but according to the phase of the moon.

514. GROWN-UP although some understand "dried", others "green." It should also be understood that there is an affinity between humans and plants; for we say "grown-up herb" as well as, "in the flower of age."

WITH THE JUICE OF BLACK POISON "black" either "harmful" because men become black after being poisoned: or else because herbs are "of black juice," i.e. sap. They say, moreover, that, by circumlocution, the rural poppy is meant.

et matri praereptus amor.
ipsa mola manibusque piis altaria iuxta,
unum exuta pedem uinclis, in ueste recincta,
testatur moritura deos et conscia fati
sidera; tum, si quod non aequo foedere amantis
curae numen habet iustumque memorque, precatur.
  Nox erat et placidum carpebant fessa soporem
corpora per terras, siluaeque et saeua quierant

516. ET MATRI PRAEREPTVS AMOR secundum Plinium, qui dicit in *Naturali historia* [8.165] pullos equinos habere in fronte quandam carnem, quam eis statim natis adimit mater; quam si quis forte praeripuerit, odit pullum et lac ei denegat; Iuuenalis *cui totam tremuli frontem Caesonia pulli / infudit.* [*Sat* 6.616-7] et merito suspicantur amorem creari ex carne, sine qua mater non alit ex se creatum.

517. IPSA MOLA farre et sale. ordo autem est: ipsa Dido mola et piis manibus, id est puris, deos testatur.

518. VNVM EXVTA PEDEM quia id agitur ut et ista soluatur et inplicetur Aeneas.

IN VESTE RECINCTA quia, ut supra diximus, [ad 2.134] in sacris nihil solet esse religatum, praecipue eius quae amore uult solui.

519. CONSCIA FATI SIDERA id est planetas, in quibus fatorum ratio continetur.

520. SI QVOD NON AEQVO FOEDERE AMANTIS CVRAE NVMEN HABET ordo est: tunc numen precatur, si quod curae habet amantes non aequo foedere. *si quod* autem bene dubitat utrum res malae habeant praepositas postestates. sensus autem hic est: [aut] 'Αντέρωτα inuocabat, contrarium Cupidini, qui amores resoluit aut certe cui curae est iniquus amor, scilicet ut inplicet non amantem.

521. IVSTVMQVE MEMORQVE ut expugnetur qui est causa discordiae.

522. NOX ERAT protenditur ista descriptio ad exaggerationem uigiliarum Didonis.

523. SILVAEQVE secundum eos qui dicunt omnia quae crescunt animalia esse.

and snatched away from the mother, the love [charm] is sought out. The queen herself, now resolute on death, having one foot bare, her robe ungirt, standing by the altars with the salt cake and pious hands, makes her appeal to the gods and [520] to the stars, conscious of her fate: then, if any deity, both just and mindful, has as a concern lovers unequally yoked, him she invokes.

It was night, and weary bodies over the earth were enjoying a peaceful repose: the woods and raging

516. SNATCHED AWAY FROM THE MOTHER THE LOVE [CHARM] this is according to Pliny, who says in the *Natural History* [8.165] that foals have a certain piece of skin on their forehead that the mother removes after they are born: and if someone by chance stole it, she would hate her foal and deny it milk. Juvenal says "On whom Caesonia poured the entire forehead of the trembling foal." [*Sat* 6.616–7] And so rightly they suspect that love is created out of the flesh, without which the mother would not nourish what she bore our of herself.

517. HERSELF...WITH THE SALT CAKE of grain and salt. The word order however is this: Dido herself calls the gods to witness with salt cake and pious hands, i.e. clean.

518. HAVING ONE FOOT BARE this is done so that she might be free and Aeneas might be bound.

HER ROBE UNGIRT because, as we said above, [on 2.134] nothing is accustomed to be bound in rites, especially those of she who wishes to be free from love.

519. THE STARS, CONSCIOUS OF HER FATE i.e. the planets, in which the calculation of the fates is contained.

520. IF ANY DEITY, BOTH JUST AND MINDFUL, HAS AS A CONCERN LOVERS UNEQUALLY YOKED the word order is: then the divinity is invoked if it has as a concern in lovers unequally yoked: "if any" she rightly doubts whether evil things have control. This, however, is the meaning: [either] she invokes Anteros, the opposite of Cupid, who dissolved loves, or else him whose charge is unequal love, clearly so that she might bind the man who does not love her.

521. BOTH JUST AND MINDFUL so that he who is the cause of discord might be expunged.

522. IT WAS NIGHT this description is extended in order to exaggerate Dido's wakefulness.

523. THE WOODS according to those who say that all things that grow are animate.

aequora: cum medio uoluuntur sidera lapsu,
cum tacet omnis ager, pecudes pictaeque uolucres,
quaeque lacus late liquidos, quaeque aspera dumis
rura tenent, somno positae sub nocte silenti
[lenibant curas et corda oblita laborum].
at non infelix animi Phoenissa, nec umquam
soluitur in somnos, oculisue aut pectore noctem
accipit: ingeminant curae rursusque resurgens
saeuit amor magnoque irarum fluctuat aestu.
sic adeo insistit secumque ita corde uolutat:
'en, quid ago? rursusne procos inrisa priores
experiar, Nomadumque petam conubia supplex,
quos ego sim totiens iam dedignata maritos?
Iliacas igitur classes atque ultima Teucrum

524. AEQVORA elementa etiam animalia esse uoluerunt; unde est in septimo *aethera mulcebant cantu.* [7.34]

525. TACET AGER ea quae in agris sunt.

530. OCVLISVE AVT PECTORE NOCTEM ACCIPIT quia potest aliud esse sine alio, ut si quis dormiens mente turbetur.

531. RESVRGENS SAEVIT AMOR grauior enim est cum resurgit; sententia quasi generalis.

533. ADEO scilicet furuit; ut in hoc proposito permaneret uitandae sine dubio lucis.

534. EN QVID AGO *en* 'ecce.' et quasi demonstrantis particula est, per quam intellegimus eam multa cogitasse et sic prorupisse 'ecce, quid actura sum?' est autem comicum principium, nec incongrue amatrici datum. sic Terentius *quid igitur faciam?;* [*Eun* 46] nam haec coniunctio multa eum cogitasse significat.

RVRSVS duo significat: frequenter 'iterum,' raro 'uicissim,' id est 'mutuo,' ut hoc loco.

535. NOMADVMQVE PETAM inuidia a personis: 'petam mulier et regina nomadas?,' id est 'uagos.'

536. MARITOS futuros scilicet. est autem elocutio 'dedignor illam rem.'

537. VLTIMA IVSSA aut intellegimus Aenean ei obtulisse nauigandi facultatem, aut *Teucrum iussa* non quae ipsi iusserant sed quae eis a Ioue iussa sunt, ut *nauiget, haec summa est.* [237]

seas were still; when the stars roll in the middle of their gliding course; [525] when every field is hushed: the beasts, and speckled birds, both those that far and wide haunt the liquid lakes and those that possess the fields with rough bushes overgrown, all stretched under the silent night, [allayed their cares and every heart forgot its toil]. But not so the soul-distressed Phoenissa; not one moment [530] is she lulled to rest, nor enjoys the night with eyes or mind. Her cares redouble; and love, again arising, rages afresh and fluctuates with a high tide of passions. Thus then she persists and revolves these secret reflections in her breast: "Lo! What shall I do? Baffled as I am, shall I in turn apply to my former suitors? [535] Shall I sue for a humble match with one of the Numidians I have so often disdained as husbands? Shall I then attend the fleet of Ilium, and submit to the basest commands of the Trojan?

524. SEAS they wanted even elements to be animate, so in the seventh book, "the heavens caressed with song." [7.34]

525. EVERY FIELD IS HUSHED those things that are in the fields.

530. ENJOYS THE NIGHT WITH EYES OR MIND because one is able to be without the other, so that someone sleeping might be disturbed in his mind.

531. LOVE, AGAIN ARISING, RAGES for love is more severe when it appears again: a virtually universal statement.

533. THUS THEN of course she rages: so that she might remain in her intention surely of avoiding the light.

534. LO! WHAT SHALL I DO? "lo"; "look": as if it is a demonstrative particle, through which we understand that she has thought over many things and broken forth saying "look, what shall I do?" It is however a comical beginning and not unfittingly given to a female lover. Thus Terence says, "what therefore shall I do?" [*Eun* 46] For this conjunction means that he has thought about many things.

IN TURN means two things: frequently "again," rarely "in turn," i.e. "in return," as in this passage.

535. SHALL I SUE scorn expressed by [the status of] persons: "shall I, a woman and a queen, seek out nomads?" i.e. wanderers.

536. HUSBANDS namely, future husbands. It is, however, a statement that "I scorn that thing."

537. BASEST COMMANDS either we are to understand that Aeneas offered her the opportunity to sail or "the commands of the Trojans," not which they gave, but which they were ordered by Jupiter to do, as, "Bid him set sail. In sum; be this our message." [237]

iussa sequar? quiane auxilio iuuat ante leuatos
et bene apud memores ueteris stat gratia facti?
quis me autem, fac uelle, sinet, ratibusue superbis
inuisam accipiet? nescis heu, perdita, necdum
Laomedonteae sentis periuria gentis?
quid tum? sola fuga nautas comitabor ouantes?
an Tyriis omnique manu stipata meorum
inferar et, quos Sidonia uix urbe reuelli,
rursus agam pelago et uentis dare uela iubebo?
quin morere ut merita, es, ferroque auerte dolorem.
tu lacrimis euicta meis, tu prima furentem

538. QVIANE re uera; et est una pars orationis.

539. STAT permanet.

543. NAVTAS non Troianos; nam iniuriose dixit *nautas,* id est, adsuetos laboribus.

OVANTES laetantes. abusiue; nam proprie ouatio est minor triumphus. qui enim ouationem meretur, et uno equo utitur et a plebeis uel ab equitibus Romanis deducitur ad Capitolium et de ouibus sacrificat, unde et 'ouatio'; qui autem triumphat, albis equis utitur quattuor et senatu praeeunte in Capitolio de tauris sacrificat.

545. VIX VRBE REVELLI aut 'mox,' id est 'paulo ante,' ut *uix e conspectu,* [1.34] aut re uera 'uix,' ut diximus supra [ad 1.361]; nam nulla ratione dimitterent patriam, nisi eos aut odium Pygmalionis coegisset aut timor, ut *conueniunt quibus aut odium crudele tyranni / aut metus acer erat.* [1.361-2]

547. QVIN MORERE *quin* 'immo.' et bene omnis eius intentio tendit ad mortem; nam si procos rogare turpe est, solam sequi inpossibile et inhonestum, Tyrios trahere difficile, sola mors superest.

548. TV LACRIMIS EVICTA MEIS bene totum ei inputat, sed cum excusatione, quae Aeneae nuptias suasit, sed uicta lacrimis, ut *sinum lacrimis impleuit obortis. Anna refert.* [30-1]

TV PRIMA FVRENTEM Vrbanus hoc diuidit, licet alii iungant, et uult hunc esse sensum: tu persuasisti ut nuberem, uicta lacrimis meis. tu etiam nunc me his oneras malis; nam me olim occidissem nisi te deserere formidarem.

And that, because I am well rewarded for having lent them my assistance, and in their grateful hearts a just sense of my former kindness remains? [540] But, suppose I had the will, who will put it in my power, or receive into their proud ships me, the object of their hate? Ah! Lost one, are you unacquainted with, are you still to learn, the perfidiousness of Laomedon's race? What then? Shall I steal away by myself to accompany the triumphant crew? Or, attended by my Tyrians and all my people in a body, [545] shall I pursue them and again drive them out to sea, and order those to spread their sails to the winds, whom, with much ado, I forced from Tyre? Nay, rather die, as you deserve, and end your woes with the sword. You, sister, subdued by my tears, and my distracted mind

538. BECAUSE indeed, and it is one part of speech.

539. REMAINS stays.

543. CREW rather than Trojans: for she says "crew" insultingly, i.e. men accustomed to toil.

TRIUMPHANT rejoicing. Incorrectly, for an ovation is properly a small triumph. He who merits an ovation rides a single horse and is led by the plebs or Roman knights to the Capitoline, where he makes a sacrifice of sheep (*oves*), hence ovation: he who triumphs, however, employs four white horses, with the senators preceding him to the Capitoline, and makes a sacrifice of bulls.

545. WITH MUCH ADO, I FORCED FROM TYRE either "soon," i.e. shortly before, as, "soon out of sight" or indeed "scarcely," as we said above, [on 1.361] for they abandoned their country for no reason, unless the hatred of Pygmalion drove them or fear, as, "they came together with them or the cruel hatred of the tyrant or there was intense fear." [1.361–2]

547. NAY, RATHER DIE "nay rather," indeed. It is also appropriate that all her intention is toward death, for if it is shameful to beg for suitors, impossible and disgraceful to follow them alone, and difficult to drag along the Tyrians, then only death remains.

548. YOU, SUBDUED BY MY TEARS she appropriately ascribes everything to her, but with a justification: she encouraged her marriage to Aeneas, but "subdued by my tears," as, "she filled the rounds of her eyes with welling tears. Anna replies." [30–1]

YOU FIRST...MY DISTRACTED MIND Urbanus separates this (though others join them), and he wants the sense to be: you, subdued by my tears, persuaded me to marry. Now, too, you oppress me with these evils, for I would have killed myself long ago if I did not fear to abandon you.

his, germana, malis oneras atque obicis hosti.
non licuit thalami expertem sine crimine uitam
degere, more ferae, tales nec tangere curas;
non seruata fides cineri promissa Sychaeo.'
   Tantos illa suo rumpebat pectore questus:
Aeneas celsa in puppi iam certus eundi
carpebat somnos rebus iam rite paratis.
huic se forma dei uultu redeuntis eodem

549. OBICIS HOSTI 'ob' naturaliter breuis est, sicut et 're' et 'ad,' sed plerumque producuntur hac ratione: 'obicio' 'reicio' 'adicio' 'i' habent uocalem sequentem, quae per declinationem potest in consonantis formam transire, ut 'obieci' 'reieci'; ergo etiam antequam transeat, interdum fungitur officio consonantis et praecedentem longam facit.

551. MORE FERAE Plinius in *Naturali Historia* [8.43] dicit lyncas post amissos coniuges aliis non iungi. multi *fere* aduerbium uolunt, ut sit sensus: more scilicet, quo iam uiduitatem ferre consueuerat. 'crimen' autem bene, ut supra *potui succumbere culpae.* [19]

552. SYCHAEO pro 'Sychaeio.'

554. CERTVS EVNDI indubitabiliter profecturus.

555. CARPEBAT SOMNOS hoc est quod et paulo post culpat Mercurius. sed excusatur his rebus: nam et certus eundi fuerat et rite cuncta praeparauerat. aut certe prooeconomia est, ut possit uidere Mercurium.

556. FORMA DEI bene non 'deus,' sed *forma;* raro enim numina sicut sunt possunt uideri. unde et sequitur *uultu redeuntis eodem;* nam licet *redeuntis* dicat, id est 'eius qui possit agnosci,' tamen non 'faciem' dicit, sed 'uultum,' qui potest saepe mutari.

EODEM 'o' semper longum est, quia 'eodem' ablatiuus est semper. 'eadem' autem et producit et corripit; nam et nominatiuus est, ut 'eadem mulier fecit,' et ablatiuus, ut 'eadem faciente muliere.'

you first oppressed with these woes and exposed me to the enemy. [550] Might I not have led an unwedded life without fault, like a wild animal, and have avoided such cares? I have violated the faith I plighted to the *manes* of Sychaeus."

Such heavy complaints she poured forth from her heart. Aeneas, determined to depart, [555] was enjoying sleep in the lofty stern, since all things were now ready. The appearance of the god, returning with the same aspect,

549. EXPOSED ME TO THE ENEMY *ob* is naturally short, just as both *re* and *ad*, but they often are lengthened for this reason: *obicio*, *reicio*, and *adicio* have the vowel *i* following, which is able to change its form into a consonant as the word is inflected, as in *obieci*, *reieci*; therefore even before it changes it behaves like a consonant and makes the preceding syllable long.

551. LIKE A WILD ANIMAL Pliny says in the *Natural History* [8.43] that lynxes, after they have lost their mates, do not take another. Many read the adverb *fere* instead of *ferae*, so the sense would be: like one who had just become accustomed to widowhood. "Fault" is also appropriate, as above, "to this fault I might give way." [19]

552. SYCHAEUS for "Sychaeius."

554. DETERMINED TO DEPART doubtlessly about to go forth.

555. WAS ENJOYING SLEEP this is the thing for which shortly after Mercury reproaches him. But the sleep is excused by these things: for he had been both determined to depart and he had thoroughly prepared everything: or else it is a previous arrangement, so that he is able to see Mercury.

556. THE APPEARANCE OF THE GOD fittingly not the god, but rather the appearance: for divinities can rarely be seen just as they are. So it follows, "returning with the same aspect"; for although he says "[of the god] returning", i.e. of one who can be known, nevertheless he does not say "face" but "appearance," which can often be changed.

SAME The *o* of *eodem* is always long, because *eodem* (with long *o*) is always ablative; however the *a* in *eadem* can be either long or short, for it is both nominative, as in "the same woman did it," and ablative, as in "as the same woman was doing it."

obtulit in somnis rursusque ita uisa monere est,
omnia Mercurio similis, uocemque coloremque
et crinis flauos et membra decora iuuenta:
'nate dea, potes hoc sub casu ducere somnos,
nec quae te circum stent deinde pericula cernis,
demens, nec Zephyros audis spirare secundos?
illa dolos dirumque nefas in pectore uersat,
certa mori, uarioque irarum fluctuat aestu.
non fugis hinc praeceps, dum praecipitare potestas?
iam mare turbari trabibus saeuasque uidebis
conlucere faces, iam feruere litora flammis,
si te his attigerit terris Aurora morantem.
heia age, rumpe moras. uarium et mutabile semper
femina.' sic fatus nocti se immiscuit atrae.
Tum uero Aeneas, subitis exterritus umbris,
corripit e somno corpus sociosque fatigat:
'praecipites uigilate, uiri, et considite transtris;

557. VISA MONERE EST bene *uisa;* non enim re uera est.

558. OMNIA MERCVRIO SIMILIS aliud enim est idem esse, aliud simile esse; ergo non est certus Aeneas.

VOCEMQVE quia orationis est deus; Horatius 'Mercuri facunde.' [*Carm* 1.10.1]

COLOREMQVE ET CRINIS FLAVOS ideo et perustus et flauus Mercurius introducitur, quia satis uicinus est soli praeter ceteras stellas.

559. ET MEMBRA DECORA IVVENTAE quia palaestrae deus est; Horatius *catus et decorae / more palaestrae.* [*Carm* 1.10.3-4] 'iuuentae' autem 'aetatis,' a 'iuuenta.' sane figura est: similis membra uocemque coloremque.

562. ZEPHYROS uentos; de Africa enim Zephyro nauigare non poterat.

563. NEFAS IN PECTORE VERSAT ne non timeret amatricem, bene addidit *certa mori,* item *uarium et mutabile semper femina.* [569]

565. PRAECEPS festinus.

567. CONLVCERE propter *ferte citi flammas.* [594]

571. VMBRIS ut supra *forma dei.* [556]

572. CORRIPIT omen est futurae tempestatis.

573. PRAECIPITES ut supra Mercurius *non fugis hinc praeceps?* [565]

appeared to him in his sleep and thus again seemed to admonish him; in every thing resembling Mercury, in voice, complexion and golden locks, and comely youthful limbs: [560] "Goddess-born, can you indulge in sleep at this juncture? Infatuated, not to see what dangers in a moment may beset you, nor listen to the breathing of the friendly Zephyrs! She, bent on death, is revolving guileful purposes wickedness in her breast and fluctuates with a tide of angry passions. [565] Will you not fly hence with precipitation, while thus to fly is in your power? Forthwith you shall behold the sea in commotion with her oars and torches fiercely blaze; forthwith the shore lighted up with flames, if the morning reach you lingering on these coasts. [570] Come then, quick, break off delay: woman is a fickle and ever changeable thing." This said, he mingled with the sable night.

Then, indeed, Aeneas, in consternation at this sudden apparition, snatches his frame from the couch and rouses his companions: "Awake, my mates, precipitously, and plant yourselves on the benches;

557. SEEMED TO ADMONISH HIM and "seemed" is well said: for it is not in fact true.

558. IN EVERY THING RESEMBLING MERCURY for it is one thing to be the same and another to be similar: therefore Aeneas is unsure.

IN VOICE because he is god of speech. Horace, "eloquent Mercury." [*Carm* 1.10.1]

COMPLEXION AND GOLDEN LOCKS Mercury is therefore introduced as tanned and blond because he is quite the closest to the sun, aside from certain stars.

559. COMELY YOUTHFUL LIMBS because he is the god of the gymnasium. Horace, "clever and in the style of the beautiful gymnasium" [*Carm* 1.10.3–4] However [supply] "in age" to "youthful," from youth. The image is of similar limbs, voice, and complexion.

562. ZEPHYRS winds: for it was not possible to sail from Africa with the Zephyr.

563. IS REVOLVING WICKEDNESS IN HER BREAST so that he would not fear his lover, he has well added "bent on death." Likewise "woman is a fickle and ever changeable thing." [569]

565. WITH PRECIPITATION with haste.

567. BLAZE because "having been roused, take up torches."

571. APPARITION as above, "the appearance of the god." [556]

572. SNATCHES an omen of the storm to come.

573. PRECIPITOUSLY as Mercury says above [565], "fly hence with precipitation?"

soluite uela citi. deus aethere missus ab alto
festinare fugam tortosque incidere funes
ecce iterum stimulat. sequimur te, sancte deorum,
quisquis es, imperioque iterum paremus ouantes.
adsis o placidusque iuues et sidera caelo
dextra feras.' dixit, uaginaque eripit ensem

576. ECCE ITERVM STIMVLAT phantasia est ad sociorum terrorem; sic in sexto *deus, ecce deus.* [6.46]

SANCTE DEORVM aut distingue *sancte,* aut secundum Ennium dixit *respondit Iuno Saturnia sancta dearum.* [*Ann* 1.53]

577. QVISQVIS ES atqui supra dixit *omnia Mercurio similis;* [558] sed sciendum est secundum Tullium in libris *De deorum natura* [*DND* 3.22.56] tres esse Mercurios: superum, terrenum, inferum. ergo *quisquis es* aut quicumque de tribus. aut certe ad Iouem spectat, id est 'quisquis es qui praecipis,' ut in nono *quisquis in arma uocas,* [9.22] cum Irin uidisset, id est 'quicumque Irin misisti.' plane illud occurrit quod ait *deus aethere missus ab alto,* [574] ubi et Iouem conplectitur et supernum Mercurium. sed potest et hoc loco, ut diximus, quasi phantasiam facere propter socios, et *quisquis es* ideo dicere, quia, licet uiderit, non tamen re uera nouit esse Mercurium; unde ait supra et *forma* et *uultu* [556] et *uisa monere est.* [557].

ITERVM PAREMVS quia iam paruerat praeparatione nauigiorum.

578. SIDERA CAELO DEXTRA FERAS hoc est uentos, qui ex ortu siderum aut prosperi aut aduersi sunt. sic in *Georgicis praeterea tam sunt Arcturi sidera nobis;* [*G* 1.204] nec enim *sidera* dicit re uera, cum Arcturus una sit stella. ergo *dextra sidera* uentos uel tempora.

instantly unfurl the sails. A god, dispatched from the high heavens, [575] once more prompts me to hasten my departure and cut the twisted cables. We follow you, O holy one of the gods, whoever you are, and once more obey your commands [with joy]. Ah! Be present, lend us your propitious aid, and light up friendly stars in the heavens." He spoke and snatches his keen

576. ONCE MORE PROMPTS the apparition is intended to frighten his comrades; thus we find later [6.46], "The god, behold, the god!"

O HOLY ONE OF THE GODS either punctuate after "holy one," or [he says "holy one of the gods,"] in the manner of Ennius, who said, "Saturnian Juno, holy one of the gods." [*Ann* 1.53]

577. WHOEVER YOU ARE yet he said above, "in every thing resembling Mercury." [558] But it must be understood that, as Cicero writes in the books *On the Nature of the Gods* [*DND* 3.22.56], there are three Mercuries: celestial, earthly, and infernal. Therefore, "whoever you are" means either whichever one of these three, or else he refers to Jupiter, i.e. "whoever you are who gives the command," as in the ninth book, "whoever you are that calls me to battle" [9.22] when he had seen Iris i.e. "whoever you are who had sent Iris." Clearly, what he said has happened, "A god, dispatched from the high heavens" [574], which involved both Jupiter and the celestial Mercury. But in this passage, as we said, it is possible to make a virtual apparition on account of his comrades, and for this reason to say, "whoever you are" because, although he saw it, he nevertheless did not know that it really was Mercury: for this reason he says above, "appearance" and "aspect" and "seemed to admonish." [556]

WE ONCE MORE OBEY because he had already obeyed as to the preparations for sailing.

578. LIGHT UP FRIENDLY STARS IN THE HEAVENS that is, the winds, which from the rising of the stars are either fortuitous or adverse. Thus in the *Georgics*, "we must watch the stars of Arcturus." [*G* 1.204] Yet he does not really mean "stars," since Arcturus is only one star: therefore "friendly stars" are either the winds or the weather.

fulmineum, strictoque ferit retinacula ferro.
idem omnes simul ardor habet, rapiuntque ruuntque;
litora deseruere; latet sub classibus aequor;
adnixi torquent spumas et caerula uerrunt.
Et iam prima nouo spargebat lumine terras
Tithoni croceum linquens Aurora cubile.
regina e speculis ut primum albescere lucem
uidit et aequatis classem procedere uelis,
litoraque et uacuos sensit sine remige portus,
terque quaterque manu pectus percussa decorum,
flauentesque abscissa comas, 'pro Iuppiter, ibit
hic' ait 'et nostris inluserit aduena regnis?

584. PRIMA...AVRORA designatio temporis est, non diei descriptio; unde infert, *ut primum albescere lucem / uidit;* [586-7] sic in duodecimo *cum primum crastina caelo puniceis inuecta rotis Aurora rubebit.* [12.76] et bene hanc primum inducit uidisse crepusculum, quae quasi amatrix tota uigilauerat nocte; sic in *Bucolicis* de amatore *nascere praeque diem ueniens age, Lucifer, almum.* [*E* 8.17]

NOVO LVMINE secundum Epicureos, qui stulte solem de atomis dicunt constare et cum die nasci, cum die perire.

585. TITHONI CVBILE Tithonus frater Laomedontis fuit. hunc Aurora amatum in caelum leuauit, quem longinquitas uitae in cicadam conuertit; Horatius *longa Tithonum minuit senectus.* [*Carm* 2.16.30]

586. ALBESCERE LVCEM hypallage est; luce enim albescunt omnia, non lux albescit.

587. AEQVATIS VELIS feliciter plenis, sine motu aliquo.

590. PRO IVPPITER aut irascentis exclamatio est, ut in Terentio *pro supreme Iuppiter;* [*Adel* 196] aut certe testatur Iouem, quem in Aeneae inuocauit aduentu, ut *Iuppiter, hospitibus nam te dare iura loquuntur.* [1.731]

591. IBIT ET INLVSERIT ibit et inludet, tempus pro tempore. et sic dixit *certantque inludere capto.* [2.64]

[580] flashing sword from the sheath and cuts the hawsers with the drawn steel. The same eagerness at once seizes them all: they bale, they hurry away; they have quitted the shore; the sea lies hidden under the feet; they with exerted vigor upturn the foaming billows and sweep the azure deep.

[585] And now Aurora, leaving Tithonus' saffron bed, first sowed the earth with new-born light: soon as the queen from her watchtowers marked the dawn whitening and the fleet setting forward with balanced sails and perceived the shore and vacant port without a rower; thrice and four times smiting her fair bosom and [590] tearing her golden locks: "O Jupiter! Shall he go?" she says, "and shall this stranger have mocked my kingdom?

584. AURORA...FIRST an indication of the time, not a description of the day: for this reason he writes [586–7], "soon as the queen ... marked the dawn whitening." Thus in the twelfth book, "When tomorrow's Aurora, carried by her scarlet car, first reddens the sky." [12.76] And the poet portrays well that she has first seen the twilight, like a lover who stayed awake all night. Thus a lover sings in the *Eclogues*, "Arise then, O morning star, coming before the favorable day." [*E* 8.17]

NEW-BORN LIGHT according to the Epicureans, who foolishly say the sun is composed of atoms, and with the day is both born and dies.

585. TITHONUS' BED Tithonus was the brother of Laomedon. Aurora lifted him into heaven as her lover, turned him into a cicada due to the length of his life. Horace, "A long old age diminished Tithonus" [*Carm.* 2.16.30].

586. THE DAWN WHITENING this is hypallage: for everything grows white in the light, light does not become white.

587. WITH BALANCED SAILS filled abundantly, without any rippling.

590. O JUPITER either an exclamation of rage, as in Terence, "O Jupiter above!" [*Adel* 196], or else she is invoking Jupiter, whom she invoked upon the arrival of Aeneas, "Jupiter, for they say that you keep the laws of hospitality." [1.731]

591. SHALL HE GO AND SHALL . . . HAVE MOCKED "shall he go and shall he mock," one tense for another. Thus had the poet said, "they vied to mock the captive." [2.64]

non arma expedient, totaque ex urbe sequentur,
deripientque rates alii naualibus? ite,
ferte citi flammas, date tela, impellite remos!
quid loquor? aut ubi sum? quae mentem insania mutat?
infelix Dido, nunc te facta impia tangunt.
tum decuit, cum sceptra dabas. en dextra fidesque,
quem secum patrios aiunt portare Penates,
quem subiisse umeris confectum aetate parentem!
non potui abreptum diuellere corpus et undis
spargere? non socios, non ipsum absumere ferro
Ascanium, patriisque epulandum ponere mensis?
uerum anceps pugnae fuerat fortuna. fuisset:
quem metui moritura? faces in castra tulissem,
implessemque foros flammis, natumque patremque
cum genere extinxem, memet super ipsa dedissem.

592. NON ARMA EXPEDIENT furentis haec uerba sunt, ut ipsa paulo post *quae mentem insania mutat?;* [595] nam haec a sana non procedunt, ut imperet absentibus, *ferte tela,* [594] cum sola sit.

593. NAVALIBVS de naualibus, ubi stant naues.

595. AVT VBI SVM numquid in coetu sum?

597. CVM SCEPTRA DABAS ut *ac dominum Aenean in regna recepit.* [214]

FIDESQVE subaudi 'en' etiam in sequentibus; aut certe 'hic est quem dicunt portare deos.' sane 'en' nominatiuo melius iungitur, ut *en Priamus.* [1.461]

602. IPSVM ASCANIVM aut qui est causa nauigationis, ut *quem regno Hesperiae fraudo,* [355] aut ad patris dolorem, ut *qui nati coram me cernere letum fecisti.* [2.538]

EPVLANDVM PONERE quod fecit Procne occiso Ity filio propter stuprum sororis.

604. IN CASTRA classes, ut *nos castra mouemus.* [3.519]

605. FOROS tabulata nauium, ab eo quod incessus ferant. et est generis masculini, numeri tantum pluralis.

606. CVM GENERE EXTINXEM morte Aeneae et Ascanii; et est syncope.

MEMET SVPER IPSA DEDISSEM satis amatorie.

Will they not make ready arms, and pursue from all the city? And will not others tear my ships from the docks? Run quick, fetch flames, fetch weapons, ply the oars. [595] What am I saying? Or where am I? What madness turns my brain? Unhappy Dido! Are you then at length stung with the fact of his foul impious deeds? Then it had become you so to act, when you imparted [to him] your scepter. Is this the honor, and the faith! This [the man] who, they say, carries with him his country's gods! Who bore on his shoulders his father spent with age! [600] Might I not have torn in pieces his mangled body and strewn it on the waves? Might I not with the sword have destroyed his friends, Ascanius himself, and served him up for a banquet at his father's table? But the fortune of the fight was doubtful. Grant it had been so: thus resolute on death, whom had I to fear? I might have hurled firebrands into his camp, [605] filled the gangways with flames, extirpated the son, the sire, with the whole race, and flung myself upon the pile.

592. WILL THEY NOT MAKE READY ARMS? these are the words of one infuriated, as she herself says shortly after, "what madness turns my brain?" [595] For such commands do not come from a sane woman, to command those who are not there—"Fetch weapons!"[594]—when she is alone.

593. THE DOCKS from the docks, where the ships are moored.

595. OR WHERE AM I am I still in a union?

597. WHEN YOU IMPARTED TO HIM YOUR SCEPTRE as, "[she] has taken Aeneas into her kingdom for her lord." [214]

AND FAITH supply "*en*" even to the lines following this one: or else, "this is the one whom they say carried the gods." Of course "*en*" is better used with a nominative, as, "Look—it's Priam!" [1.461].

602. ASCANIUS HIMSELF either because he is the cause of their sailing away, as, "whom I cheat of the Hesperian crown," [355] or for the purpose of aggrieving his father, as, "You have made me see the death of my son before my very eyes." [2.538]

SERVED HIM UP FOR A BANQUET which Procne did after slaying her son Itys because of the rape of her sister.

604. INTO HIS CAMP fleets, as, "We strike the camps" [3.519].

605. GANGWAYS [*FOROS*] the boards of ships, a term derived from the fact that they bear (*ferant*) those going aboard; it is masculine in gender and plural in number.

606. I MIGHT HAVE EXTIRPATED WITH THE WHOLE RACE with the deaths of Aeneas and Ascanius; it is also syncope.

FLUNG MYSELF sufficiently in the manner of a lover.

'Sol, qui terrarum flammis opera omnia lustras,
tuque harum interpres curarum et conscia Iuno,
nocturnisque Hecate triuiis ululata per urbes,
et Dirae ultrices et di morientis Elissae,

607. SOL iam utitur inprecationibus, hoc est, deuotionibus; unde et 'deuotor' et 'deuotrix' dicitur qui inprecatur. non autem 'terrarum flammis,' sed 'opera terrarum.' et bene inuocat Solem, cui supra [58] per numen Liberi sacrificauit.

608. INTERPRES CVRARVM aut quas patior, aut generaliter curarum coniugalium interpres, hoc est, media et conciliatrix. Cicero, *quique interpretes corrumpendi iudicii solent esse.* [*Verr* 1.12.36]

CONSCIA IVNO siluit rem turpem; sic supra *et pronuba Iuno.* [166]

609. NOCTVRNIS non *triuiis*, sed per nocturnum tempus.

VLVLATA PER VRBES Proserpinam raptam a Dite patre Ceres, cum incensis faculis per orbem terrarum requireret, per triuia eam uel quadriuia uocabat clamoribus. unde permansit in eius sacris ut certis diebus per compita a matronis exerceatur ululatus, sicut in Isidis sacris, ubi est imitatio inuenti Osiridis, quem dilaniatum a Typhone eius fratre uxor Isis per totum orbem requisisse narratur; Iuuenalis, *plangentis populi currit derisor Anubis.* [*Sat* 6.534] Hecaten autem causa inuocat ultionis. unde etiam Furias uocat, sed usurpatiue modo 'Diras' dixit; nam 'Dirae' in caelo, 'Furiae' in terris, 'Eumenides' apud inferos, unde et tres esse dicuntur; sed haec nomina confundunt poetae. 'ultrix' uero, hoc est Tisiphone; nam Graece τίσις ultio dicitur.

610. DII MORIENTIS ELISSAE aut Manes dicit, unde est *uos o mihi Manes / este boni, quoniam superis auersa uoluntas;* [12.646-7] aut certe ἀναιρετικούς dicit, id est, Martem et Saturnum, qui intercidunt uitae rationem, si radiis suis ortum geniturae pulsauerint: Horatius *te Iouis impio / tutela Saturno refulgens / eripuit uolucresque fati / tardauit alas* [*Carm* 2.17.22-25]—et bene *tardauit*, quia necessitas fati inpediri potest, non penitus eludi; sic Vergilius *nec fata uetabant / stare decemque alios Priamum superesse per annos.* [8.398-9]

You, Sun, who with your flaming beams survey all works on earth, and you, witness Juno, the agent of these my cares; Hecate, with howlings through the cities, in the "crossroads", by night; [610] and you avenging Dirae and gods of dying Elissa,

607. SUN now she uses curses, that is, incantations (*devotiones*): for this reason, those who curse are called "devoter" and "devotress." This line should be read not "with your flaming beams of the earth," but "all works on earth." And she does well to invoke the Sun, to whom she had previously sacrificed through the divinity of Liber [58].

608. AGENT OF THESE MY CARES either I am now suffering, or generally as agent of my marital cares, that is the mediator and conciliator. Cicero, "those who are accustomed to act as mediators in corrupting the seat of judgment." [*Verr* 1.12.36]

WITNESS JUNO she does not speak of the disgraceful affair; thus above, *pronuba Juno* [166]

609. BY NIGHT not modifying crossroad', but meaning throughout the night hours.

HOWLINGS THROUGH THE CITIES when Ceres was searching with lighted torches all over the earth for Proserpina, stolen by father Dis, she shouted for her at forks in the road and crossroads. For this reason it remains part of her rites that on certain days howling is carried out by the matrons at the crossroads, just as in the rites of Isis, when there is a re-creation of the finding of Osiris, whom his wife Isis is said to have sought throughout the whole world after he had been torn to pieces by his brother Typhon; Juvenal, "Anubis runs mocking the mournful people." [*Sat* 6.534] However she calls upon Hecate for the sake of vengeance, and for this reason, too, she calls the Furies, improperly called the Dirae; for the "Dirae" are in the sky, "Furies" on earth, "Eumenides" among the dead. For this reason they are said to be three in number, although poets confuse these names. The woman who seeks vengeance is indeed Tisiphone, for vengeance is called *tisis* in Greek.

610. GODS OF DYING ELISSA either he says ghosts, and for this reason he writes, "You ghosts, be good to me, since the gods' good will has been taken from me." [12.646–7] Or else she speaks of the deadly stars, i.e. Mars and Saturn, which destroy the plan of life if their rays should strike the rising of one's birth star; Horace, "The gleaming protection of Jove snatched you from baleful Saturn and slowed Fate's swift wings." [*Carm* 2.17.22–25] And he rightly says "slowed," because, although Fate is able to be impeded, it cannot be entirely eluded. Thus Virgil, "The Fates did not prevent [Troy] to stand for another ten years nor Priam to survive." [8.398]

accipite haec, meritumque malis aduertite numen,
et nostras audite preces. si tangere portus
infandum caput ac terris adnare necesse est,
et sic fata Iouis poscunt, hic terminus haeret:
at bello audacis populi uexatus et armis,
finibus extorris, complexu auulsus Iuli,
auxilium imploret, uideatque indigna suorum
funera; nec, cum se sub leges pacis iniquae
tradiderit, regno aut optata luce fruatur,
sed cadat ante diem, mediaque inhumatus harena.

611. MERITVMQVE MALIS ADVERTITE NVMEN quod mali merentur.

612. AVDITE PRECES inprecationes dicit; nam non sunt preces, ut paulo post *inprecor arma armis.* [629]

613. ADNARE ut in primo *huc pauci uestris adnauimus oris,* [1.538] id est 'per tempestatem uenimus.' et bono colore futura praedicit.

614. FATA IOVIS participium est, non nomen.

TERMINVS HAERET si hoc est inmutabile.

615. AVDACIS POPVLI Rutulorum, sicut semper inducuntur; alibi *audacis Rutuli ad muros.* [7.409]

616. FINIBVS EXTORRIS extra suas terras remotus. et significat quando Euandri et Tarchonis petivit auxilium.

617. INDIGNA SVORVM FVNERA Pallantis dicit et ceterorum.

618. PACIS INIQVAE ut supra diximus, [ad 1.6] propter perditam linguam, habitum, nomen, quae solet uictor inponere, sicut postulat Iuno. [12.823]

620. SED CADAT ANTE DIEM Cato dicit iuxta Laurolauinium, cum Aeneae socii praedas agerent, proelium commissum, in quo Latinus occisus est, fugit Turnus; et Mezentii auxilio conparato uictus quidem est ab Aenea, qui tamen in ipso proelio non conparuit. Ascanius postea Mezentium interemit. alii dicunt quod uictor Aeneas, cum sacrificaret super Numicum fluuium, lapsus est nec eius cadauer inuentum est; unde dictum est *mediaque inhumatus harena.* postea dictus est inter deos receptus. *ante diem* autem *ante fati necessitatem;* et bene quod passura est optat Aeneae, ut ipse, *sed misera ante diem.* [697]

receive these my words; in justice to my wrongs, turn to me your divine regard and hearken to my prayers. If it must be, and Jove's sayings so require, if this be his determination, that the execrable traitor reach the port and swim to land: [615] yet harassed, at least, by war and the hostilities of an audacious people, expelled from his own territories, torn from the embraces of Iulus, may he sue to others for relief and see the ignominious deaths of his friends; and, after he shall have submitted to the terms of a disadvantageous peace, let him neither enjoy his crown nor the wished-for light, [620] but die before his time, and [lie] unburied in the midst of the sandy shore.

611. AND IN JUSTICE TO MY WRONGS, TURN TO ME YOUR DIVINE REGARD because the wrongs [done to her] deserve attention.

612. HEARKEN TO MY PRAYERS she says curses: for they are not prayers, as shortly after, "Let them take this curse, that…their arms …be opposed…to one another." [629]

613. SWIM as in the first book, "Some of us safely swam to your shores," [1.538] i.e. "we arrived during a sea storm." And she predicts the future vividly.

614. JOVE'S SAYINGS *fata* is a participle, not a noun.

IF THIS BE HIS DETERMINATION if it is unchangeable.

615. OF AN AUDACIOUS PEOPLE of the Rutulians, as they are always depicted; elsewhere, "toward the wall of the audacious Rutulian." [7.409]

616. EXPELLED FROM HIS OWN TERRITORIES carried off beyond his lands. And this signifies the time when he sought help from Evander and Tarchon.

617. THE IGNOMINIOUS DEATHS OF HIS FRIENDS he speaks of Pallas and the others.

618. OF A DISADVANTAGEOUS PEACE as we said above [on 1.6], due to the loss of language, traditional dress, and name, things which the victor usually imposes; thus, "Juno demands." [12.823]

620. BUT DIE BEFORE HIS TIME Cato says that, when Aeneas' comrades were seeking plunder near Laurolavinium [i.e., Lavinium], a battle ensued, during which Latinus was killed and Turnus fled; and joining forces with Mezentius' army, he was conquered by Aeneas, who himself, however, did not enter into the battle. Ascanius afterward slew Mezentius. Others say that the victorious Aeneas, when he was sacrificing above the river Numicus, fell in, and that his body was never found; for this reason it is said "unburied in the midst of the sandy shore." Afterward he is said to have been received among the gods. "Before his time," however, is before the inevitability of fate: this is well-put, because she hopes for Aeneas that which she herself is about to suffer, dying "unhappily before her time" [697].

haec precor, hanc uocem extremam cum sanguine fundo.
tum uos, o Tyrii, stirpem et genus omne futurum
exercete odiis, cinerique haec mittite nostro
munera. nullus amor populis, nec foedera sunto.
exoriare aliquis nostris ex ossibus ultor,
qui face Dardanios ferroque sequare colonos,
nunc, olim, quocumque dabunt se tempore uires.
litora litoribus contraria, fluctibus undas
imprecor, arma armis; pugnent ipsique nepotesque.'
Haec ait, et partis animum uersabat in omnis,
inuisam quaerens quam primum abrumpere lucem.
tum breuiter Barcen nutricem adfata Sychaei;

621. CVM SANGVINE FVNDO quasi inprecationes ipsas suo consecraret cruore.

622. TVM VOS, O TYRII non sunt mandata, sed inprecationes, ut dissentiant omnibus rebus, sicut et factum est; nam si mandata sunt, quomodo *genus futurum*?

623. EXERCETE id est 'fatigate.'

624. NEC FOEDERA SVNTO quia rupta sunt tertio. *sunto* autem 'sint'; et fit propter metrum, addita 'o' tertiae personae numeri pluralis modi indicatiui, ut 'amanto' 'docento' 'legunto,' 'nutriunto.' Vrbanus dicit uerbo eum iuris usum propter odia hereditaria.

625. EXORIARE exoriatur; et ostendit Hannibalem.

EX OSSIBVS secundum Anaxagoran, qui homoeomerian dicit, id est omnium membrorum similitudinem, esse in rebus creandis, id est ex ossibus, ex sanguine, ex medullis; nam omnia pro parte sui transeunt in procreationem. Lucretius *nunc ad Anaxagorae ueniamus homoeomerian.* [*DRN* 1.830]

628. FLVCTIBVS VNDAS propter illud quod in foederibus cautum est, ut Corsica esset media inter Romanos et Carthaginienses.

629. PVGNENT IPSIQVE NEPOTESQVE potest et ad ciuile bellum referri.

632. BREVITER festinatione mortis; simul nectit causam morarum et ipsi et sorori.

These are my prayers; these the last words I pour forth with my blood. You, too, O Tyrians, with irreconcilable enmity, pursue his offspring and all his future race, and present these offerings to my shade: let no amity or treaties between the two nations subsist. Arise some avenger from my bones who may persecute those Trojan fugitives with fire and sword, now, hereafter, at whatever time power shall be given. Let them take this curse from me, that their shores, their waves, their arms and ours, may still be opposed to one another; and may they themselves and posterity, too, be still in war engaged."

She spoke and every way turned her soul, seeking, as soon as possible, to break off the hateful light. Then briefly thus she addressed Barce, the nurse of Sychaeus

621. I POUR FORTH WITH MY BLOOD as if she consecrated the curses themselves with her blood.

622. YOU, TOO, O TYRIANS these are not commands, but curses, that these peoples might disagree on all matters, as in fact happened. For how could she give commands to "all his future race?"

623. PURSUE i.e. harass.

624. NO TREATIES SUBSIST [*SUNTO*] because they are broken for a third time. *Sunto,* however, is *sint*: and the *o* is added because of the meter to the third person plural of the indicative mood, as in *amanto*, *docento*, *legunto*, *nutriunto*. Urbanus says that the poet uses this legal phrasing because of the traditional hatred.

625. ARISE let one arise, also meaning Hannibal.

FROM MY BONES according to Anaxagoras, who says that, in the creation of things there is homoeomeria (a likeness of all elements), i.e. from bones, from blood, from marrow: for all things in procreation come over for their own part. Lucretius, "Now let us now come to the homoeomeria of Anaxagoras." [*DRN* 1.830]

628. THAT THEIR SHORES, THEIR WAVES due to the fact that precaution was taken in treaties that Corisca might be non-aligned between the Romans and the Carthaginians.

629. POSTERITY TOO BE STILL IN WAR ENGAGED this can also recall the Civil War.

632. BRIEFLY due to her rushing to die: likewise she contrives for herself and her sister a reason for delay.

namque suam patria antiqua cinis ater habebat:
'Annam cara mihi nutrix huc siste sororem;
dic corpus properet fluuiali spargere lympha,
et pecudes secum et monstrata piacula ducat:
sic ueniat; tuque ipsa pia tege tempora uitta.
sacra Ioui Stygio, quae rite incepta paraui,

634. HVC SISTE huc adduc, ut *et cum grege sistit ad aram.* [8.85] hinc et 'sistatur' dicimus, id est 'adducatur'; nam 'stare' aliud est. nec aliter possumus dicere quam 'sta hic,' 'siste huc.' fallit autem plerumque uerbi similitudo, quia dicimus 'sto' et 'sisto' cum diuersa significent.

635. SPARGERE LYMPHA sacrificantes diis inferis aspergebantur, ut *spargens rore leui et ramo felicis oliuae,* [6.230] superis abluebantur, ut *donec me flumine uiuo abluero;* [2.719] modo autem inferis sacrificat, ut 'sacra Ioui Stygio.' [638]

636. PIACVLA purgationes; alias 'sacrilegia.'

637. SIC VENIAT ne praemitteret aut praecederet.

TEGE corona, ut et ipsa tardaret.

638. IOVI STYGIO hoc est, Plutoni. et sciendum Stoicos dicere unum esse deum cui nomina uariantur pro actibus et officiis. unde etiam duplicis sexus numina esse dicuntur ut, cum in actu sunt, mares sint, feminae, cum patiendi habent naturam; unde est *coniugis in gremium laetae descendit.* [*G* 2.326] ab actibus autem uocantur, ut 'Iuppiter' iuuans pater, 'Mercurius' quod mercibus praeest, 'Liber' a libertate. sic ergo et modo Iouem 'Stygium' dicit inferis sacrificatura, ut alibi *Iunoni infernae dictus sacer.* [6.138] hinc est Iouis oratio *caelicolae, mea membra, dei, quos nostra potestas officiis diuisa facit.*

QVAE RITE INCEPTA ordo est: sacra quae paraui animus est rite perficere.

(for the dark grave lodged in her native country): "Dear nurse, present her hither to me my sister Anna; [635] bid her make haste to sprinkle her body with running water and bring with her the victims and the things for expiation of which I told her: thus let her come; and you yourself cover your temples with a holy fillet. I have a mind to finish the sacrifice begun with proper rites, which I have prepared for Stygian Jupiter

634. PRESENT HITHER TO ME bring to this place, just as, "he presented [the sow with] its young before the altar." [8.85] Hence we also say "present her hither" (*sistatur*), i.e. "let her be led forth": for "stand" (*stare*), is another thing altogether. We are not able to put it any differently than "stand here" and "present [somebody] here." The similarity of these words however deceives many, because we say "*sto*" and "*sisto*" although they have different meanings.

635. SPRINKLE WITH [RUNNING] WATER those performing sacrifices to the gods of the underworld were sprinkled (*aspergebantur*), as, "sprinkling them with the light dew from a fruitful olive branch." [6.230] Those performing sacrifices to the celestial gods were cleansed (*abluebantur*), as, "until I cleanse myself in running water." [2.719] Now, however, she is sacrificing to the infernal gods, thus "rites … for Stygian Jupiter." [638]

636. EXPIATION acts of cleansing; in another context, this word means wicked actions.

637. THUS LET HER COME lest she send her before this time or that she herself come forth.

YOU YOURSELF COVER with a crown, so that she herself could delay.

638. STYGIAN JUPITER that is Pluto. And it must be understood that the Stoics say that there is one god, whose names vary according to the activities and responsibilities. For this reason the divinities are even said to be of double gender, so that when they are in action, they are male. They are female when they have a nature for being acted upon, for which reason, " [With fruitful rain the sky god] falls into the lap of his joyful spouse." [*G* 2.326] But the gods are named for their actions, so that "Jupiter" is the helpful father (*iuvans pater*); "Mercury" because he is preeminent in commerce (*merces*); "Liber" due to liberty. Therefore, since she is about to sacrifice to the underworld gods, she names Stygian Jupiter, just as elsewhere, "[the bough] said to be sacred to Juno of the underworld." [6.138] And hence the speech of Jupiter, "O heaven-dwelling gods, my limbs, whom our power makes divided by duties."

BEGUN WITH PROPER RITES, WHICH I HAVE PREPARED the word order is thus: the rites which I have prepared, it is my intention is to carry out properly.

perficere est animus, finemque imponere curis,
Dardaniique rogum capitis permittere flammae.'
sic ait: illa gradum studio celerabat anili.
at trepida et coeptis immanibus effera Dido
sanguineam uoluens aciem, maculisque trementis
interfusa genas et pallida morte futura,
interiora domus inrumpit limina et altos
conscendit furibunda rogos ensemque recludit
Dardanium, non hos quaesitum munus in usus.
hic, postquam Iliacas uestes notumque cubile
conspexit, paulum lacrimis et mente morata,
incubuitque toro, dixitque nouissima uerba:
'dulces exuuiae, dum fata deusque sinebant,

639. CVRIS amoribus.

640. DARDANIIQVE ROGVM CAPITIS in quo eius imago fuerat.

641. STVDIO ANILI aut pro aetatis possibilitate, aut pro industria qua utuntur aniculae.

642. AT TREPIDA festina; nam moritura nihil timebat.

COEPTIS INMANIBVS EFFERA furiata saeuis cogitationibus.

644. PALLIDA MORTE FVTVRA aut pallidior quam solent homines esse post mortem, aut *pallida* omine mortis futurae.

646. FVRIBVNDA furenti similis.

647. NON HOS QVAESITVM MVNVS IN VSVS quem Aeneas non ad hunc usum reliquerat. et, ut supra diximus [ad 496], secundum Homerum uertitur munus in perniciem. tale est in *Bucolicis: hos illi, quod nec bene uertat, mittimus haedos.* [*E* 9.6]

649. ET MENTE consilio.

651. DEVSQVE SINEBAT aut Iuppiter, qui Aenean abscedere conpulit, aut amor, aut necessitas fati.

to put a period to my miseries and to commit the pyre of the Trojan to the flames." Thus she spoke; the other quickened her pace with an old woman's energy. But Dido, trembling with agitation and maddened on account of her horrid purpose, rolling her blood-red eyes, her throbbing cheeks suffused with spots, and all pale with approaching death, burst into the gate of the inner palace and, infuriated, mounts the lofty pyre and unsheathes the Trojan sword: a present not provided for such purposes as these. Here, after she had viewed the Trojan vestments and the familiar bed, having wept and considered awhile, she threw herself on the bed and spoke her last words: "You dear remains, while the god and the Fates permitted,

639. TO MY MISERIES to her loves.

640. THE PYRE OF THE TROJAN the pyre upon which there was an image of Aeneas.

641. WITH AN OLD WOMAN'S ENERGY referring either to the ability of one her age, or to an old woman's customary industry.

642. BUT TREMBLING hastening; for she was not at all afraid, although she was about to die.

MADDENED ON ACCOUNT OF HER HORRID PURPOSE made wild by grim thoughts.

644. ALL PALE WITH APPROACHING DEATH either very pale, as people usully look after death: or "pale," as an omen of her impending death.

646. INFURIATED similar to one who is furious.

647. A PRESENT NOT PROVIDED FOR SUCH PURPOSES AS THESE which Aeneas had left behind not for this use: and, as we said above [on 496], according to Homer, the gift has turned into a means of destruction. Thus in the *Bucolics*, "We send him these kids (and a curse on him!)" [*E* 9.6]

649. CONSIDERED her plan.

651. WHILE THE GOD PERMITTED either Jupiter who compelled Aeneas to leave, or love, or the inevitability of fate.

accipite hanc animam, meque his absoluite curis.
uixi et quem dederat cursum Fortuna, peregi,
et nunc magna mei sub terras ibit imago.

653. VIXI excusat uitae abruptionem, quia dicit Plato magna poena adfici animas eorum qui uitam ante tempus relinquunt. ET QVEM DEDERAT CVRSVM FORTVNA PEREGI non natura nec fatum. tribus enim humana uita continetur: natura, cui ultra centum et uiginti solstitiales annos concessum non est; fato, cui nonaginta anni, hoc est tres Saturni cursus, exitium creant, nisi forte aliarum stellarum benignitas etiam tertium eius superet cursum; fortuna, id est casu, qui ad omnia pertinet quae extrinsecus sunt, ut ad ruinam, incendia, naufragia. bene ergo dixit *Fortuna;* sic Cicero in *Philippicis multa mihi inminere uidebantur praeter naturam praeterque fatum,* [*Phil* 1.10] id est gladii Antonii ex casu.

654. SVB TERRAS IBIT IMAGO bene 'imaginem' dixit. ualde enim quaeritur apud philosophos quid illud sit quod inferos petat. nam tribus constamus: anima, quae superna est et originem suam petit; corpore, quod in terra deficit; umbra, quam Lucretius sic definiuit, *spoliatus lumine aër.* ergo umbra, si ex corpore creatur, sine dubio perit cum eo, nec est quicquam reliquum de homine quod inferos petat. sed deprehenderunt esse quoddam simulacrum quod ad nostri corporis effigiem fictum inferos petit, et est species corporea quae non potest tangi, sicut uentus; hinc in sexto *corpora uiua nefas Stygia uectare carina.* [6.391] hanc autem rem etiam Homerus requirit simulacro Herculis apud inferos uiso. [*Od* 11.601 ff.] et sciendum simulacra haec esse etiam eorum qui per apotheosin di facti sunt; unde aut uisi esse apud inferos aut illuc descendisse dicuntur: Horatius de Libero *te uidit insons Cerberus aureo / cornu decorum.* [*Carm* 2.19.29-30] sciendum tamen abuti poetas et confuse uel simulacrum uel umbram dicere.

receive this soul and free me from these cares. I have lived and finished the race which fortune has given me. And now my image shall descend illustrious below:

653. I HAVE LIVED she justifies the cutting short of her own life, because Plato says that great punishments are visited upon the souls of those who depart from life before their time.

AND FINISHED THE RACE WHICH FORTUNE HAS GIVEN ME not which nature or fate has given me. For human life is comprised of these three things: of nature, to which no more than one hundred and twenty solar years is given; of fate, to which ninety years (which is three revolutions of Saturn) bring about an end, unless by chance the good influence of other stars endure past its third revolution; and of fortune, i.e. chance, which pertains to all those things that come from without, such as destruction, fire, and shipwreck. Therefore she is right to say "fortune"; thus Cicero in the *Philippics*, "Many things were seeming to threaten me outside of the regular course of nature and even of fate," [*Phil* 1.4.10] i.e. the chance encounters with Antony's assassins.

654. MY IMAGE SHALL DESCEND BELOW she rightly says image. It is intensely debated among the philosophers, what it might be that goes to the underworld. For we are made up of three things: of spirit, which is heavenly and seeks its place of origin; of body, which is placed within the earth; and of shadow, which Lucretius defines as, "air deprived of the light" [cf. *DRN* 4.364–9]. Therefore if a shadow is created out of the body, without doubt it dies with it, so that nothing remains of a person that might go to the underworld. But they have insisted that there is a certain simulacrum, which, being made in the likeness of our body, goes to the underworld, and that it is a bodily image that cannot be touched, just like the wind. Thus in the sixth book, "It is impermissible to carry a living body in this Stygian ferry." [6.391] But even Homer grapples with this issue when the simulacrum of Hercules is seen among the dead [*Odyssey* 11.601 ff.]. And it must be understood that these are the simulacra of those who were made into gods by apotheosis, hence they are said either to be seen among the dead or to have descended to the underworld. So Horace writes of Liberus [Bacchus], "Cerberus looked upon you, bearing your golden horn, and did not harm you." [*Carm* 2.19.29] It must be understood, however, that poets misuse the terms and indiscriminately refer to both simulacra and shadows.

urbem praeclaram statui; mea moenia uidi;
ulta uirum, poenas inimico a fratre recepi;
felix, heu nimium felix, si litora tantum
numquam Dardaniae tetigissent nostra carinae.'
dixit, et os impressa toro 'moriemur inultae,
sed moriamur' ait. 'sic, sic iuuat ire sub umbras:

655. VRBEM PRAECLARAM STATIVI non est contrarium illi loco *pendent opera interrupta;* [88] nam, licet paululum aliquid superesset, quantum ad ipsam pertinet fecerat, ut *urbemque paratam,* [75] item paulo post *urbemque tuam.* [683] et re uera ciuitati quid superest factis muris, templo, portu, theatro?

MEA MOENIA VIDI a me facta. et pertinet ad adfectum, ut 'quam uestrae fecere manus.' [3.498]

656. VLTA VIRVM puniendo eius interfectorem; nam ideo addidit *poenas inimico a fratre recepi.* et re uera nulla auari maior est poena quam amittere pecuniam propter quam commiserat scelus. bene autem *recepi,* quasi debitas. ergo hoc dicit 'feci illud et illud; felix nimirum fuissem, si tantum Aeneas Carthaginem non ueniret.' alii haec quasi per interrogationem uolunt accipi, ut nihil dicat esse perfectum: 'numquid urbem statui? numquid ulta sum uirum? numquid a fratre poenas recepi? felix tamen fuissem, si uel hoc tantum contingeret ut Carthaginem non ueniret Aeneas.' et hanc uarietatem gignit hic sermo *tantum;* nam ad utrumque admittitur. tamen melior est sensus superior, quem non nulli sic exponunt propter *pendent opera interrupta,* [88] ut ordo sit 'urbem praeclaram et mea moenia statui uidi,' hoc est, 'uidi dum statuerentur.'

659. OS INPRESSA TORO adplicito ore ad lectulum; aut quasi amatrix, ut *stratisque relictis incubat;* [82] aut certe quasi peritura insensibili rei dat sensum et sic ad lectulum loquitur ut ad hastam Turnus *te Turni nunc dextra gerit,* [12.97] Mezentius ad equum *Rhoebe, diu, res si qua diu mortalibus ulla est.* [10.861]

660. SIC, SIC quasi interrogatio et responsio: 'et placet sic inultam perire? placet.' et hoc eam se loco intellegimus percussisse; unde alii dicunt uerba esse ferientis.

[655] I have raised a glorious city, have seen my own walls, have avenged my husband, and exacted punishment from an unnatural brother; happy, alas! Truly happy, if only the Trojan keels had never touched my shores!" She spoke, and pressing her lips to the bed, "Shall I die unrevenged? [660] But let me die," she says, "thus, thus with pleasure I descend to the shades below.

655. I HAVE RAISED A GLORIOUS CITY this does not contradict that statement, "The towers begun cease to rise," [88] for although a small amount remained, she had done as much as was her concern, as, "the prepared city," [75] likewise shortly after, "your city." [683] And in truth what else does a city need once it has walls, a temple, a gate, a theater?

HAVE SEEN MY OWN WALLS created by me: and it pertains to emotion, as, "which your own hands have built." [3.498]

656. AVENGED MY HUSBAND by punishing his murderer, for which reason she added "and exacted punishment from an unnatural brother." And there is truly no greater punishment for a greedy man than to lose the money for which he had committed a crime. However she says "exacted" well, as though the punishments were debts to be exacted. Therefore she is saying this: "I have done this and that. I would have been truly happy, if only Aeneas had never come to Carthage." Others wish these verses to be understood as though they represented an inquiry so that nothing she might say had been completed: "Have I raised a city? Have I avenged my husband? Have I exacted punishment from an unnatural brother? Nevertheless I would be happy, if only it had happened that Aeneas had not come to Carthage." And the word "only" causes this difference: for either meaning is admissible, although the former sense is better. There are those who (due to the verse "the works … are discontinued" [88]) read the syntax in this way: "I have seen a glorious city and my walls to be established," that is, "I have seen them while they were being established."

659. PRESSING HER LIPS TO THE BED having touched her lips to the bed: either as if she were a lover, as, "she presses the couch he had left," [82] or else, as if she were about to die, she imputes reason to an object without reason, and thus speaks to the bed, just as Turnus spoke to his spear, "Now the hand of Turnus holds you," [12.97] or as Mezentius spoke to his horse, "Rhoebus, we have lived long, if anything for mortals is long." [10.861]

660. THUS, THUS, as if part of a question and answer: "Is it pleasing to die unavenged, thus? It is." And at this point we understand that she has struck herself, for which reason some say that these are the words of her stabbing herself.

hauriat hunc oculis ignem crudelis ab alto
Dardanus et nostrae secum ferat omina mortis.’
dixerat, atque illam media inter talia ferro
conlapsam aspiciunt comites, ensemque cruore
spumantem, sparsasque manus. it clamor ad alta
atria; concussam bacchatur Fama per urbem.
lamentis gemituque et femineo ululatu
tecta fremunt; resonat magnis plangoribus aether,
non aliter, quam si immissis ruat hostibus omnis
Carthago aut antiqua Tyros, flammaeque furentes
culmina perque hominum uoluantur perque deorum.
audiit exanimis, trepidoque exterrita cursu
unguibus ora soror foedans et pectora pugnis
per medios ruit, ac morientem nomine clamat:

661. HAVRIAT HVNC OCVLIS IGNEM aut uideat omina tempestatis futurae, aut certe satisfaciat suae crudelitati.

663. INTER TALIA per talia, ut *hunc inter fluuio Tiberinus amoena.* [7.30]

665. SPARSASQVE MANVS aut perfusas sanguine aut morte resolutas.

667. FEMINEO VLVLATV proprio feminarum; Horatius *et illa non uirilis eiulatio.* [*Epo* 10.17]

670. ANTIQVA TYROS uel nobilem dicit, uel illud ostendit quia Carthago ante Byrsa, post Tyros dicta est, post Carthago a Cartha oppido, unde fuit Dido, inter Tyron et Beryton.

672. AVDIIT EXANIMIS ‘territa’; nam, ut diximus [ad 1.484], ‘exanimatus’ mortuus est.

673. ORA SOROR FOEDANS cruentans, sanguine foedans.

674. NOMINE CLAMAT aut Didonem uocat, ut supra diximus, [ad 36] Poenorum lingua uiraginem; nam Elissa dicta est, sed uirago est uocata cum se in ignem praecipitauit. aut *nomine clamat* ‘nominat,’ sicut et Homerus dicit ἔκ τ’ ὀμόμαζεν. aut certe uero nomine, ut solent dolentes, ut *hunc ego te, Euryale, aspicio,* [9.481] item *mater, Cyrene mater;* [*G* 4.321] hinc et ibi ait *et te crudelem nomine dicit.* [*G* 4.356] et multi quaerunt quomodo procedat hoc, cum eius nomen nusquam sequatur. sed tractum est a iure, ubi dicitur nihil interesse utrum quis unum filium habens dicat ‘fili, heres esto’ an ‘Titi, heres esto’; ergo dicendo *hoc illud germana fuit* [675] quasi nomen dixit. sane sciendum bene eum perturbate integrum non dedisse sermonem.

Let the cruel Dardanian from the sea drink in with eyes this fire and take everything of my death with him." She spoke, and in the midst of these remarks, her attendants perceive her fallen on the sword [665] and the weapon stained with foaming gore and her hands besmeared. The outcry reaches the lofty palace; Rumor wildly flies through the alarmed city; the houses ring with lamentations, groans, and female yells, and the sky resounds with loud shrieks: just as if all [670] Carthage, or ancient Tyre, in the hands of the invading enemy, were falling to the ground and the furious flames were rolling over the tops of houses and temples. Her sister was breathless at the news and with trembling haste, all aghast, disfiguring her face with her nails, and [beating] her bosom with her hands, rushes through the midst of the crowd and calls her dying [sister] by name:

661. LET HIM DRINK IN WITH EYES THIS FIRE either let him see the omens of the coming storm or else let him make amends for his cruelty.

663. IN THE MIDST OF THESE REMARKS throughout these remarks, as, "in its midst the Tiber with its lovely river." [7.30]

665. HER HANDS BESMEARED either drenched in blood or relaxed in death.

667. FEMALE YELLS yelling such as women make. Horace, "what an unmanly wailing!" [*Epod* 10.17]

670. ANCIENT TYRE either he calls Tyre "noble," or he points this out because Carthage was first called Byrsa, then Tyre, and then Carthage, named for the town of Cartha, where Dido was from, between Tyre and Beirut.

672. BREATHLESS AT THE NEWS terrified, for as we have said [on 1.484], *exanimatus* [without animation, lifeless] means dead.

673. HER SISTER...DISFIGURING HER FACE bloodying, disfiguring with blood.

674. CALLS HER BY NAME either she calls "Dido," which, as we said above [on 35], means "heroic woman" in the Punic language (for her name is Elissa), but she is called a heroic woman because she has thrown herself into the fire. Or "calls her by name" means she named her: just as Homer often says, "to call by name." Or else she calls her by her real name, as mourners are accustomed to do, thus we find, "Is this you I look upon, Euryalus?" [9.481] or "O mother, mother Cyrene" [*G* 4.321] as well as later, "he calls you by name, cruel one." [*G* 4.356] There are many who question how this works out, since her name is not used in the following verses. But this is treated according to the law, where there is said to be no difference between someone having a son saying, "Son, be my heir," or "Titius, be my heir." Therefore by saying, "O sister, was this your meaning?" [675], it is as if she said her name. Of course it must be understood that he appropriately has not given the distraught woman's entire speech.

'hoc illud, germana, fuit? me fraude petebas?
hoc rogus iste mihi, hoc ignes araeque parabant?
quid primum deserta querar? comitemne sororem
spreuisti moriens? eadem me ad fata uocasses:
idem ambas ferro dolor, atque eadem hora tulisset.
his etiam struxi manibus, patriosque uocaui
uoce deos, sic te ut posita, crudelis, abessem?
exstinxti te meque, soror, populumque patresque
Sidonios urbemque tuam. date uulnera lymphis
abluam et, extremus si quis super halitus errat,
ore legam.' sic fata, gradus euaserat altos,
semianimemque sinu germanam amplexa fouebat
cum gemitu, atque atros siccabat ueste cruores.

676. HOC ROGVS ISTE MIHI adludit ad historiam.

677. QVID PRIMVM DESERTA QVERAR? conqueritur cur relicta sit nec ad par exitium conuocata.

COMITEMNE SORORem deest 'illudne, quod spreuisti comitem sororem?' et semiplene loquitur.

680. STRVXI MANIBVS subaudis 'rogos.'

PATRIOS DEOS Saturnum et Iunonem.

681. POSITA exanimata; Statius *positusque beata / morte pater.* [*Theb* 8.651-2]

683. DATE aut 'aquam', aut 'date', id est 'permittite.' lauare autem cadauera satis proximis concedebatur; unde queritur mater Euryali *nec uulnera laui ueste tegens.* [9.487]

685. ORE LEGAM Cicero in *Verrinis: ut extremum filiorum spiritum ore excipere liceret.* [*Verr* 2.5.118]

GRADVS EVASERAT ALTOS 'ascenderat,' rogi scilicet, qui pro qualitate fortunarum fiebant; unde in sexto ait *caeloque educere certant.* [6.178]

687. CRVORES usurpauit; nam nec 'sanguines' dicimus numero plurali nec 'cruores.'

SICCABAT autem 'exprimebat.'

[675] "O sister, was this your meaning? Did you practice thus to deceive me? Was this what I had to expect from that pyre, those fires and altars? Abandoned! Where shall I begin to complain? Did you disdain a sister for your companion in death? Had you invited me to the same fate, one distress and one hour had snatched us both away by the sword. [680] Did I raise [that pyre] with these very hands, and with my voice invoke our country's gods that I should cruelly absent myself from you, thus stretched out upon it. Ah sister! you have involved yourself and me, your people, your Tyrian nobles, and your city, in one common ruin. Give, that I may clean her wounds with water and catch with my lips, [685] if there be yet any straggling remains of breath." This said, she mounted the high steps and in her bosom embracing, cherished her expiring sister with sighs and dried up the drops of black bloods with her robe.

676. WAS THIS WHAT I HAD TO EXPECT FROM THAT PYRE she alludes to the story.

677. ABANDONED! WHERE SHALL I BEGIN TO COMPLAIN? a complaint about why she has been abandoned and was not summoned to a similar death.

A SISTER FOR YOUR COMPANION this is missing because she speaks incompletely: "What is the reason that you disdained a sister for your companion?"

680. DID I RAISE WITH THESE VERY HANDS supply "pyres."

OUR COUNTRY'S GODS Saturn and Juno.

681. STRETCHED OUT UPON lifeless; Statius, "his father is stretched out in blissful death." [*Theb* 8.651]

683. GIVE either give me water or "grant me." A relative was given the right of washing the corpse, hence Euryalus' mother laments that she did not "cleanse his wounds while covering with a cloak." [9.487]

685. CATCH WITH MY LIPS Cicero in the *Verrines*, "to be permitted to catch the dying breath of their sons." [*Verr* 2.5.118]

SHE MOUNTED THE HIGH STEPS "she had climbed," namely the steps of the funeral pyre, which was constructed in accordance with the quality of her station; so in the sixth book he says, "they struggle to heap up [his pyre] to the sky." [6.178]

687. DROPS OF BLOODS he has misused it, for we say neither "bloods" nor "gores" in the plural.

DRIED UP moreover, "wrung out."

illa, graues oculos conata attollere, rursus
deficit; infixum stridit sub pectore uulnus.
ter sese attollens cubitoque adnixa leuauit;
ter reuoluta toro est, oculisque errantibus alto
quaesiuit caelo lucem, ingemuitque reperta.
Tunc Iuno omnipotens, longum miserata dolorem
difficilisque obitus, Irim demittit Olympo,
quae luctantem animam nexosque resolueret artus.
nam quia nec fato, merita nec morte peribat,
sed misera ante diem, subitoque accensa furore,

689. SVB PECTORE per transitum dicit uulneris locum.

691. TER REVOLVTA TORO EST aut 'saepius,' aut promanteusis est propter bella Carthaginis.

692. INGEMVITQVE REPERTA atqui dixit *inuisam quaerens quam primum abrumpere lucem;* [631] sed ostendit morientes sua inprobare desideria, ut in sexto *quam uellent aethere in alto / nunc et pauperiem et duros perferre labores.* [6.436-7]

693. TVNC IVNO OMNIPOTENS aut pronuba aut inferna.

694. DIFFICILESQVE OBITVS quia supererat uita ei quae casu, non aut fato aut natura, moriebatur; ut *nam quia nec fato, merita nec morte peribat,* [696] id est, naturali.

IRIM DEMITTIT OLYMPO ut et supra diximus, [ad 3.46] trahit hoc de *Alcesti* Euripidis, qui inducit Mercurium ei comam secantem quia fato peribat mariti. sane sciendum hoc ideo nunc fieri quia certis consecrationibus solebant homines facere ut muniti essent aduersus fortunae inpetus nec poterant mori nisi exauctorati illa consecratione; unde circa Didonem ista seruantur.

697. SED MISERA ANTE DIEM non est contrarium quod dicit in decimo *stat sua cuique dies;* [10.467] nam, ut saepe diximus, secundum sectas loquitur, et hoc secundum alios, illud secundum alios dictum est. quamquam grammaticae responsioni possit sufficere *omnia uincit amor, et nos cedamus amori.* [*E* 10.69]

She, trying to lift her heavy eyes, again sinks down. The wound, deep fixed in her breast, hisses. [690] Thrice leaning on her elbow, she made an effort to raise herself up; thrice, she fell back on the bed and with swimming eyes sought light in the heavens, and, finding it, heaved a groan.

Then all-powerful Juno, in pity to her lingering pain and uneasy death, sent down Iris from heaven [695] to release the struggling soul and the tie that bound it to the body: for, since she neither fell by fate nor deserved death, but unhappily before her time, and maddened with sudden rage,

689. IN HER BREAST the poet reveals in passing the place of the wound.

691. THRICE LEANING ON HER ELBOW either "very often": or it is a prophesy, because of the wars of Carthage.

692. FINDING IT, HEAVED A GROAN and he says, "seeking, as soon as possible, to break off the hateful light" [631] thus showing how those who are dying reject the things they need, as in the sixth book, "How willingly would they [who had committed suicide] now endure poverty and hard labor in the upper world." [6.436–7]

693. THEN ALL-POWERFUL JUNO either as goddess of marriage or of the underworld.

694. UNEASY DEATH because she who died by happenstance, not by fate or nature, had life remaining, as, "since she neither fell by fate nor deserved death," [696] i.e. in a natural way.

SENT DOWN IRIS FROM HEAVEN as we also said above [on 3.496], he took this from the *Alcestis* of Euripides, who depicts Mercury cutting Alcestis' hair because she died in fulfillment of her husband's fate. Of course it must be understood that this happens now because people usually perform particular rituals so that they might be protected against the onslaught of fortune and they are unable to die unless they are released by that ritual: hence these things are performed with regard to Dido.

697. BUT UNHAPPILY BEFORE HER TIME this verse does not contradict what he says in the tenth book, "to each is his own day established." [10.467] For, as we have often said, the poet speaks according to [philosophical] schools, saying one thing according to some and another thing according to others. Although it is possible a grammatical answer is enough, "love conquers all and let us yield to love." [*E* 10.69]

nondum illi flauum Proserpina uertice crinem
abstulerat, Stygioque caput damnauerat Orco.
ergo Iris croceis per caelum roscida pennis,
mille trahens uarios aduerso sole colores
deuolat et supra caput adstitit: ‘hunc ego Diti
sacrum iussa fero, teque isto corpore soluo:’
sic ait et dextra crinem secat: omnis et una
dilapsus calor, atque in uentos uita recessit.

698. FLAVVM CRINEM matronis numquam flaua coma dabatur, sed nigra; unde Iuuenalis *et nigro flauum crinem abscondente galero.* [*Sat* 6.120] huic ergo dat quasi turpi.

699. CAPVT DAMNAVERAT necdum eam morti destinauerat.

700. IRIS ROSCIDA quia cum nubibus est, quae rore non carent.

701. ADVERSO SOLE bene naturalem rem expressit; Iris enim nisi e regione solis non fit, cui uarios colores illa dat res, quia aqua tenuis, aër lucidus, et nubes caligantes inradiata uarios creant colores.

703. CORPORE SOLVO quia ait supra *nexosque resolueret artus.* [695]

704. OMNIS ET VNA uno impetu effusa est uita, id est anima.

705. DILAPSVS CALOR secundum eos qui dicunt animam calorem esse, qua recedente corpus friget, ut *corpusque lauant frigentis et ungunt.* [6.219]

IN VENTOS VITA RECESSIT anima, ut in sexto *quemque sibi tenues nascentem arcessere uitas.* [immo *G* 4.224] et dicendo ‘in uentos’ aut eos sequitur qui animam aërem dicunt, hoc est ‘in materiam suam rediit,’ aut certe eos qui dicunt animam perire cum corpore, ut intellegamus ‘euanuit’ *in uentos recessit,* ut in nono *sed aurae omnia discerpunt.* [9.312]

Proserpina had not yet cropped the blonde hair from the crown of her head and condemned her to Stygian Pluto. [700] Therefore dewy Iris, drawing a thousand various colors from the opposite sun, shoots downward through the sky on saffron wings and alighted on her head: "I, by command, bear away this lock sacred to Pluto and disengage you from that body. She said, and cut the lock with her right hand: [705] at once all the body's warmth was extinguished, and life vanished into air."

698. BLONDE HAIR blonde hair was never attributed to a matron, but black hair was, hence Juvenal, "concealing her blond hair with a black wig." [*Sat* 6.120] Therefore [Virgil] gives her blonde hair as if she were disgraceful.

699. CONDEMNED HER it had not yet been her destiny to die.

700. DEWY IRIS because she is within the clouds, which do not lack dew.

701. FROM THE OPPOSITE SUN he has expressed the natural matter well. For Iris [a rainbow] does not appear except in the vicinity of the sun: this phenomenon produces its colors when mist, clear air, and dark clouds illuminated by the sun's rays produce various colors.

703. DISENGAGE YOU FROM THAT BODY because he said above, "the tie that bound it to the body." [695]

704. AT ONCE ALL her life, i.e. soul, poured forth in a single discharge.

705. THE BODY'S WARMTH WAS EXTINGUISHED according to those who say that the soul is warmth, and with its departure, the body grows cold, as, "They wash and anoint the cold body." [6.219]

LIFE VANISHED INTO AIR that is the soul, as in Book Six, "each thing, at its birth, draws its little bit of life." [actually *G* 4.224] By saying "into air," he is either following those who say that the soul is air, that is, "the soul returns to its material of origin" or else following those who say that the soul dies with its body, as we might understand "she vanished into thin air," as in Book Nine, "but the winds scatter everything." [9.312]

Notes

1. For the meaning of "comic" here, see W. S. Anderson, "Servius and the 'Comic Style' of *Aeneid* 4," *Arethusa* 14 (1981): 115–125.

2. *Inventio*, "invention," refers to the way in which factual information can be rendered into plausible legal argumentation, and so, more generally, it can be understood to mean "contrivance." Servius claims that Virgil here makes Dido's argument appear uncontrived.

4. Servius refers several times in this book to *excusatio*, the rhetorical defense in which a defendant admits that the substance of an accusation is valid, but offers a justification for the admitted action. As Quintilian writes, "When all other defenses are impossible, *excusatio* remains."[1]

8. Several manuscripts have the reading *unanimem*, as does Horace *Serm* 1.3.31. Thilo notes that three of the manuscripts and the Servius text in the editions by Stephanus and Fabricius read *locuturam* instead of *locutura*.

9. Servius here gives two different meanings for the form *insomnia*. See the discussion of Robert J. Getty, "Insomnia in the Lexica," *American Journal of Philology* 54 (1933): 1–28, esp. 5–7 for discussion of Servius' evidence. *Terret*, the variant mentioned by Servius, is recorded only in the corrections of one ninth-century manuscript of Virgil (Bern 184).

10. Servius means that *succedo* can be formed either with *sub* and the accusative or, as here, with dative.

18. Servius' point here concerns the impersonal verb *pertaedet*, "it tires out," and the participle *pertaesum* used by Virgil. Servius' remark that *pertaesum* is a participle not derived from a verb is based on the rule, explained in a commentary on the grammarian Aelius Donatus, that participles were formed from the first-person forms of verbs. Since *pertaedet* is an impersonal verb, it appears only in the third person.

30. Servius' alternate definition of *sinus* as "eyelid" is not found in any previous author, but this comment was used by Isidore of Seville in *Etymologiae* 11.39.

33. The Julian Law mentioned in Servius' citation refers to legislation initiated by the Emperor Augustus in 18 BC that encouraged married couples to have children.

35. Servius seems to mean that the imperative form of *esse* (to be), *esto*, can be used in an adverbial sense, like "Be that as it may…"

1. Quintilian, *Inst. Or.* 7.4.13, *Hinc quoque exclusis excusatio superest.*

37. Servius implies here that *Africa* is derived from *Afer* and follows the pattern of being longer than the word from which it is derived. His comment on 2.601 noted that *Lacaenae* is shorter than *Laconica,* the word from which it is derived.

52. In a long and fascinating note on the derivation of Orion's name in the comment on 1.535, Servius accounts for the short first syllable by saying that the hero's name derives from the Greek name, *Ourion,* and when the *u* was dropped the initial *o* became short.

54. DS here mentions the variant *impenso* (at great cost), for *incensum.* The text of this line is uncertain. Servius reads:

His dictis incensum animum inflammavit amore

and cites a parallel passage from Horace; DS mentions the alternative:

His dictis impenso animum inflammavit amore

and cites a parallel from Terence. The editions of Hirtzel and Mynors read:

His dictis impenso animum flammavit amore

Austin[2] has an excellent discussion of the manuscript tradition and the consequences of the variants, deciding, along with most modern commentators, for *incensum.* Although the best manuscripts of Virgil read *flammavit,* the best manuscripts of Servius read *inflammavit.*

56. Commenting on 2.225, Servius wrote, "It is called a *delubrum* (shrine) which housed many deities under one roof, because under one roof there is washing, as with the Capitoline, in which Minerva, Jupiter, and Juno are housed."[3] Servius probably means a literal washing of rain through the single *impluvium* of the roof.

Bidentes refers to the age of the sheep when they receive their permanent pair of front teeth. Readers interested in ovine dentition are referred to James Henry's note in *Aeneidea* (1878) II, 594–596, and the remarks of Pease ad loc.

58. "Liber's spouse" refers to the myth of Ariadne, the daughter of King Minos who escaped with Theseus from Crete; before proceeding to Athens, Theseus' ship landed first on Naxos, where Ariadne, having fallen asleep under a tree, was left behind. Dionysus (Liber) found her and took her away to be married.

59. Curitis = Quiritis, a cult title of Juno, "protector of spear-throwers," from an old Sabine word, *cures,* "spear." Servius refers here to the Roman wedding custom of parting the bride's hair with a *hasta,* "spear." See Plutarch, *Roman Questions,* 87, and *Life of Romulus,* 29.

2. Roland G. Austin, *Aeneidos liber quartus P. Vergili Maronis edited with a commentary,* (Oxford; New York, 1963).

3. *Delubrum dicitur quod uno tecto plura conplectitur numina, quia uno tecto diluitur, ut et Capitolium, in quo Minerva, Iuppiter, Iuno.*

61. Translating *nomen* as adjective may seem odd, but derives from the way grammarians analyzed the language. There were eight parts of speech according to late-antique grammarians: nouns, pronouns, verbs, adverbs, participles, conjunctions, prepositions, and interjections.[4] What we call adjectives were classified as nouns, *nomina.*

73. Dittany is an herb that grows on Mount Dicte in Crete (hence its name) and is believed to have healing qualities. Virgil is more explicit about wounded animals seeking this plant at 12.414–415.

77. *Convivia* were festive banquets, generally held in the evening and rarely ending before dark. The *prandium* was a simpler midday meal, to which guests were not normally invited. It would be unusual to start feasting or drinking earlier in the day, but, as Servius' citation shows, a man in exile might very well remedy his situation by turning to drink in the afternoon. The eighth hour is early afternoon (eight hours after dawn).

80. DS adds "Or 'dim moon' means night, because it does not always rise, nor at the same hour. 'Alternately' since the sun shines in the day, the moon at night. Or does the moon hold back its light, setting and hiding itself?"[5]

82. The verb *mereo* means "to earn"; it also appears as a deponent verb, *mereor.* In military slang, the phrase *merere stipendium* and *mereri stipendium* are used to mean "to serve for pay," i.e., "to serve as a soldier." Here, Servius' remark also indicates there may have been a change in the pronunciation of the dipthong *ae* from Virgil's time to his own.

95. Servius' point is that when referring to groups of mixed gender by using the masculine *duorum* instead of the feminine *duarum.*

105. *Olli* is an archaic form of *illi,* as Servius' first suggestion makes clear; the second suggestion, that it could be used adverbially, may be by analogy with *ex illo,* so used at 1.623 and 2.169. Austin has a good discussion of this line, ad loc.

106. Servius seems to be saying that although the reading *adverteret* (to Libya) has better support in the manuscripts, the meaning of *averteret* (from Libya) fits the text. The weight Servius gives *adverteret* is doubly odd because none of the extant early manuscripts of Virgil have that reading.

112. Here Servius offers a choice between *foedera* (nominative and accusative plural) and *foedere* (ablative singular). The meaning in the plural would be simply "sign treaties" and in the singular "joining the people with a treaty." The older manuscripts all read *foedera.*

4. See, for example, Donatus, *Ars Minor, GL* vol. 4 p. 355 "Partes orationis quot sunt? Octo. Quae? Nomen pronomen verbum adverbium participium coniunctio praepositio interiectio."

5. "Aut ideo nox "obscura luna," quia nec semper nec eadem hora oritur. "Vicissim" autem ideo, quia per diem sol lucet, illa per noctem: ergo apparens diurnum lumen, id est solis, reprimit. An ipsa luna suum lumen reprimit, occidens et se obscurans?"

120. See note on line 61.

174. The meaning of this line hinges on whether the pronoun is *quo* (agreeing with *malum*, "evil") or *qua* (agreeing with *fama*, "rumor"). In the first case, the line would mean that rumor is not the same as evil, which is the fastest of all things; in the second case, the line would mean that rumor is the swiftest of all evils. Servius holds tenaciously to his belief that because this line is a *definitio* of evil, the correct reading must be *quo* and that the first case is true. The manuscripts, testimonia, and modern editions all point in the other direction, however.

Definitio is a rhetorical term, used to refer to the larger group of which an item is a part. Cf. Cicero, *Topica* 5.26–7.32.

198. The point of Servius' note is that *Garamantide nympha* can be taken to mean either the nymph whose name in Garamantis, or a nymph who is a Garamantian.

203. DS makes this reading clearer: "Surely the phrase *amens animi* puts a nominative in place of a genitive." His soul is not mad, Servius seems to indicate, but he is mad of soul.

211. Cicero (*Inv* 1.98) explains that the *conquestio* comes at the conclusion of a speech and is intended to secure the audience's sense of mercy.

212. Servius here refers to the legend of Carthage's being enclosed within the space of a bull's hide, on which see 1.366–367.

214. On the Roman procedure of *coemptio*, the fictitious sale of bride to groom that symbolizes the transfer of her person from her father's family to that of her new husband, see remarks in *OCD*, 3rd ed., 920 (s.v. *manus*) and, more fully, Jane F. Gardner, *Women in Roman Law and Society* (Bloomington and Indianapolis, 1986), esp. 11–13.

233. Servius notes that the Latin preposition *super*, like the Greek *hyper*, means "over" in a physical sense and "upon" in a more figurative sense.

246. Servius here refers to a legend concerning Atlas' fear that a "son of Jupiter" would steal the golden apples of his tree; the son in question turned out to be not Perseus but Hercules. See Ovid, *Met* 4.631–662. The name *Telamo(n)* for Atlas is recorded only by Servius (cf. on 1.741).

250. The Lucretius text now accepted is *ubi in campos albas descendere ningues.*

261. Pliny does not specifically mention that there are many kinds of jasper, though cf. Aulus Gellius, *Noctes Atticae* 2.26.11.

276. Most modern editions read *debetur.*

281. Servius suggests understanding this use of the concessive conjunction *quamquam* to mean, "although he burns to leave, he is awed and does not."

291. The Serenus cited here may be the poet Serenus Sammonicus (d. AD 212), although this same line is attributed to Annianus by Terentianus Maurus in his didactic poem *De litteris, de syllabis, de metris* 2001–2004 (*Grammatici Latini* vol. 6, ed. H. Keil [1874], 123).

323. Different manuscript traditions have Vergil reading different books to Augustus, but Charles Murgia has convincingly reconstructed them as Books One, Four, and Six.

335. Servius' meaning appears to be that Aeneas' speech is more effective because it is constructed of negations.

336. The Harvard Servius lists the Sallust parallels as Iug. 95.4; Hist. 1.77; 13 Maur.

340. The argument from necessity to which Servius refers here is elaborated upon by Quintilian, who notes that in lieu of a better rhetorical defense, "We may blame necessity, as when a soldier overstays his leave, he may say that he was delayed by floods, or by ill-health."[7]

345. Modern editions of Horace read *habebat* for *agebat.*

350. Servius points out that the grammatical way to say "it is right for us to do something" requires the pronoun in the dative (*nobis*) rather than the nominative (*nos*), which is why he says the line should be read as though the impersonal *fas est* introduced the clause with *nos* as its subject.

364. Here Servius uses *status* in a rhetorical sense, on which Cicero notes (*Topica* 25.93), "The refutation of an accusation is called *status* in Latin." Also see Quintilian's discussion, *Inst. Or.* 3.6.1.

373. "Also, it (*eiectum*) should be separated." Servius argues that a comma should follow *eiectum* and that *litore* should be taken with *egentem* so that the line reads, "an outcast, needing a shore." Most modern editors disagree, though James Henry, *Aeneidea* (1878) II, 719–722, stoutly defended Servius' position.

379. The atheistic author to whom Cicero refers (*DND* 1.63) is Diagoras.

383. Austin notes on this line that Dido "might be a Greek accusative form, but it is more probably a vocative."

384. Urbanus was a Virgilian commentator active after the second century AD.

390. Modern editions read *parantem* for *uolentem*, but Servius has just quoted it (*ad* 388) this way.

400. Modern editions of the *Georgics* read *volat* for *volans* at 3.201.

419. In rhetoric, an acyrology is an impropriety of speech. Servius' point here is that Virgil has improperly written *sperare* for *timere*. See further

[7] Quintilian, *Inst. Or.* 7.4.14: *Aut necessitatis, ut cum miles ad commeatus diem non adfuit et dicit se fluminibus interclusum aut*

Quintilian, *Inst. Orat.* 8.2.3.

426. Aulis is a town on a peninsula, not an island, though it was frequently mistaken for one by Latin writers, on which see Oberhummer, *RE* 2 (1896) 2409.

427. Mynors reads *cinerem* in this line, Hertzel and Williams read *cineres* along with Servius.

432. After quoting Servius, Pease ad loc. notes "which is what we might indicate by putting beautiful in quotation marks."

435–6. These lines, the climax of Dido's speech, in which she asks a final favor, are the subject of various interpretations complicated by textual questions. Conington calls it the most difficult line in Virgil. The first question is who grants the favor, and here the text can read *dederis*, "you (Anna) will give" or *dederit*, "he (Aeneas) will give." The second is whether to read *cumulata* (agreeing with *morte*) or *cumulatam* (agreeing with *veniam*). Mynors and Hirtzel read *dederit*, the reading of Virgil's literary executors, Tucca and Varius, that Servius rejects.

443. Servius and two ninth-century manuscripts read *alte* instead of *altae* in this line. The adjective would modify *frondes* in the next line, but Servius seems to imply the adverb modifies *it*. See discussion of Pease ad loc.

446. Servius reads *radicem*, the modern texts accept *radice* citing *G* 2.292.

462. The problem in this line is that a feminine adjective (*sola*) is modifying a masculine noun (*bubo*). Servius' solution is that a feminine noun (*avis*) is understood in apposition to *bubo*. The cryptic last sentence of the comment seems to mean that when *oscines* are silent, they indicate good fortune, when they cry, ill fortune, and likewise when *praepetes* fly, they indicate good fortune, when they sit, ill. Servius explains the difference between *oscines* and *praepetes* in his commentary on 3.361: "Birds are either *oscines* or *praepetes*: *oscines* predict the future with their song, *praepetes* give augury with flight."[8]

466. See Servius' comment on 9 above.

471. Servius' last comment seems to be indicating a play on words: *agitatus* (the perfect participle of *agito*) can mean agitated, but the related verb *ago* can mean "to play a role."

504. By "marked," *notatus*, Servius refers to the placing of *notae*, signs used to indicate, among other things, possibly corrupt verses.

510. Servius' point here is that the adverb *ter* modifies *tonat*, not *centum*.

534. On the comic beginning of this line, see Anderson's article cited in the note on line 1.

535. In this note, Servius draws out the implications of Virgil's regular refer-

8. *Aves aut oscines sunt, aut praepetes: oscines, quae ore futura praedicunt; praepetes, quae volatu augurium significant.*

ence to Numidians as *Nomades*, i.e. nomads.

572. Servius apparently means that the description of Aeneas' fitful waking foreshadows the description of Dido's sudden withdrawal from him in the Underworld (*cum corripuit sese*, 6.472).

573. It is unclear whether *praecipites* in Virgil's text is proleptic, or if it should be taken as a vocative, addressed to the subject of *vigilate*. See comments of Austin ad loc.

577. Servius indicates that this sentence, depending where one puts the comma, might read either, "O holy one of the gods, whoever you are," or "O holy one, whoever you are of the gods."

597. Austin notes ad loc., "Virgil was the first to use this demonstrative *en* with a nominative."

602. The story referred to here is that of Procne, Philomela, and Tereus, best known from Ovid's version, *Met* 6.424 ff.

605. Servius gives the etymology of *forus, -i*, m., (gangway) from the verb *fero* (to bear).

607. Perhaps Servius meant to refer to verse 4.58, where Liber as well as Phoebus Apollo, god of the sun, are invoked.

610. Servius' citation of 8.398 does not include the word *Troiam*, although it is the subject of *stare* in the indirect statement. (Our translation assumes that he meant to include it.)

614. Servius maintains that *fata* here is not "the Fates," but rather the perfect participle of *for, fari* (to speak, decree). Hence *fata Iouis* would be Jove's decrees. It is worth noting that in his note on 10.628 Servius writes, *Vox enim Iouis fatum est* ("Jove's word is fate.")

624. Servius' metrical explanation of the use of *sunto* instead of *sint* is not altogether correct. *Sunto* is the more formal form of the imperative (sometimes called the second imperative), which is used frequently in laws and ritual pronunciations. (Compare English, "Thou shalt not," as opposed to "Don't.") It is true, however, that the subjunctive is ordinarily used for the first person of the second imperative.

636. *Piacula* can mean either a sinful act, or the sacrifice carried out in atonement for a sinful act. Dido's ambiguous use of the word here, handled succinctly by Servius, has been the cause of much scholarly discussion, on which see Austin *ad loc.*

665. The meaning of *sparsas manus* is debated still along the very lines Servius points out: Are the hands covered with blood or lying limp? See 21 and Austin's note on this line for further comment and bibliography.

670. Austin notes that Vergil mentions Tyre as the mother city of Carthage.

689. Virgil had not previously mentioned where Dido stabbed herself, but here, as Servius notes, we discover that it was in her breast.

691. Anna's three attempts to sit up are, Servius suggests, an indication of the three Punic Wars.

698. Servius has misquoted, and thus misrepresented Juvenal (6.120), which reads, *Sed nigrum flauo crinem abscondente galero* ("But concealing her black hair with a blond wig").

Bibliography

A complete bibliography of books and articles on Servius would run to many pages. We have chosen to present, instead, a short guide to further reading.

There are two modern editions of Servius. The first is by Georg Thilo and Hermann Hagen, *Servii Grammatici qui feruntur in Vergilii carmina commentarii,* 3 vols. (Leipzig, 1881–1902), the third volume of which also has shorter Virgil commentaries by various writers. The second, the Harvard Servius, *Servianorum in Vergilii carmina commentariorum editionis Harvardianae*, has published two volumes. The earlier volume (vol. 2, 1946) on *Aeneid* 1–2 was edited by Edward Kennard Rand *et al.*, the later (vol. 3, 1965) on *Aeneid* 3–5 was edited by Arthur Stocker and Albert Travis. The 1946 volume was harshly criticized by Eduard Fraenkel in a two-part review in the *Journal of Roman Studies* 38 (1948) 131–43 and 39 (1949) 145–54.

The best introductions to Servius and guides to previous bibliography are Peter K. Marshall, *Servius and commentary on Virgil* (Asheville, N.C., 1997); George P. Goold, "Servius and the Helen Episode," *Harvard Studies in Classical Philology* 74 (1970) 101–68; and Don Fowler, "The Virgil Commentary of Servius," in *The Cambridge Companion to Virgil,* ed. Charles Martindale (Cambridge, 1997) 73–78. For those willing to go beyond English, Thilo's preface in vol. 1 of his edition remains an excellent survey. Karl Barwick's article "Zur Serviusfrage," *Philologus* 70 (1911) 106–45, is crucial in establishing the relationship between S and DS. Emil Thomas' *Scoliastes de Virgile* (Paris, 1880) provides another excellent overview and critique of Thilo and Hagen's edition.

Robert Kaster's publications set Servius within his historical context and explore the function of the *grammaticus* in society. See especially *Guardians of Language* (Berkeley, 1988) and "Macrobius and Servius: *Verecundia* and the Grammarian's function," *Harvard Studies in Classical Philology* 84 (1980) 219–62. In addition, there are valuable comments in Alan Cameron, "The Date and Identity of Macrobius," *Journal of Roman Studies* 56 (1966) 25–38, and Anne Uhl, *Servius als Sprachlehrer* (Göttingen, 1998).

Vergil's Aeneid

Selections from Books 1, 2, 4, 6, 10, and 12

Barbara Weiden Boyd

The divinely sanctioned plight of Rome's founding hero Aeneas, a Trojan's view of the fall of Troy, the divinely finagled love affair of Aeneas and Phoenician queen Dido, Dido's angry suicide when Aeneas leaves her, their re-meeting in the Underworld, the death of Aeneas' young charge Pallas at Latin Turnus' hands, the revenge killing of Turnus by Aeneas—all these stories are found within these selections.

Student Text: (2001) Paperback, ISBN 0-86516-480-0 ***Teacher's Guide:*** (2003) Paperback, ISBN 0-86516-481-9

This volume offers Barbara Weiden Boyd's newly edited, revised, and updated selections from *Vergil's Aeneid, Books I–VI*, by Clyde Pharr (whose user-friendly format revolutionized Latin textbooks), plus additional passages from Books 10 and 12, not found in Pharr's edition. Included also are Pharr's original introduction, grammatical appendix (with two updated sections), word lists, plus the unique pull-out vocabulary. The book is designed for college and AP* classes, and for self-study.

Praise for Boyd's Vergil's Aeneid, 10 & 12: Pallas and Turnus:

The notes are more than scholarly: they are practical … Anybody can pull lines out of a work, but not everyone can bring the lines alive and make the text work the way Boyd has.

– Gaylan DuBose
Texas Classics in Action

For those students who have read and enjoyed the Aeneid using Pharr's textbook, this supplement will allow teachers to present additional passages seamlessly into the curriculum.

Sharon Kazmierski

Student Text: (1998) Paperback, ISBN 0-86516-415-0 ***Teacher's Guide:*** (1998) Paperback, ISBN 0-86516-428-2

Bolchazy-Carducci Publishers, Inc.
1000 Brown Street, Unit 101 • Wauconda, IL 60084
www.BOLCHAZY.com